Learning with Computers

D0450920

The potential of new information technologies to support learning is now widely recognised, and educational institutions at all levels have invested heavily in realising this potential. Although computers are often thought to encourage isolation, one of the clearest findings of recent research is that effective learning with computers is often a collaborative and social process.

Learning with Computers brings together a significant body of research that shows how working with others at the computer can be beneficial to learners of all ages, from the early school years to the highest levels of education. Karen Littleton and Paul Light also investigate factors such as gender that explain why some interactions are not as productive as others. The contributors draw upon a considerable range of theoretical frameworks, encompassing cognitive-developmental psychology, social psychology and contemporary situated learning approaches, focusing throughout on the role of the computer in supporting and mediating learning.

Learning with Computers will be of great interest to students and researchers in psychology, as well as those in the rapidly developing field of learning technology.

Karen Littleton is a Lecturer in Psychology at The Open University. Her previous publications include *Cultural Worlds of Early Childhood* (1998), *Learning Relationships in the Classroom* (1998), *Making Sense of Social Development* (1998) (all edited with Martin Woodhead and Dorothy Faulkner). **Paul Light** is Pro-Vice Chancellor at Bournemouth University. His previous publications include *Learning to Think* (1991) (edited with Sue Sheldon and Martin Woodhead) and *Growing up in a Changing Society* (1991) and *Becoming a Person* (1991) edited with Martin Woodhead and Ronnie Carr.

Learning with Computers

Analysing productive interaction

**Edited by Karen Littleton and
Paul Light**

London and New York

First published 1999
by Routledge
11 New Fetter Lane, London EC4P 4EE

Simultaneously published in the USA and Canada
by Routledge
29 West 35th Street, New York, NY 10001

Typeset in Times by Routledge
Printed and bound in Great Britain by Creative Print and Design
(Wales), Ebbw Vale

British Library Cataloguing in Publication Data
A catalogue record for this book is available from the British Library

Library of Congress Cataloguing in Publication Data
Learning with computers: analysing productive interactions / edited by
Karen Littleton and Paul Light.
p.   cm.
Includes bibliographical references and index.
1. Computer-assisted instruction. 2. Educational technology. 3. Group
work in education. 4. Social interaction in children. I. Littleton,
Karen. II. Light, Paul.
LB1028.5.L3886   1998
371.33'4–dc21   98–17805
                                                                           CIP

ISBN 0–415–14285–7 (hbk)
ISBN 0–415–14286–5 (pbk)

Contents

Illustrations

Figures

Tables

Contributors

Charles Crook did doctoral research at Cambridge University, was a lecturer at Durham and is now Reader in Psychology at Loughborough University. His research applies a cultural psychological approach to issues of learning and child development.

Franco de Guglielmo has a first degree in sociology from the University of Salerno (Italy), a psychology certificate from the University of Neuchâtel (Switzerland), and is a Research Assistant in Neuchâtel working on the project: 'Learning a technical profession today'.

Danièle Golay Schilter is a Research Assistant at the University of Neuchâtel, Switzerland. Her research interests include: sociocognitive interactions among peers, the teaching of secondary school mathematics and researching the dynamics of interviews. She is the author of an inquiry into the further education needs of small industries. Her current research interests focus on the observation and the analysis of learning and training situations.

Christine Howe is Professor and Head of the Department of Psychology at Strathclyde University. In addition to computer-assisted learning, she has research interests in language acquisition, children's conceptual development, gender and dialogue and collaborative problem-solving. She has published over ninety books, chapters, articles and reports including *Language Learning: A Special Case for Developmental Psychology* (Erlbaum, 1993); *Peer Interaction and Knowledge Acquisition* (Blackwells, 1993); *Group and Interactive Learning* (Computational Mechanics, 1994); *Gender and Classroom Interaction: A Research Review* (SCRE, 1997) and *Conceptual Structure in Childhood and Adolescence: The Case of Everyday Physics* (Routledge, 1998).

Kim Issroff is a Lecturer in the Higher Education Research and Development Unit at University College London. Her research interests include computer-supported collaborative learning, technology in teaching and learning in higher education and affective aspects of learning technologies.

Paul Light held a Chair in Education at The Open University, UK and a Chair in Psychology at the University of Southampton before moving to become Pro-Vice Chancellor (Academic) at Bournemouth University in 1997.

Vivienne Light has a background in creative arts, holds an MA in Education from The Open University, UK and is currently an ESRC-funded Research Fellow in the Department of Psychology, University of Southampton.

Karen Littleton is a Lecturer in Psychology at The Open University, UK and currently holds an ESRC personal research fellowship. Her research interests include collaborative learning and gender and IT.

Neil Mercer is Professor and Director of the Centre for Language and Communications at The Open University, UK. His research is mainly on language and the process of teaching and learning. He wrote *Common Knowledge: The Development of Understanding in the Classroom* (Methuen Routledge, 1987) with Derek Edwards. He is also the author of *The Guided Construction of Knowledge: Talk Amongst Teachers and Learners* (Multilingual Matters, 1995).

Patricia Murphy is Director of the Centre for Curriculum and Teaching Studies at The Open University, UK. Her research on science and gender arising from the APU assessment programme is well known. Her most recent book, co-edited with Caroline Gipps, is *Equity in the Classroom: Towards an Effective Pedagogy for Girls and Boys* (Falmer/UNESCO, 1996).

Jean-François Perret is a Senior Lecturer at the University of Neuchâtel, Switzerland and Head of the Education Sector of the Centre 'New Technologies and Learning' at the University of Fribourg. He has conducted several large-scale assessments of curricula. He is also the author of several books (on the teaching of mathematics and of music; on curricula; on school books). His research work is particularly focused on the representations that teachers and learners develop of the activities in which they are engaged.

Anne-Nelly Perret-Clermont is Professor of Psychology at the University of Neuchâtel, Switzerland. Her research interests are in the social psychology of learning and development. She has edited books on social relationships and cognitive growth; on education in the pluricultural Swiss context; and on the historical and social background of Jean Piaget's youth. Her present research projects are centred on the social psychological dimensions of the impact of new information technologies on vocational programmes and on distance learning.

Roger Säljö is Professor of Psychology of Education at Göteborg University, Sweden. His research interests include communication, human learning and development within a sociocultural perspective and in particular issues of how people learn by developing and appropriating technologies of various kinds.

Eileen Scanlon is Reader in Educational Technology and Director of the Computers and Learning Research Group at The Open University, UK. Her research interests include collaborative learning, and science education at all levels, from primary to adult learning.

Andrew Tolmie is a Lecturer in Psychology at the University of Strathclyde. His research interests include computer-assisted learning and collaborative activity; uses of these to promote conceptual development and the acquisition and transfer of skills; and the contribution of dialogue to children's understanding of emotion and theory of mind.

Geoffrey Underwood is Professor of Cognitive Psychology at the University of Nottingham. His research on the acquisition of skill in readers, musicians, drivers, and crossword experts has been described in a number of books, most recently *Reading and Understanding* (Blackwells, 1996) and *Implicit Cognition* (Oxford University Press, 1996).

Jean Underwood is Professor of Psychology at Nottingham Trent University and is a member of the ESRC Centre for Research in Development, Instruction and Training, University of Nottingham. Her research on children's use of classroom computers has been described in a number of books, most recently *Computers and Learning* (Blackwells, 1990), *Computer Based Learning: Potential into Practice* (Fulton, 1994), and *Integrated Learning Systems: Potential into Practice* (Heinemann, 1997). She is the Editor of the journal *Computers and Education*.

Rupert Wegerif is a Research Fellow in the Centre for Language and Communications in the School of Education, The Open University, UK. He has written a number of articles, chapters and reports on the use of IT to support learning through communication. His research focuses on the relationship between new media and conversational reasoning. He is editor, with Peter Scrimshaw, of the book *Computers and Talk in the Primary Classroom* (Multilingual Matters, 1997).

Acknowledgements

The production of this book was made possible by the award of personal ESRC Research Fellowships to both Karen Littleton and Paul Light.

Heartfelt thanks are due to Carole Kershaw. Without her support and assistance, the task of editing this book would have been considerably greater.

Figure 3.1 and 3.3 are reproduced with permission from Carfax Publishing Limited, Abingdon. The figures originally appeared in: Tolmie, A. and Howe, C. (1993) 'Gender and dialogue in secondary physics', *Gender and Education* 5: 191–209. Figure 3.2 is reproduced with permission from Elsevier Science Limited, Oxford. The figure originally appeared in: Howe, C., Tolmie, A., Anderson, A. and MacKenzie, M. (1992) 'Conceptual knowledge in physics: the role of group interaction in computer-supported teaching', *Learning and Instruction* 2: 161–183.

1 Introduction

Getting IT together

Paul Light and Karen Littleton

Computers and children's learning

In one guise or another, computers have become almost ubiquitous over the last quarter of the twentieth century, and one of the things that is clear about the twenty-first century is that computers will play an increasingly significant role in both our leisure environments and our working lives. Consequently, learning to live and work with computers must figure amongst the more obvious 'attainment targets' of any contemporary educational curriculum. In parallel with this (and potentially independent of it) there is the issue of what the computer has to offer as a technology for supporting education more generally. What, if anything, can computers offer as adjuncts to (or even substitutes for) classroom education?

One vision of the place of computers in education (perhaps the predominant one in the early days) saw the computer as a perfect vehicle for carefully tailored contingent instruction, whereby each student could be taught at his or her own level and pace. Psychologists and educationalists who favoured an associationist model of learning saw the possibility that the computer might succeed where the teaching machines of the 1950s had failed (Light, 1997). Meanwhile critics of the new educational technology bewailed the impending 'dehumanisation' of the teaching/learning process.

A great deal of software developed for school use has indeed adopted essentially this approach; breaking desired learning goals into small steps and relying on reward, repetition and contingent incrementation of difficulty levels to impart various skills. Such 'drill and practice' software has been especially popular in the area of elementary arithmetic, where rote learning has long held a place. The computer takes the place of the teacher, in asking the questions and giving feedback to the learner. Typically, such software takes little from the learner's response to each question other than whether it is correct or not.

From this starting point the obvious direction of development, as greater computational power becomes available in the classroom, is to emulate more of the human teacher's capabilities. We can see this reflected in the move towards 'Intelligent Tutoring Systems' which 'model' each learner on the basis of patterns of response, and shape a teaching strategy accordingly. Progress in this direction has been frustratingly slow, and thus far only a few extremely expensive systems with very restrictive domains of application can claim much success.

In practice, though, computers in schools are more often than not used by pairs or small *groups* of children rather than by individuals (Wegerif and Scrimshaw, 1997). This pattern has doubtless been shaped in part by resource constraints, and perhaps also by children's apprehensiveness about working with new technology on their own. Increasingly, however, there is also a positive belief on the part of teachers that *interacting around* the computer can be a particularly productive way of learning. Indeed it is widely held that some of the clearest benefits of classroom computer use arise from the fact that they lend themselves so well to collaborative modes of use (Crook, 1994).

There is a good deal of research evidence to support this proposition, as we shall see throughout this volume. In a wide range of situations involving working with computers, pairs or small groups of children not only appear to perform tasks better than individuals, but also to learn more from doing so. This is true even with types of software developed specifically for individual use, such as the drill and practice software (Mevarech *et al.*, 1991) or Intelligent Tutoring Systems (e.g. Woolf, 1988).

What are the bases of this intellectually productive interaction? What features of the computer hardware or software contribute to or influence it? Are there circumstances in which such interactions around the computer are *un*productive or even *counter*productive? What research methods are available to explore these issues, what assumptions do they make and what problems do they pose? This introduction will offer an overview of some of the broader issues involved, while the contributions which follow will pursue particular approaches in greater depth.

Cognitive approaches: peer facilitation of individual learning

There are clearly lots of possible ways in which working with others might be helpful in approaching a task, and other ways in which the presence of others might prove a hindrance. Some of these can be approached from the standpoint of the cognitive or information-processing resources which partners might bring to the interaction.

Where several people work on a problem together, whatever it is, there is an obvious sense in which there are greater cognitive resources available for its solution than if a single individual is faced with the same problem. Thus, for example, even if the group members have got equally good memories, it is likely that some will spot and remember some items of relevant information and others will remember other items. Likewise one child may have a particular talent for a given aspect of the task, another for another aspect. With a computer task, one child may have more experience of the type of software involved, another may have better keyboard skills and so on.

Advantages accruing to groups as a result of these factors may not depend to any significant extent on any form of productive interaction beyond that required to let each contribute according to his or her strengths. In fact group performance might be optimised by marginalising the less able member(s) of the group and letting the more able member(s) complete the task. Whether learning outcomes at the level of the *individual* will be enhanced or damaged by this kind of group work is an open question. Benefit is possible, even for the child who has been reduced to the role of observer. Undoubtedly there are circumstances in which it is more instructive to observe a successful solution to a problem than to participate in an unsuccessful one. Equally clearly, there are circumstances in which less actively involved group members may simply 'switch off', or 'free ride' on the performance of their partners.

Such analyses make minimal assumptions about *interactions* between the partners working together at the computer, but of course such interactions will take place. They may embody conflicts of various kinds. A computer keyboard does not lend itself particularly well to being shared, and a 'mouse' even less so. There may well be conflicts about who does what. There may also be conflicts about the best approach to solving the problems presented by the task itself. The potentially productive role of conflicting perspectives on the task is highlighted in one particular tradition of research in this field, namely the neo-Piagetian approach. Though this work largely antedated the advent of computers, it is an approach that finds echoes in contemporary research involving productive interactions around computers, and has had considerable influence methodologically.

Piaget himself saw children's active construction of their own understanding as fundamental to their cognitive growth, and viewed peer interaction as a peculiarly potent source of progress (Piaget, 1932). According to Piaget, the young child cannot treat adults' ideas on their own merits, because of the differences of status involved. Disagreements with other *children* serve much more effectively to highlight alternatives to the child's own point of view. The alternatives can be considered 'on equal terms', and since the resulting conflicts of opinion demand resolution, the children involved are effectively prompted towards higher-level solutions which incorporate the partial insights reflected in their varying initial positions.

This model of peer facilitation of children's understanding is linked to Piaget's particular account of the genesis of 'operational thinking' in the early school years. However, via the work of Doise and colleagues in Geneva in the 1970s and 80s, it has come to exert a rather wider influence. Doise and Mugny (1984) and Perret-Clermont (1980) set out to demonstrate that individual progress in understanding could be fostered by 'sociocognitive conflict'; that is, exposure to the conflicting ideas of peers in the context of paired or small-group problem solving.

The typical design adopted in their studies involved individual pre-tests and post-tests, separated by a period of practice on the task undertaken either individually (the 'control' condition) or in pairs/groups (the 'experimental' condition). The key research question was thus not whether groups would do better on the task than individuals, but whether children who have had a chance to work on the task in groups will make greater individual progress than those who have not.

Where, as was often the case, greater individual gains were apparent in the experimental than in the control group, the explanation offered was couched in terms of sociocognitive conflict. The resolution of this conflict was conceived of in essentially individualistic terms. It might not even happen during the session itself, but perhaps later. Howe *et al.* (1992) offer evidence that progress made as a result of peer interaction may not be apparent in individual performance until perhaps several months later. Moreover, Doise demonstrated that the other child who supposedly held the conflicting point of view did not need to be physically present at all, as long as the conflicting views were introduced *as being* those of another child. Here again, then, a social process of sorts is involved, but the role of actual interaction is minimal.

The three-step (individual pre-test/group or individual treatment/individual post-test) design adopted by Doise and colleagues has been widely adopted in research on peer facilitation of computer-based learning, as we shall see in this volume. So too has the use of rather brief and circumscribed (not to say contrived) tasks. These features, especially when taken together with the rather self-contained nature of much computer-based interaction and the convenience of computer-based data collection, offer ideal conditions for experimental methods. The individualistic, cognitive level of analysis has thus come to be associated with the adoption of experimental methods of research in this field. This association is reflected in a variety of ways and degrees in several chapters of the present volume.

We have noted that an emphasis on the productive potential of conflict marks much of the research in this field (Howe and Tolmie, Chapter 3; Scanlon, Issroff and Murphy, Chapter 5). However, the emphasis in much of this research is not so much on the child's exposure to conflicting points of view, but rather on the socially mediated processes of conflict resolution. Concepts such as 'argumentation' and 'negotiation' move us toward a much more fundamentally *social* model of productive interaction, to which we turn in the next section.

Sociocognitive approaches: the joint construction of understanding

The approaches which we want to introduce in this section have in common a concern with the negotiation of *meaning* in collaborative problem solving. The focus is upon the ways in which the presence of partners influences the child's perception of the task and of the situation. More specifically, attention is given to the processes whereby learners can jointly construct an understanding of a task in such a way as to facilitate its solution.

To the hard-nosed cognitive psychologist, a task is a task is a task. It might involve solving the Towers of Hanoi, or a quadratic equation, or transposing a piece of music, but it can be defined essentially from the outside. Its meaning is determinate. To the social psychologist, life is typically more complex. Tasks, whether on the computer or off it, are usually susceptible of a variety of 'readings'. Areas of indeterminacy might include whether we are supposed to be doing the task as fast as possible or as carefully as possible, whether we are going to look stupid if we get it wrong, whether it is a 'fun game' or 'boring school stuff', and so on. All of these meanings are potentially negotiable. The very fact of having a partner may make some of these readings of the task more or less likely (e.g. a task may be more likely to be construed as a *test* if each child works separately than if they work together). Moreover, the presence of a partner affords the opportunity to negotiate an agreed attitude to the task and the situation.

At another level, the solution of the task may in turn involve building some kind of mental representation of 'what the problem is'. Developmental and educational psychologists influenced by Vygotsky have tended to focus upon the processes whereby the problem is interpreted and a strategy for solution is adopted. Vygotsky (1978) saw these processes as highly susceptible of social influence, though unlike Piaget he focused mainly upon interactions between partners who differed markedly in their levels of ability.

Using the concept of a 'zone of proximal development', Vygotsky offered a sketch of the ways in which a more experienced partner could extend at the margins the competences of a less experienced child. Newman *et al.* (1989) use the more attractive term 'construction zone' to refer to that area of potential development just beyond what the child can achieve unassisted.

This 'social constructivist' approach has been adapted by a number of contemporary researchers to encompass the situation of children of more or less the same level of ability working on a task collaboratively (e.g. Forman and McPhail, 1993, cited in Forman and Larreamendy-Joerns, 1995). Mercer and Wegerif (Chapter 6) offer an analysis largely in this vein, though they see it as going well beyond Vygotsky. Whereas Vygotsky saw social processes as constitutive of individual knowledge, Mercer and Wegerif argue that classroom knowledge needs to be construed as intrinsically social. In the present context, their emphasis is on talk, and its role in building 'common knowledge' amongst children sitting together at the computer. In contrast to studies in the neo-Piagetian tradition, the emphasis is upon the interaction *per se*, and the evidence it offers for group productivity, rather than simply on *individual* pre- and post-tests.

Videotaping, computer logs and transcripts have been the principal resources for this kind of analysis, and the challenge has been to find the analytic approaches which best illuminate 'what it is that really matters' in effective interactions. Thus, for example, Howe and Tolmie (Chapter 3) have explored a variety of aspects of discourse amongst students working on computer-supported collaborative science tasks in an essentially quantitative fashion, using coding schemes and correlations with learning gains as their principal investigative tools. By contrast, Mercer and Wegerif (Chapter 6) adopt a more qualitative approach, and are less directly concerned with individual learning outcomes. From analysis of primary school children's talk in the context of collaborative computer work they distinguish three different types of talk ('disputational', 'cumulative' and 'exploratory') and address the potentials for learning inherent in each of these.

The social constructivist approach has tended to be mainly concerned with the role of overt, observable processes of interpersonal interaction in shaping the child's response to cognitive tasks. The emphasis tends to fall very heavily on talk. This suffers the limitation that shared experience is often tacit, unspoken. Indeed one of the virtues of shared community experience is that it renders unnecessary certain types of routine forms of communication. For research observers, such tacitly shared experience creates problems because, typically, researchers will not be party to the sharing process and thus they will be hard pressed to detect its influence.

The problem of 'observability' poses itself in other areas too. Thus far, we have had rather little to say about the ways in which the presence of other children (or indeed of adults) can influence the child's response to the task in affective and motivational terms. Here, social psychological analyses in terms of such processes as social facilitation and social comparison have more to offer (see Littleton, Chapter 11).

Up to this point, we have talked about 'children' (or even 'learners') in a very generic fashion. However, there are obviously both group and individual differences to contend with, as well as the impact of such differences upon the patterns and productivity of interaction. Gender differences in response to collaborations with classroom computers are addressed by Underwood and Underwood (Chapter 2) and Howe and Tolmie (Chapter 3), and both chapters point to the fact that there may be significant differences in the ways boys and girls collaborate around the computer. There may also be special features in between-group as compared to within-group interactions, as suggested by the results of research discussed in both of these chapters on mixed gender groupings at the computer. Individuals also differ in the ways in which they respond to the computer and to co-operative modes of working (Forman and Larreamendy-Joerns, 1995). Such differences in response may themselves be conditioned by the previous experiential histories of the individuals concerned (Scanlon, Issroff and Murphy, Chapter 5; Crook, Chapter 7).

Classrooms and computers

Experimental research typically requires the use of very self-contained experimental tasks, and in the case of learning with computers this usually involves children working for one or more relatively short sessions on a purpose-built or 'off the shelf' piece of software. However, it is not at all clear that such tasks offer an adequate model of children's day-to-day learning environment. Learning (whether with the computer or otherwise) is normally a more continuous and extended process.

Moreover, many experimental studies, including our own (Barbieri and Light, 1992; Light *et al.*, 1994), have involved a particular and limited model of collaboration in which the partners are enjoined to work together intensively at the computer. Collaborative experiences are typically more than just brief localised sessions of joint activity. And as Crook (Chapter 7) observes, the productivity of interactions observed within such sessions may arise from previous interactions which comprise a broader social context in which they are located. Classrooms are communities, framed by their distinctive physical locations and social rules, and the patterning of social action and interaction is shaped over considerable periods of time.

In a more limited time-frame, Issroff (Chapter 4) illustrates graphically the way in which patterns of interaction change over time, again helping to establish the importance of the temporal dimension of productive interaction. As Underwood and Underwood (Chapter 2) point out, many forms of collaboration or co-operation are possible. A typical situation might be one in which a group of children parcel out the elements of a task between themselves, and in which only part of the task involves the computer. More extended and naturalistic classroom-based studies may offer a better opportunity to reflect these more varied and extended aspects of co-operative learning using computers than do experimental studies (Scanlon *et al.*, Chapter 5).

Even observational studies in the classroom, however, frequently involve fairly circumscribed observations. As Crook (Chapter 7) points out, they may effectively decouple the computer activity from the broader context of classroom life. As computers become better integrated into the curriculum, it becomes more and more important to understand the way in which they function as part and parcel of the everyday school situation. It is an open question how far the processes of productive interaction with which we are concerned can be understood in isolation from the wider 'cultural niche' that is the classroom.

Then again, it is clear that a great deal of what is learned using computers is learned outside the classroom; at home, in vocational training settings, and at work. The final chapters of this volume will widen our focus in some of these directions, raising both the question of how productive interaction around the new technology is shaped by the context, and at the same time drawing attention to the ways in which the technology itself is changing what and how we need to learn.

Chapters by Light and Light (Chapter 10) and Golay Schilter *et al.* (Chapter 8) extend the examination of computer-based interaction to encompass higher and vocational education, and to interaction through as well as around computers. Säljö (Chapter 9) takes a broader perspective again, on technologies generally as well as computers in particular. His argument is that the computer itself needs to be seen as a 'cultural tool', an embodiment of social practice and process, capable of mediating social relationships in new ways.

But if this is true of technologies in general, what if anything is special about computers? The advent of the computer as an educational tool has certainly coincided with a renewed and lively research interest in productive processes of interaction in learning. How far is this just a coincidence? What evidence do we have that interacting around computers has educational potentialities above and beyond those of interacting in other learning settings? These are amongst the questions addressed throughout this volume, in terms of the facility of the computer for supporting interaction (Howe and Tolmie, Chapter 3; Mercer and Wegerif, Chapter 6), and the possibility of 'laying down tracks' in the computational environment (Crook, Chapter 7). Direct comparisons of interaction in computer and non-computer environments are fraught with difficulties (though see Scanlon, Issroff and Murphy, Chapter 5). As we move from interactions *around* the computer towards interactions *through* computers (i.e. networked communications, computer-supported collaborative work, etc.) we rapidly reach a stage where these kinds of direct comparison are impossible anyway. Computers increasingly afford *new* possibilities for collaborative learning which are different in kind from those available in other contexts. Their advent may hopefully not only promote new forms of collaborative activity amongst learners, but also illuminate the nature of our human capabilities as collaborative learners.

References

Barbieri, M. S. and Light, P. (1992) 'Interaction, gender and performance on a computer-based problem solving task', *Learning and Instruction* 2: 199–214.

Crook, C. (1994) *Computers and the Collaborative Experience of Learning*, London: Routledge.

Doise, W. and Mugny, G. (1984) *The Social Development of the Intellect*, Oxford: Pergamon.

Forman, E. and Larreamendy-Joerns, J. (1995) 'Learning in the context of peer collaboration: a pluralistic perspective on goals and expertise', *Cognition and Instruction* 13: 549–564.

Howe, C., Tolmie, A. and Rodgers, C. (1992) 'The acquisition of conceptual knowledge in science by primary school children: group interaction and the understanding of motion down an incline', *British Journal of Developmental Psychology* 10: 113–130.

Light, P. (1997) 'Computers for learning: psychological perspectives', *Journal of Child Psychology and Psychiatry* 38: 1–8.

Light, P., Littleton, K., Messer, D. and Joiner, R. (1994) 'Social and communicative processes in computer-based problem solving', *European Journal of Psychology of Education* 9(1): 93–109.

Mevarech, Z., Silber, O. and Fine, D. (1991) 'Learning with computers in small groups: cognitive and affective outcomes', *Journal of Educational Computing Research* 7(2): 233–243.

Newman, D., Griffin, P. and Cole, M. (1989) *The Construction Zone: Working for Cognitive Change in Schools*, Cambridge: Cambridge University Press.

Perret-Clermont, A-N. (1980) *Social Interaction and Cognitive Development in Children*, London: Academic Press.

Piaget, J. (1932) *The Moral Development of the Child*, London: Routledge.

Vygotsky, L. S. (1978) *Mind in Society*, Cambridge, MA: Harvard University Press.

Wegerif, R. and Scrimshaw, P. (eds) (1997) *Computers and Talk in the Primary Classroom*, Clevedon: Multilingual Matters.

Woolf, B. (1988) 'Representing complex knowledge in an intelligent machine tutor', in J. Self (ed.) *Artificial Intelligence and Human Learning*, London: Chapman and Hall.

2 Task effects on co-operative and collaborative learning with computers

Jean Underwood and Geoffrey Underwood

Introduction

Current learning theorists appreciate that cognitive solutions are only a partial answer to our understanding of the learning process and that there is a social dimension to the construction of knowledge (see Brown, 1990). If this is so, how and under what circumstances may social interaction guide cognitive development? Rogoff (1990) has outlined a number of key questions concerning the nature of learning in a social context. What do children gain from social interaction and under what circumstances do those gains occur? What aspects of children's social interaction contribute to children's advances? How do variations in the nature of the group affect the nature of the interaction and therefore what learning takes place? Does it matter whether the partners are adults or peers, whether there are varying levels of expertise or of status within the group, or to what extent partners share in decision making? Are there any differences in the role of the interaction depending on the age of the children?

A review of the evidence suggests that when pairs of children solve a problem together they think more effectively than when they work alone (Kruger, 1993). When children work in groups there are benefits to be gained, but group work also carries risks. These risks are particularly high for certain combinations of children, and may be further exacerbated by the use of a computer as the medium of instruction. Not all of the evidence supports the view that group work results in improved performance. Nevertheless it is this interaction between the social structure of the group, the computer as a possible 'other' person within the group, and the task in hand, that has been the focus of our work. This chapter will outline the research that we have conducted on the question of social interaction and learning, with an emphasis on the influence of the gender composition of the learning group and upon the analysis of dialogue that is associated with task performance.

For some time now we have been investigating the learning outcomes that take place when children, mainly in pairs, work with and around computers, and endeavouring to answer some of the questions Rogoff has articulated.

This work has two defining foci: an emphasis on co-operative and collaborative working and an emphasis upon predictive models of learning outcomes. Evidence from our own controlled interventions in schools, and those of other researchers, has provided insight into the social and cognitive circumstances of effective collaborations with computers.

The introduction of computers into the educational equation has produced strong responses and had profound effects. The intensity of the argument over the value of individual versus group working is intensified when computers are part of the learning environment. The computer is not simply another educational resource. Some evaluation studies have found only limited gains for individualised learning although these findings are not universal and may be task dependent. There are strongly expressed concerns that there may be negative psychosocial effects for students working individually at the computer. Wragg clearly articulates this discomfort: 'the majority of parents do not want their children to learn by sitting at a screen all day long. Most normal adult behaviour is interactive – and you get some strange people if they've been up in the attic staring at a computer screen from the age of 5 to 16' (Picardie, 1995, p. 11). Wragg is articulating the fear of individualised instructional packages now commonly termed Integrated Learning Systems (Underwood *et al.*, 1996a). Although it is accepted that the computer can support many different modes of teaching and learning there is a growing body of evidence to show that children are more likely to work collaboratively when working on computer tasks than they are on standard classroom tasks, as long as the tasks allow for some level of co-operation and collaboration (see Hawkins *et al.*, 1982; Clements and Nastasi, 1985; and Underwood and Underwood, 1990).

Computers can support, and are supporting, a range of teaching and learning styles. This renewed focus on the role of social interaction has led to an increasing interest in collaborative and co-operative learning and new technologies can be a key to such social interaction. Pea (1993) has argued that some uses of technology 'enhance' education by making the achievement of 'traditional' objectives more efficient, for example in mathematics and science. But technology can shift the goals of education. One example would be how the use of calculators has shifted the focus of mathematics towards estimation and the meaning of operations and away from the mechanics of the arithmetic operations themselves. Co-operative working with technology also brings about shifts in our objectives. Instead of asking students to write individual essays we can ask them to produce newspapers and multi-media presentations involving graphics, sound and text. Instead of asking students to produce work for presentations to the teacher, we can ask them to produce a resource, a data file perhaps, to be used by other students. We might even ask them to produce a learning pack for their peers. These new goals are too great for any one student to meet, and co-operative work is essential if we are to take the opportunities on offer with classroom computers.

Co-operative or collaborative learning

The term 'co-operative learning' refers to learning environments in which small groups of students work together to achieve a common goal. The nature of the co-operation between the participants may differ within and between these learning environments. Currently terms such as group work, co-operative and collaborative learning are used very loosely in the literature. Here they refer to learning environments in which small groups, two to six learners, work together to achieve a common goal. In achieving that common goal, however, the members of the group may choose to take responsibility for sub-tasks and work co-operatively, or they may 'collaborate' by working together on all parts of the problem. If the learners collaborate and share in the decision-making process the level of social interaction is necessarily high, but this is not necessarily so for co-operative workers. It may be that some tasks are more likely to engender collaborative rather than co-operative strategies as we shall show from our own studies, but it is equally likely that the characteristics of the social group may predispose the members to one mode of learning rather than another.

The social underpinning of co-operative learning emphasises that learning under positive contact conditions can facilitate interpersonal relationships which may in turn have positive effects on student motivation, self-esteem and academic learning. Such positive effects have been shown across all age ranges, ethnic groups, classes and abilities and are most developed when full collaboration rather than simple social co-operation ensues. The cognitive view of co-operative learning emphasises cognitive processes such as conflict resolution, hypothesis testing, cognitive scaffolding, reciprocal peer tutoring and overt execution of cognitive and meta-cognitive processes and modelling.

Students can serve as a resource for each other. When problems are well defined and the computer serves as a tutor, the students often play the role of motivational facilitator, providing psychological support for one another. On the other hand, when the problem is ill defined and the computer serves as a simulator or information-processing tool the students may co-construct solutions and resolve conflicts by collaborative discussions. Some collaborating groups may be efficient because of conflict-based mechanisms (as predicted by a Piagetian model) and others due to co-constructive processes, as described by Vygotsky (1978).

Examples of the conflict-resolution model of learning are to be found in the work of Howe and her colleagues (1992), who have shown that when pairs of students differ not only in their predictions about problem outcomes but also in their underlying conceptual understanding, then collaboration facilitates learning. O'Malley (1992) has extended Howe's work to computer and learner interactions and has shown that when a computer agent makes different predictions then the human learner is more likely to show evidence of conceptual change than they do when that agent either makes similar predictions or reveals similar conceptions.

Learning in groups and with peers may be a more effective way of achieving some educational goals (e.g. conceptual change) than individualised instruction. There is a great deal of evidence which demonstrates that both peer tutoring and peer collaboration can facilitate learning and development. However, we are only just beginning to identify the components of effective peer interaction.

The value of discussion

Some educators have expressed concern over the amount of discussion that takes place when children work in groups. Too much talking is thought to get in the way of learning. However, the analysis of verbal interactions reassures and informs us that, with the appropriate group organisation, discussion not only becomes task oriented but is also associated with improved performance. By examining children's discussions as they work together we can gain insights into how social interaction affects learning.

Discussion in a group may occur at many different levels. At its richest it will result in the development of Teasley and Roschelle's (1993) *joint problem space* (jps) where the participants use language and action to establish shared knowledge, to recognise divergence from that shared knowledge, and to rectify misunderstandings that impede work. Not all group discussion leads to such rich and fruitful collaboration, in some instances discussion may simply express the etiquette of turn taking or, in dysfunctional groups, may be directed to non-task derogatory comments.

In any group that effectively collaborates, the members of the group will be able to introduce knowledge and ideas to the other members and will in turn be able to accept information from their partners. Further mechanisms will be in place to monitor on-going activity for evidence of divergence of meaning or of goal, and to repair any divergence that might impede the progress of the collaboration.

Factors affecting style of working

A number of factors influence the effectiveness of co-operative learning. These include individual differences such as gender, group size and ability mix, subject domain, task type and organisation (see Underwood and Underwood, 1990; Underwood, 1994). Our own work has focused on gender differences in collaborative learning environments. Informal observations of one computer writing class of 13-year-olds showed that most of the boys worked individually at a machine while girls worked in groups, despite the fact that this was a group writing project. This was as much a function of the boys 'charging' into the room and commandeering the newest machines as of the girls choosing to work at one machine. The girls worked in a collaborative manner around the computer, actively editing text being input by one of their group. The boys, who had not managed to acquire sole rights to a machine, were therefore obliged to work in a co-operative mode, with each boy in the group taking his turn to write while the other members of the group played around and disturbed the rest of the class.

In our more formal interventions we have found that gender is a very significant controlling variable in group effectiveness, with girls showing a greater willingness to collaborate, that is working actively together on solving the task, than boys and this collaboration has resulted in commensurate learning gains. A difference in the nature of interactions was also observed by Underwood *et al.* (1990) with boy/girl pairs showing little signs of collaboration and indeed not even co-operating as much as single gender pairs. Howe *et al.* (1992) report a similar problem for boy/girl pairs failing to communicate during a physics problem-solving task. To some extent this reluctance to discuss a problem, and jointly work within the problem space, can be addressed by giving the children appropriate instructions. Using the TRAY task, Underwood *et al.* (1993a) explicitly instructed half of the pairs to collaborate, and told the other children that their individual contribution was most valued. The mixed pairs continued to perform less well than single gender pairs, and they also showed little benefit from the instructions to collaborate. Girl/girl pairs worked collaboratively whatever instructions they were given, and the largest gains were shown when the boys were told to work together. The benefits of the collaboration instructions were seen in pairs who discussed the problem and agreed upon a joint action.

Mixed pairs tend not to co-operate or to compete, but work independently. Such pairings may be involved in turn taking within the activity, for example each child having access to the mouse in order to explore the contents of the screen. This was our observation with some of the pairs as they worked through one of Brøderbund's Living Books ('Arthur's Teacher Trouble'). This was at best a very low level co-operation, with little or no conversational exchange. Often mixed groups are less well behaved and can be a particularly dangerous combination, characterised by males commandeering the keyboard or the mouse leaving the females as spectators. This is not because females have any inherent disabilities or phobias about using computers (at least, not until after they have had unpleasant confrontations with a computer bully), but because the boys see themselves as the rightful and superior users of the technology. This attitude is summed up by the overheard remark: 'After all, classroom computers are little more than extended games machines, and who has ever seen a girl out-performing a boy on "Street Fighter"? . . . And this is why Nintendo isn't making "Game Girls". . . . ' Whatever the reasons, classroom observations have repeatedly reported girls sitting towards the back in computer classes, boys sitting with the right hand nearest the mouse, and girls being bullied away from control of the machine even though they express interest and then frustration at not being allowed to contribute (Culley, 1988; Barbieri and Light, 1992; Beynon, 1993). This influence is seen in the low level of co-operation between members of mixed-gender groups.

Comparisons between groups and individuals working on the same task suggest productivity advantages for small groups of children, but the effectiveness of the work is sometimes associated with the composition of the group (Fletcher, 1985; Chi *et al.*, 1989; Underwood *et al.*, 1990; Howe *et al.*, 1992). In our previous investigation of children working in pairs on a cloze problem-solving task with the infant TRAY program, we found that mixed-gender pairs were outperformed on a number of measures (Underwood *et al.*, 1990). A study of young children's programming with a floor turtle found a different pattern of results, however, with girl/girl pairs at a disadvantage (Hughes and Greenhough, 1989). Yelland's (1995) attempted replication of this result, though initially successful, went on to show that the poor performances of girl-only pairings disappeared over time and equally significantly depended upon the criteria for success. Girls were slower but less error prone, and on this basis could be considered to be more successful than the boy-only pairs.

In general when pairs of children solve a problem together, they think more effectively than when they work alone, but this may not be true for all tasks and for all gender combinations. The evidence from our work on problem-solving tasks such as TRAY (a cloze task) or KidSim (a graphical-programming environment) conforms to this view. At first sight working in groups appears less likely to affect children's learning with less problem-oriented but equally interactive programs such as Living Books (a multi-media reading-development application). Further, from our observations of the same children with TRAY and with a floor turtle there were indeed differences in the nature of co-operation during performance (Underwood *et al.*, 1993b). This leads to the suggestion that the task is an important factor in levels of co-operation and in learning outcomes. Here we examine how different tasks support or encourage different levels of interaction. The absence of group-facilitation effects may be associated with any one specific task but does it afford the opportunity for individuals to interact with other members of the group?

Levels of co-operation and learning outcomes

A key aim of our work has been to identify the characteristics of co-operative and collaborative working that can be used to predict performance. What kinds of discussion are associated with performance enhancement? In our own controlled interventions in schools we have analysed the dialogue between the children within our groups to establish the level of co-operation or collaboration between the children. Each statement of the dialogue between children as they negotiate their way through the task has been categorised according to the Bales (1950) Interaction Analysis schedule that breaks discussion into four main types – group agreement, offers suggestions/answers, asks for suggestions/answers, and group disagreement. Within each of these four categories there are three sub-types, making twelve possible statement categories in all:

Positive socio-emotional comments

>A1 shows solidarity (e.g., offers a reward)
>A2 shows tension release (e.g., jokes)
>A3 agrees (e.g., concurs, complies)

Task-specific help

>B4 gives a suggestion (e.g., a direction)
>B5 gives an opinion (e.g., evaluates)
>B6 gives orientation (e.g., clarifies or repeats)

Task-specific requests

>C7 asks for orientation (e.g., requests information)
>C8 asks for an opinion (e.g., requests an evaluation)
>C9 asks for a suggestion (e.g., requests possible ways of acting)

Negative socio-emotional comments

>D10   disagrees (e.g., withholds help; shows passive rejection)
>D11   shows tension (e.g., withdraws)
>D12   shows antagonism (e.g., deflates other's status)

These classifications undoubtedly have their problems. There are difficulties in classifying some comments within the four broad categories, with some ambiguity between D10 and D11, for example. On the other hand, some of the categories seem to be too narrow in some situations, and B4, for example, may need to be further divided according to the focus of the suggestion being made. Furthermore, it can be argued that the Interaction Analysis was designed for the classification of comments in free discussion and that it has limited validity for groups working with a tool such as a computer. We have found little difficulty in using it with our pairs of children, however, and have found the task-specific help (B statements) and the task-specific requests (C statements) to be particularly valuable indicators of problem-focused discussion. For some studies we have needed to augment the Interaction Analysis to take account of who has use of the mouse and who has use of the keyboard, in recognition of the uneven distribution of power within a pair. The Bales classification is valuable, all the same, and can not only be used to predict successful task performance, but can also be used to help us understand the process by which dialogue facilitates the group's coming to grips with a task. Gillies and Ashman (1996) have also found a modified version of the Bales classification to be valuable in their analysis of co-operative group learning in classrooms.

   We have found a number of differences between the pairs using this analysis (Underwood and Underwood, 1995) and this is pointing towards an explanation of some of the performance differences. For example, in the version of the TRAY task where all pairs of children were told to collabo-rate, the girl/girl pairs offered more suggestions than the other pairs, particularly offering more evaluation and analysis. So far as negative socio-emotional comments were concerned, the boy/girl pairs offered them more often than the other pairs, suggesting that they were disagreeing with each other more, and showing tension and antagonism. These results are in general agreement with other observations in the literature, with boy/girl pairs tending to talk less about the task and with one partner dominant, especially with the boy partner taking control of the keyboard/mouse.

Our observations of children's discussions while they were programming with KidSim, a graphical-programming environment, found a number of relationships with specific components of the programming task. We have described some of the problems of having children write programs elsewhere (Gilmore *et al*, 1995; Underwood *et al.*, 1996b). Briefly, these problems fall into the categories of repetitive rule-writing, failing to debug the program, rules that are too specific by virtue of having too large a spotlight, and system specific problems (system speed, system crashes). The children had little difficulty in using the program, and this is indicated by our need to use time-to-complete as the dependent measure in the programming exercise, because all groups succeeded. As in the previous TRAY studies, the nature of the discussions between children was related to task performance. Barbieri and Light (1992) have reported relationships between discussions of planning, the integration of information and negotiation between group members and performance in a spatial problem-solving task. This study also found that discussion of the task predicted performance. The total amount of time necessary to complete a given programming exercise showed a simple correlation with the number of statements per second in which the pairings gave opinion/analysis, expressed feelings and wishes, but the regres-sion analysis also highlighted the importance of tension-releasing statements on good performance. An example of dialogue from one group illustrating these statements is as follows:

		Bales Category
Ian	That and that . . . goes . . . and that one's gotta go there though 'cos otherwise he's just gonna not know what to do.	B5
Tom	Which one's that? Let's have a look.	C8
Ian	Have we done everything else?	B5
Tom	Right.	A3
Ian	Do I get a go?	B5
Tom	You can't do it.	D12
Ian	It's 'cos . . . it's when you do this . . .	D11
Tom	Ha ha.	A2

As with the TRAY task, statements of antagonism (D12) lead to reduced performance with the programming task, in this case the measure being increased time to solve the problem at hand. However, the most successful account of performance was with rule testing in which pairs who felt able to express opinions and to analyse the situation (B5) and expressed agreement and understanding (A3) outperformed other groups. The following extract illustrates a discussion during rule testing:

Bales Category

Duncan	. . . along the ground, so we need to stretch it down one, don't we?	B5
Steven	Yeh.	A3
Julian	Click on that.	B4
Duncan	Elastic man!	A2
Steven	Why isn't it grabbing?	C8
Julian	'Cos you need to click that.	B5

The clear result from this study is that when children work in groups around a computer their discussions are task-oriented. The amount of time spent testing programmed rules was predicted almost entirely by two categories of dialogue – the number of opinions expressed and the number of affirmative comments. Very little of the discussion during rule testing concerns anything but the evaluation of those rules. Offering opinions and suggestions also accounted for most of the variance in total programming time, and in time spent writing the rules. The common feature of these relationships is that the discussion is reflecting the needs of each task.

Lee (1993) adds to our understanding of effective group work. Her work is with children of 9 to 12 years of age working on the problem-solving adventure game 'Where in the world is Carmen Sandiego?'. Her children worked in groups of four with one of the following gender structures:

- All girl (4Gs) or all boy (4Bs)
- Girl dominated foursome (3Gs:1B)
- Boy dominated foursome (1G:3Bs)
- Equal ratios (2Gs:2Bs)

Lee found major differences in the nature of the interaction between the children in single-sex groups. In girl-only groups there was increased overall interaction, a willingness to ask for help and just as importantly a willingness to provide that help. This was not so for the all-boy groups, but the boys in mixed gender groups talked more and asked for and received support for the group. Disturbingly the girls in mixed-gender groups talked less and, in male-dominated groups (1G:3Bs), were unlikely to receive help from the group. Any help that the girls in these groups did receive tended to be inadequate.

A final important point is that girls made far fewer negative emotional statements than boys in Lee's study. Boys were particularly prone to make negative comments in all-boy groups, but when a girl was present the number of negative comments declined and in the female-dominated group (3Gs:1B) no negative comments were made at all by either sex! This contradicts one of our findings but may be explained by the size of the groups. In mixed pairs the boy can dominate but it is less easy for a single boy to dominate a mixed foursome. The girls gain strength from each other.

The findings in the KidSim study are very similar to those of our TRAY studies and of Lee's adventure game. In these three problem-solving environments, pairs who talked constructively together, introducing knowledge and ideas to the other member and accepting information from their partner, outperformed those who did not. In the TRAY environment this was more likely to be girl-only groups, although boys would and could co-operate if encouraged to do so. Mixed-gender pairings were not able to interact. Organisational constraints meant that there were no mixed-gender pairings available to the KidSim study.

The third task we set children was to work in pairs through the Brøderbund CD-ROM storybook by Mark Brown, 'Arthur's Teacher Trouble' (Underwood and Underwood, 1996). The twenty-four screen-pages of the storybook follow the main character, Arthur, through a school spelling competition. At the start of each screen-page part of the text of the story is displayed and read aloud. In addition, a rich illustration of an appropriate part of the text is displayed. The user may then interact with different aspects of the display by a mouse-click. Both words and illustrations can be activated by clicking on them. Clicking on a word results in its pronunciation, either in isolation or together with other words. Clicking on a feature of the illustration results in an animation. Most of the objects in the illustration could be activated in this way – characters may provide dialogue or perform actions, and objects such as doors, toys and cookies perform some animated action.

The 'Arthur' program is highly interactive but less problem-oriented than our other tasks. An analysis of the dialogue between the pairs of children revealed that all-girl pairings showed more tension release by joking and laughing than did the other pairs (A2). Pairs of girls also asked each other for information and orientation more than did the other pairs (C7). Again we used multiple regression analyses to predict story comprehension on the basis of dialogue and screen interaction while working with the storybook. For the boy/boy pairs, there were three predictor variables in the order clicks on characters, clicks on animated features and clicks on words, but the quality of the dialogue did not contribute to performance outcomes. The regression analysis applied to the data from the girl/girl pairs failed to enter any predictor variables, and the regression equation for the mixed pairs found only one predictor, the extent of tension displays and comment indicating withdrawal (D11).

The above results are at variance with our findings in numerous TRAY studies and in the KidSim study, and also with other research in the field. One explanation could be that the task itself does not benefit from group collaboration, and that the main interaction is between child and screen rather than between members of the group. Further regression analyses used to predict performance on a story-recall task, which took place three weeks after completion of the intervention, revealed that predictors included screen interactions, dialogue and comprehension scores. There were no successful predictors for the boy/boy pairs or for the mixed pairs. However, the performance of girl/girl pairs was successfully predicted by three variables: Bales A1 (shows group solidarity), Bales B4 (gives suggestion), and comprehension score.

The robust recall of story events during free recall was especially noticeable in the stories written by girls who had been in girl/girl pairs. Furthermore, when girls worked on the storybook with boys their free recall was on a par with that of the boys. Accounting for this effect is not straightforward. The stories were written by individual children working in a quiet classroom. The CD-ROM storybook interactions were completed several weeks previously, and yet some aspect of the paired interaction appears to be associated with recall of the storybook. There were no gender pairing effects in the screen interactions – single-gender and mixed-gender pairs tended to click on similar screen features. There were also no gender-pairing effects in the comprehension task. The Bales analysis did reveal differences between the gender pairs while they were working with the storybook, however, and this may provide a clue as to why girls' memories are influenced by their working partner. Pairs of girls joked and laughed more than other pairs, and were also more likely to ask each other for information than the other pairs. They were more relaxed about working with a partner, they regarded their partner as a source of advice and information, and this had an outcome in their superior recall of the storybook. The regression analysis also found a relationship between the dialogue features of girl/girl pairs and their story recall, with dialogue indicating group solidarity and dialogue giving suggestions, both of which aided the prediction of story recall.

Conflict, co-operation or collaboration?

Children working in groups have significantly different experiences depending on their gender and the group composition. There may also be an influence of task. All our activities required the learners to participate actively but it was in the more problem-oriented tasks, such as TRAY, that children gained success through sharing their plans and ideas. In the non-problem-oriented tasks, such as Arthur, learners needed only to agree an etiquette of task behaviour for task completion to take place, that is they needed to co-operate but not necessarily to collaborate.

The recurring observation from natural classroom tasks is that boys see the computer as being in their domain, but classroom experiments find that in single-gender groups the girls perform as well if not better than boys. In our experience it is when boys and girls are paired together that they are most likely to perform poorly. Kruger's analysis of collaborative styles helps us to understand the dynamics of group interactions and their effects upon thinking skills. Her studies of paired reasoning showed that the nature of the discussion influenced subsequent performance. Pairs that offered suggestions to a problem, and considered each other's suggestions, did better in an individual test of reasoning administered later. In particular, it was the consideration of rejected solutions that was associated with the development of thinking.

Discussion provides the opportunity to compare ideas, and to evaluate suggestions, something that our girl/girl pairs were doing with little encouragement from us. Lee's girl foursomes were equally effective. In the case of our boy/girl pairs there was little discussion and unimpressive performance. If the girls in a foursome feel that they have group support as in a female-dominated group (3Gs:1B) then quality discussion can take place. The most effective thinkers justify their own ideas and also take account of their partner's suggestions, with the eventual rejection of failed solutions being the best indicator of new understanding.

Now that we know what current patterns of performance look like, and how children tend to discuss problems when working around a computer, we can encourage the kind of interaction that will result in the development of their powers of thinking. When we have observed mixed pairs working successfully together each child has been comfortable in offering suggestions and in analysing and evaluating each other's suggestions. This sense of trust and ease of working is very important if children are to feel safe in taking those risks inherent in opening up their thinking to the peer group and hence gaining that all-important feedback on their problem-solving strategies.

References

Bales, R. F. (1950) *Interaction Process Analysis*, Cambridge: MA: Addison-Wesley.

Barbieri, M. S. and Light, P. H. (1992) 'Interaction, gender and performance on a computer-based problem solving task', *Learning and Instruction* 2: 199–213.

Beynon, J. (1993) 'Computers, dominant boys and invisible girls: or, "Hannah, it's not a toaster, it's a computer!"', in J. Beynon and H. Mackay (eds) *Computers into Classrooms: More Questions than Answers*, London: Falmer Press.

Brown, J. S. (1990) 'Towards a new epistemology for learning', in C. Frasson and G. Gauthier (eds) *Intelligent Tutoring Systems: At the End Crossroads of AI and Education*, Norwood, NJ: Ablex Publishing.

Chi, M. T. H., Bassok, M., Lewis, M. W., Reimann, P. and Galser, R. (1989) 'Self-explanations: how students study and use examples in learning to solve problems', *Cognitive Science* 13: 145–182.

Clements, D. H. and Nastasi B. K. (1985) 'Effects of computer environments on social emotional development: Logo and computer aided instruction', *Computers in the Schools* 1: 11–31.

Culley, L. (1988) 'Girls, boys and computers', *Educational Studies* 14: 3–8.

Fletcher, B. C. (1985) 'Group and individual learning of junior school children on a microcomputer-based task: social or cognitive facilitation', *Educational Review* 37: 251–261.

Gillies, R. M. and Ashman, A. F. (1996) 'Teaching collaborative skills to primary school children in classroom-based work groups', *Learning and Instruction* 6: 187–200.

Gilmore, D. J., Pheasey, K., Underwood, J. and Underwood, G. (1995) 'Learning graphical programming: an evaluation of KidSim™', in S. Arnesen, K. Nordby and D. Gilmore (eds) *Interact 95: Proceedings of the 5th IFIP Conference on HCI*, London: Chapman Hall.

Hawkins, J., Sheingold, K., Gearhart, M. and Berger, C. (1982) 'Microcomputers in schools: impact on the social life of elementary classrooms', *Journal of Applied Developmental Psychology* 3: 361–373.

Howe, C., Tolmie, A., Anderson, A. and Mackenzie, M. (1992) 'Conceptual knowledge in physics: the role of group interaction in computer-supported teaching', *Learning and Instruction* 2: 161–183.

Hughes, M. and Greenhough, P. (1989) 'Gender and social interaction in early LOGO use', in J. H. Collins, N. Estes, W. D. Gattis and D. Walker (eds) *The Sixth International Conference on Technology and Education* vol. 1. Edinburgh: CEP.

Kruger, A. C. (1993) 'Peer collaboration: conflict, co-operation or both?', *Social Development* 2: 165–182.

Lee, M. (1993) 'Gender, group composition and peer interaction in computer-based co-operative learning', *Journal of Educational Research* 9: 549–577.

O'Malley, C. (1992) 'Designing computer systems to support peer learning', *European Journal of Psychology of Education* 7: 339–352.

Papert, S. (1981) *Mindstorms: Children, Computers and Powerful Ideas*, Brighton: Harvester Press.

Pea, R. D. (1993) 'Practices of distributed intelligence and designs for education', in G. Salomon (ed.) *Distributed Cognitions: Psychological and Educational Considerations*, Cambridge: Cambridge University Press.

Piaget, J. (1952) *The Origins of Intelligence in Young Children*, New York: IUP.

Picardie, J. (1995) 'Have traditional schools had their day?', *The Independent on Sunday Review*, 2 April.

Rogoff, B. (1990) *Apprenticeship in Thinking: Cognitive Development in a Social Context*, New York: Oxford University Press.

Sutton, R. (1991) 'Equity and computers in the schools: A decade of research', *Review of Educational Research* 61: 475–503.

Teasley, S. and Roschelle, J. (1993) 'Construction of a joint problem space', in S. P. Lajoie and S. J. Derry (eds) *Computers as Cognitive Tools*, Hillsdale, NJ: Lawrence Erlbaum Associates.

Underwood, G. (1994) 'Collaboration and problem solving: gender differences and the quality of discussion', in J. Underwood (ed.) *Computer Based Learning: Potential into Practice*, London: David Fulton Publishers.

Underwood, G., Jindal, N. and Underwood, J. (1993a) 'Gender differences and effects of co-operation in a computer-based language task', *Educational Research* 36: 63–74.

Underwood, G., McCaffrey, M. and Underwood, J. (1990) 'Gender differences and effects of co-operation in a computer-based language task', *Educational Research* 32: 44–49.

Underwood, G., Underwood, J. and Turner, M. (1993b) 'Children's thinking during collaborative computer-based problem solving', *Educational Psychology* 13: 345–357.

Underwood, G., Underwood, J., Pheasey, K. and Gilmore, D. (1996b) 'Collaboration and discourse while programming the KidSim microworld simulation', *Computers and Education* 26: 143–151.

Underwood, J. and Underwood, G. (1990) *Computers and Learning: Helping Children Acquire Thinking Skills*, Oxford: Blackwells.

—— (1995) 'When do groups work? Effective collaborations with classroom computers', *NFER Topic* 14: 1–6.

—— (1996) 'Gender differences in children's learning from interactive books', in B. Robin, J. D. Price, J. Willis and D. A. Willis (eds) *Technology and Teacher Education Annual*, Charlottesville, VA.: AACE

Underwood, J., Cavendish, S., Dowling, S., and Lawson, T. (1996a) 'Integrated Learning Systems: a study of sustainable learning gains in UK schools', in J. Underwood and J. Brown (eds) *The Case for Integrated Learning Systems*, London: Heinemann.

Vygotsky, L. (1978) *Mind in Society: The Development of Higher Psychological Processes*, Cambridge, MA: Harvard University Press.

Yelland, N. (1995) 'Logo experiences with young children: describing performance, problem-solving and social contexts of learning', *Early Childhood Development and Care* 109: 61–74.

3 Productive interaction in the context of computer-supported collaborative learning in science

Christine Howe and Andrew Tolmie

Introduction

The research which we outline in this chapter seeks to identify crucial aspects of productive interaction within computer-based science work, and to examine how the computer itself might play a role in promoting these. Our interest in these issues stems from efforts within the educational literature to marry interaction and science, which led us initially to conduct studies in non-computing contexts. These studies exerted a vital influence on our thinking, and when we came to consider the potential role of computers, it was because of a desire to investigate in greater detail types of activity and styles of interaction which we already had reason to think were productive for science learning. Since the lessons of our earlier work were so influential, it is with a brief account of these that we begin. Thereafter, we shall describe our computer-based research in two parts, the first focusing on two studies which gave us a strong lead on the nature of productive interaction, and the second on two studies which cement a point emerging from the first part, that action in shared space can sometimes be as important for learning as social interaction.

Background research in non-computing environments

The issue of interaction and science first appeared in the educational literature more than ten years ago. Its emergence can be traced to the realisation that students come to science teaching with strong conceptions about the phenomena they will be studying (Driver and Erickson, 1983; Driver *et al.*, 1985), conceptions which are at variance with the received wisdom of science and which undermine its learning. A common example is the notion that objects move because they have forces imparted to them which they gradually expend, an idea which contradicts Newton's laws of motion. It quickly became recognised that shifting prior conceptions was a crucial task for teachers, and there was extensive discussion as to how this should be achieved. Several perspectives were brought to bear, but the one associated with Piaget undoubtedly carried the greatest weight. Particularly significant was Piaget's (1985) notion that conceptual growth depends on 'equilibration', that is the reconciliation of conflict between prior and newly experienced conceptions. This implies that students should be provided with ideas which conflict with their existing ones, but which, by virtue of not being too advanced, can be related to them; and that interaction between students ought to be productive, so long as conceptions differed and tasks were structured to draw differences out.

During the 1980s, attempts were made to apply Piagetian ideas about interaction to teaching programmes in science (Champagne *et al.*, 1983; Gilbert and Pope, 1986; Nussbaum and Novick, 1981). These programmes were thought to have succeeded, insofar as relatively good ideas were generated by students during the course of their discussions. However the impact of these ideas on the students' individual understanding was never evaluated, and this was a major limitation. In the first place, the education system is ultimately concerned with the learning of individuals, and not with group products. In the second, the Piagetian theory which the programmes espoused emphasised the *reconciliation* of new and existing ideas, meaning that progressive group products carried no guarantee of individual change. In recognition of these points, we began our research relating to science with three studies focusing on the implications for individual learning of interaction between students with differing conceptions (Howe *et al.*, 1990; Howe *et al.*, 1992b).

The three studies each involved administering individual pre-tests to over 100 primary school pupils aged 8–12 years, to ascertain their prior conceptions regarding the topics to be covered. In two studies the topic was object flotation; in the third it was motion down an incline. Based on their pre-test responses, the pupils were assigned to groups of four, such that prior conceptions within the group were either very similar or markedly different. The groups then worked together on tasks which were presented to them via workbooks and which had been carefully designed to draw prior conceptions out during the course of interaction and to ensure that differences of opinion were fully explored. Individual post-tests were administered to group participants several weeks after the group tasks, to ascertain the impact of the group experience upon individual understanding. The post-test performance of pupils who had worked in differing groups was consistently better than that of pupils who had worked in similar groups, although these pupils had not differed at pre-test. However, there were no discernible differences between the differing and similar groups in terms of group task ideas, and in any event these ideas were most often inferior to those observed during the post-tests with the pupils from differing groups.

On the face of it, these results were highly encouraging for the Piagetian perspective. When conceptions differed, interaction between students was productive as regards individual learning. Moreover, the lack of relation between group task and post-test performance not only signalled the dangers of using the former as the criterion of success; it also implied that individual learning was a protracted and largely private affair, consistent with the concept of equilibration. However, the studies were one degree removed from ordinary teaching experience in terms of both context and materials, and this raised questions about the generalisability of the results. On reflection, the issue of context seemed unproblematic: whilst there was no direct evidence that equivalent results would have been obtained had group activities parallel to ours been embedded in routine lessons, the teaching programmes (cited above) which stimulated our studies were classroom-based and teacher-led, and the associated patterns of interaction appeared to have been very similar to what we observed. The issue of materials was potentially more thorny. Although the combination of groups and workbook-based tasks undoubtedly has real-world parallels (Bennett, 1985), we were aware of an increasing tendency to use computer-based tasks for science teaching (Redish and Risley, 1990), in part because these are more practical for demonstrating and manipulating complex phenomena. Whilst work around computers naturally tends to involve groups (Jackson *et al.*, 1986; McAteer and Demissie, 1991), what was unclear from our point of view was the extent to which the presence of a computer would impinge upon or alter the productive elements of the interaction.

This in turn pointed up the fact that we were not actually sure what those elements were, given the absence of relation in our first three studies between group task ideas and subsequent learning. Did this mean that group interaction was only tangentially related to learning, perhaps acting as a catalyst to post-group activities, or did it mean that it was relevant but via a more subtle route than idea generation *per se*? The study of motion down an incline provided evidence against the first possibility: when questioned during the post-tests about their follow-up 'research' (reading about motion, trying things out or asking other people), most pupils denied doing anything, and the few exceptions did not stand out in terms of pre- to post-test change. The implication is that group interaction itself must have been the main force for change. If this were so, then detailed research was needed to demonstrate *how* it has its effects, using controlled circumstances to identify systematic variations in interaction, and looking for relationships between these and individual learning.

Putting these points together, the idea of research into collaborative science work around the computer had definite appeal. On the one hand, it presented a challenge to demonstrate the generalisability of our concepts regarding productive interaction. On the other, computer-based activity provided more controlled conditions for examining interaction than the use of workbooks: with a computer it is possible to ensure that key stages of a task cannot be jumped, by requiring specific responses to be made before access to the next screen is granted. Moreover, if we could identify the crucial elements of productive interaction obtained in computing contexts, this held out the possibility that active support for these could subsequently be deliberately built into software design. The research to be detailed in the next section attempted to address all these points.

Productive interaction and computer-based science

The research reported below had two specific aims: to explore a) whether individual learning is facilitated in computer environments by interaction between students whose conceptions differ; and b) whether the benefits are directly attributable to the interaction, and if so how. Because data relevant to the first aim have been reported in depth elsewhere (Howe *et al.*, 1992a; Howe *et al.*, 1995), we will focus here on the second aim only. Suffice it to say that the research gave unqualified support to the benefits of interaction where conceptions differ, the results obtained using workbooks being shown to generalise to computer environments. To meet the second aim, it was necessary to relate individual learning to interactive experiences. Thus the two studies maintained the individual pre-test/group task/individual post-test design of their predecessors, with learning gauged via pre- to post-test change. In addition, though, an exhaustive coding was made of task-relevant interaction occurring during the group session. The support for Piaget provided by our previous studies influenced our approach to coding, and directed us to hypotheses as to which features of interaction might prove productive. However, we were open to other possibilities, and in order to ensure any conclusions drawn were robust, we sought *correlational* evidence that interactive features were directly associated with pre- to post-test change.

Study I took object fall as its topic (Tolmie and Howe, 1993; Howe *et al.*, 1995) and Study II took relative speed (Howe *et al.*, 1992a). Both topics lie in an area where, due to the ephemeral nature of real-world motion, computers are particularly favoured for purposes of teaching (Redish and Risley, 1990), thus enhancing the face validity of using computers within the research and also the practical applicability of the results obtained. In both studies, the individual pre-tests were administered to over 100 participants, these being 12–15-year-old pupils in Study I and arts, science and social science undergraduates in Study II. The Study I pre-tests were presented in written form. They started with 'prediction' problems relating to objects which moved in horizontal, pendular or circular directions and then began to fall (see Figure 3.1). Examples included a golf ball rolling over a cliff, a conker falling from a string, sparks flying off a Catherine Wheel and a crate being dropped from a plane. The pupils were asked to draw the paths that the objects would follow from starting to fall until hitting the ground. Next came 'explanation' problems, which utilised four prediction scenarios but asked the pupils to indicate the forces that would be operating at the point of fall. The Study II pre-tests involved a series of computer-presented problems (see Figure 3.2). For these, the undergraduates watched two trains move across a screen, one at constant speed and one at variable, and predicted at which of three points the speeds would be the same. The distance-time information that was crucial for correct decisions could be obtained from a 'Help' facility but, whether this was accessed or not, the undergraduates were quizzed as to how they arrived at an answer.

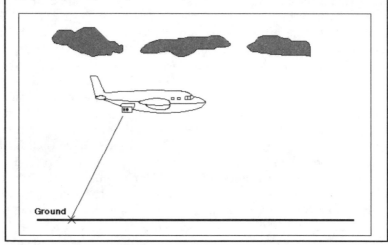

When there is an emergency and people are desperately short of food, aeroplanes bringing relief do not always land. Instead, they fly low without losing speed and drop the food in heavy crates. Suppose the plane pictured below was travelling in the direction shown and dropped a crate from its hatch. Indicate where the crate would be when it hit the ground, and show the path it would follow as it fell through the air. Use X to show where the crate would end up and remember to show the path from the hatch to the ground.

Ground

Figure 3.1 Example of paper-and-pencil prediction problem in Study I plus typical response

Pre-test responses were then scored. With Study I, responses to the prediction problems were awarded 'prediction scores' from 0 to 5, the correct response (a parabolic path in the direction of the pre-fall motion) scoring 5. Responses to the explanation problems were awarded 'conception scores' from 0 to 6 according to the number of relevant forces (for example, gravity and wind resistance) specified and used appropriately. With Study II, prediction scores were obtained from decisions about where the speed was the same, these decisions being awarded either 1 or 0 depending on whether or not they were correct. Conception scores were obtained from the justifications which the undergraduates offered for making decisions, and ranged from 0 to 5, with high scores depending on reference to distance travelled per unit time. The emphasis of the studies was on conceptual growth, and thus the conception scores were identified as focal with regard to pre- to post-test change. However, both conception and prediction scores were considered when the students were subsequently assigned to groups. For both studies, grouping meant pairing, with forty-one pairs in Study I and forty-eight in Study II. The pairs were formulated such that they were similar on both conception and prediction scores, similar on one score and different on the other, or different on both scores.

The pairs worked on the group tasks between five and eight weeks after the pre-tests. The tasks were computer-presented, and consisted of a series

a) Initial problem display

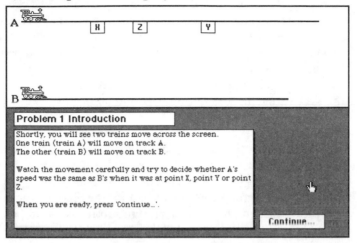

b) Display of distance/time information

Figure 3.2 Extracts from computer-based pre-test for Study II

of problems with a predict–test–explain format of the kind employed in our non-computerised studies, so as to provide as close a parallel between the two contexts as possible. Each problem related to a pre-test item, and began by asking the pairs to compare the predictions they had made previously. This involved returning pre-test answer booklets in Study I and preparing printouts of pre-test decisions in Study II. After comparing, the pairs were requested to discuss and agree joint predictions, and input these by clicking on-screen. They were then given feedback as to accuracy, a trace of the correct path for Study I (see Figure 3.3) and 'Well done, that's the correct answer' or 'Sorry that's the wrong answer' for Study II. Finally, they were asked to discuss why things turned out the way they did. The group tasks were introduced by research workers who remained for the first few items, ensuring that the procedure was grasped and the software could be operated. Thereafter, the pairs were left on their own, with a videotape running to record their interaction.

All group participants were given individual post-tests, these taking place one to two weeks after the tasks in Study I and about three weeks after in Study II. The materials used for the post-tests and the procedures followed were identical to the pre-tests, and the post-test responses were scored using pre-test principles. As noted already, learning was to be determined with reference to pre- to post-test change, and the emphasis was upon conceptual rather than prediction growth. Thus, mean conceptual scores per problem were computed for each group participant first for the pre-test responses and then for the post-test, and pre-test means were subtracted from post-test to give measures of change. Pre- to post-test change was positive, indicating that learning had occurred and, as noted already, was particularly marked under conceptual difference.

How, then, were the effects achieved? Was the interaction between peers directly relevant and, if so, was its influence consistent with the Piagetian theory which the results ostensibly support? As noted earlier, our approach to finding out involved correlating individual pre- to post-test change with various features of the group task interaction. Full details of the features can be obtained from Howe *et al.* (1992a), and Tolmie and Howe (1993). However in brief, they reflected: (a) quality of group decisions, via 'prediction scores' for the joint predictions, and, in the case of Study II where it was more obvious, 'conception scores' (both obtained using the relevant pre- and

Comparison of joint prediction and correct solution

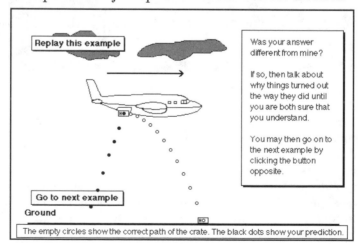

Figure 3.3 Extract from computer-based group task for Study I

post-test scales); (b) scrutiny of task materials, for example the perception of differences between pre-test predictions or between joint predictions and feedback; (c) discussion of the problems, for example the explication of underlying conceptions via references to explanatory factors, or the utilisation of prior experiences by references back to previous problems; and (d) the volume of dialogue, via total turns taken. For purposes of correlation, the prediction and conception scores were averaged across group task problems for each participating pair. The frequencies with which each of the other features occurred were totalled for each pair.

For Study I, the results initially looked disappointing: when the correlations between interactive features and pre- to post-test change were computed across all group participants, virtually none proved significant. However, as we were coding the video recordings, we were struck by perceptible differences between interactions which appeared to be associated with gender. Aware of research such as Siann and McLeod (1986) and Underwood *et al.* (1990) which suggests that gender is a major determinant of computer-based interaction, we decided to repeat the correlations taking account of gender composition. We had thirteen male pairs in our sample, twelve female and sixteen mixed, and fortunately they were more or less evenly distributed across our differing and similar combinations. When gender was taken into consideration, clear differences in the patterns of productive interaction emerged.

Pre- to post-test change in the male pairs was associated with prediction score ($r = +0.57$, df $= 21$, $p < 0.01$), and, within the group task, prediction score was directly influenced by references to conceptual material, particularly when interpreting feedback ($r = +0.46$, df $= 11$, $p = 0.06$). References to conceptual material at the feedback stage were associated in turn with the perception of differences between joint predictions and feedback ($r = +0.47$, df $= 11$, $p = 0.05$), suggesting that for the males exchanges like the following were characteristic of progress:

Alan: Well, we got that one completely wrong.

Barry: I was thinking of the speed it was travelling at. It would have had more arc and travelled up. You're saying that the weight would have pulled it straight down.

The implication is that discussions along these lines boosted prediction scores during the group task and this fed into conceptual understanding as revealed in pre- to post-test change. This means, though, that as with our earlier research in non-computer environments, it was the process of discussing and working out the answers that mattered, rather than the precise quality of that discussion.

This particular pattern did not obtain, however, with the female pairs or the mixed. With the female pairs, prediction scores were unrelated to pre- to post-test change, although references to conceptual material were. Indeed references at the feedback stage (r = +0.37, df = 20, p < 0.05) and the prediction stage (r = +0.42, df = 20, p < 0.05) were both associated with pre- to post-test change. Both also tended to be correlated with references back to the conceptual content of previous problems (in each case r = +0.48, df = 10, p = 0.06), meaning that for these groups exchanges like the following were typical of productive interaction:

Jane: I think it'll fall straight down; it's heavy.
Beth: But the crate was heavy and it didn't fall straight down.

With the female pairs, it looks then as if there was a straightforward relation between conceptual discussion and conceptual growth. However, remembering that it was the *frequency* of references to conceptual material that was related to pre- to post-change, the quality of the conceptual discussion was apparently beside the point once again. It was also beside the point in the mixed pairs, but for a different reason: here none of the interactive features were associated with pre- to post-test change, and the total number of dialogue turns was considerably reduced (Male mean of 430 turns = Female mean of 400 turns > Mixed mean of 281 turns, F = 9.50, df = 2, 70, p < 0.001). This last result appeared to reflect the fact that males and females of this age find working together an awkward social experience.

Study II was restricted to male and female pairs, with equal numbers of each gender composition. Features of group interaction were correlated significantly with pre- to post-test change for both the male and the female pairs, but unlike Study I, the patterns of correlation did not vary as a function of gender composition. In fact, as Figure 3.4 shows, the patterns were not simply equivalent but on two counts at least extremely interesting. First, group conception scores were strongly predictive of pre- to post-test change. Thus, for the first time in our research and after four studies which pointed to the contrary, we obtained evidence that group performance was playing a significant role. Second, features of interaction which were predictive of pre- to post-test change with either the male pairs or the female pairs only in Study I turned out to be predictive of pre- to post-test change with both the male and the female pairs in Study II. Differences between group predictions and feedback look from Figure 3.4 to be contexts for references to conceptual material for all groups, as they were for only the male pairs in Study I. However, references back to the conceptual content of previous problems also enter into the equation, and these were relevant only for the female pairs within Study I. Moreover, it was references back (that is, the co-ordination of ideas across problems to form a more generalised understanding) which strongly predicted group conception scores, suggesting once more that it was what the Study II groups produced from discussion that was important rather than the process of discussion *per se*. Unlike Study I, references to conceptual material played no direct part in promoting change, although such discussion, spurred on by disagreements over predictions and conceptions, must have provided the crucial context for the co-ordination of ideas.

Taking the results of the two studies together, it is clear that group inter-action played a direct role in learning. It is also clear that the computer, far from interfering with the process of interaction, actually facilitated its productive aspects by structuring discussion and providing feedback on joint solutions. At the same time, though, it appears as if there was an optimum style of interaction which spanned the two topic areas, and which was fully attained in some cases in Study II but which was never more than partially attained in Study I. This style is represented in Figure 3.4, and can be taken as what our work suggests constitutes productive peer interaction in computer-based contexts in science (and thus what software design ought to attempt to support). However, is this style essential to optimise learning? If we had only looked at same-sex pairs, we should probably have said 'yes', but Study I included mixed pairs and, as noted already, interaction in these pairs was not predictive of learning. If this were because the mixed pairs failed even to approximate the Figure 3.4 pattern, with the consequence that their learning was impaired, we might be justified in arguing that we had

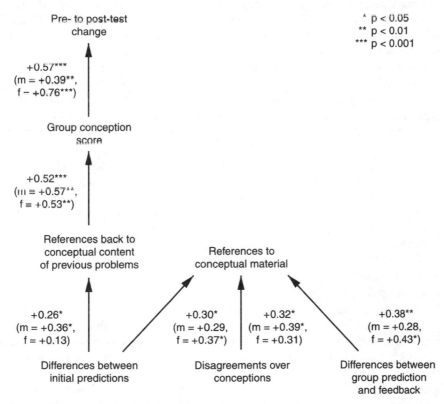

Figure 3.4 Pattern of correlation between interaction and pre- to post-test change in Study II

uncovered something essential. Unfortunately, this was not so. In the first place, the mixed pairs produced some of the intercorrelations between dialogue features which appear in Figure 3.4. For instance, disagreements over conceptions were associated with references to conceptual material ($r = +0.61$, df = 14, $p < 0.01$), which were associated to some extent with differences between initial predictions ($r = +0.36$, df = 14, $p < 0.1$), suggesting that like the male and female pairs some mixed pairs showed partial approximation to the putative ideal. The trouble was that this had no bearing on learning. In addition though, the mixed pairs in Study I did not differ from their male and female counterparts in terms of pre- to post-test change ($F = 2.14$, df = 2,70, p n.s.), meaning that their learning was not impaired.

Thus, we have what appear to be curious results. We have identified a style of interaction which benefited one set of pairs when it occurred and handicapped them when it was absent, but which had no apparent relevance to a second set of pairs who had age- and task-equivalents within the first set. Hunting for an explanation, we wondered whether the key lay within student perceptions. Perhaps the students in the first set perceived their interactions as relevant to learning, and hence paid attention to what they were saying. Perhaps the students in the second set regarded their interactions as irrelevant, noting possibly the fact already reported that dialogue was reduced and inferring an impoverished experience. We had no direct evidence to support this gloss (and still do not have any). However, we have found further signs of students varying over the significance of interaction within the learning process, which has made us think that we are along the right lines. One of these signs emerged from a study (Tolmie *et al.*, 1993) which returned to the workbook format of our earliest research. In this study, we compared the effectiveness of contrasting task designs within an overall predict–test–explain structure. One design required forced choices as part of the explanatory stage, for example choices between 'How heavy an object is doesn't matter to floating and sinking' and 'An important thing for floating and sinking is how heavy an object is'. We found that these forced choices undermined the interactive experiences entirely, almost as if the closure achieved in making the choices ended the 'cognitive work'.

This still begs an important question, however. Even if altered perceptions do explain why the mixed pairs in Study I were apparently uninfluenced by their social interaction, it remains the case that they learnt as much as the male and female pairs. What was it then that was producing this learning? If it was not the interaction, then it seems that it must have been the mental activity involved in thinking about the problems and/or the feedback. Consistent with this, there was no sign that the mixed pairs treated the entry of answers into the computer with any less care than the other groups, and yet it was typically carried out on an individual basis, turn and turn about, whilst the other looked on; in fact, for these groups the least interaction on any stage of the task took place at this point. This should not be taken to mean, however, that the task had been reduced to parallel individual activity: such explicit turn-taking would only have occurred if it had still been perceived to be shared. This implies that group activity might still have been an influence on learning in the absence of dialogue: provided interrelated actions were sufficient to create a joint focus of attention, another person's actions could be as much a cause of reflection as their statements. This suggests that group learning can take place either through verbal interaction or through action in a shared space, and that computer environments are capable of supporting *both* processes. The notion of computer support for this second element, group learning by action, is the focus of the section to follow.

Action and interaction with hypothesis-testing software

The computer support in question related to hypothesis testing, an aspect of science which another of our studies (Howe *et al.*, 1993) had shown to be extremely challenging. In that study, we found that only a small minority of 9- to 14-year-olds appreciated that to investigate ideas it is necessary to manipulate variables one by one with all other variables held constant. An equally small minority appreciated how the outcomes they predicted or observed would bear on the ideas being investigated, and, reminiscent of Study I, the ability to compare across cycles of testing and draw overall conclusions was truly exceptional. Recognising such difficulties, we developed software to support the hypothesis-testing process in two contexts, water pressure and shadow formation. This software required groups to generate ideas regarding causal variables. It then invited them to design experiments to test their ideas, and to input their decisions regarding key design features and eventual conclusions. Inappropriate decisions triggered prompting, and, whilst we anticipated some role for dialogue, it was this shaping of activity via prompting that we expected to be the mainstay of learning. The usefulness of the software was evaluated in two studies, one (Study III) focusing on the water-pressure implementation and the other (Study IV) on the shadows. Both studies compared the change from individual pre-tests to individual post-tests of pupils who worked with 'supported' software as sketched above and pupils who worked with an 'unsupported' alternative which lacked the prompting.

Pupils aged 9 to 14 years were pre-tested in both studies, with the pre-test being divided into two parts, the first establishing the variables which the pupils regarded as relevant within the topic area being considered, and the second ascertaining how they would determine if their beliefs were correct. For Study III, the first part involved a researcher demonstrating that when a stopper was removed from the side of a bottle, the water inside would spurt a particular distance. With reference to other bottles with stoppers in their sides, the pupils were quizzed as to whether hole height, bottle width, bottle shape, water frothiness and water colour would make a difference to distance travelled. For Study IV, the first part involved demonstrating that a triangle positioned at a certain distance from a lamp and a screen would project a shadow of a particular size. With reference to other triangles and distances, the pupils were quizzed as to the relevance of triangle size, triangle position, triangle colour, lamp position and lamp brightness. For both studies, the second part involved the pupils explaining: (a) which variables they *planned* to manipulate to test their beliefs regarding one of the variables from the first part; (b) how they would *manipulate* the equipment to make their test; (c) what they would *predict* when they made the manipulation and what this would tell them about their beliefs; (d) what they *observed* from testing and what this told them about their beliefs; (e) how the outcome of the present test *compared* with the outcome of previous tests relating to the variable; (f) what they would *conclude* overall regarding the variable. Subsequent to the pre-tests, the pupils' explanations to all these items were scored on scales from 1–4.

For Study III, ninety-four of 100 pre-tested pupils were assigned to twenty-five small groups (n = 3–5), with thirteen groups allocated to work with the supported software and twelve with the unsupported. For Study IV, 112 of 120 pre-tested pupils were assigned to foursomes, with fourteen groups allocated to work with the supported software and fourteen with the unsupported. Assignment to groups was at random from within a school class, as was assignment of groups to software types. The groups came one by one to a separate classroom a few weeks after the pre-tests, to be introduced to the software and the computer by a researcher who remained in the room throughout to deal with any difficulties. Regardless of software type, the groups were directed by the computer through sequences which paralleled the second part of the relevant pre-tests and which required equivalent activities on bottles or triangles present in the room (see Figure 3.5 for examples of the on-screen instructions). The groups were asked to explore the relevance of two variables in turn, and were permitted to carry out as many test cycles as they considered necessary. The software brought the activity to an end by asking the groups to draw conclusions about the variables they had investigated and to say whether or not they could draw conclusions about variables which they had not tested. Video records were made of group interaction, and coded later for a range of features. Some features, for example 'refers to previous test', were inspired by Studies I and II. Others were specific to the hypothesis-testing context, for example 'makes appropriate (or inappropriate) suggestion regarding the setting of the equipment' and 'relates activity to principles of hypothesis testing'.

At each stage of the task, the computer monitored group activity by requesting decisions to be registered on-screen. This information was saved to allow calculation of time spent on task, number of on-screen responses, time spent and number of responses made whilst deciding manipulations, total number of tests carried out, number of valid tests conducted, number of accurate reports of outcome, and number of appropriate conclusions.

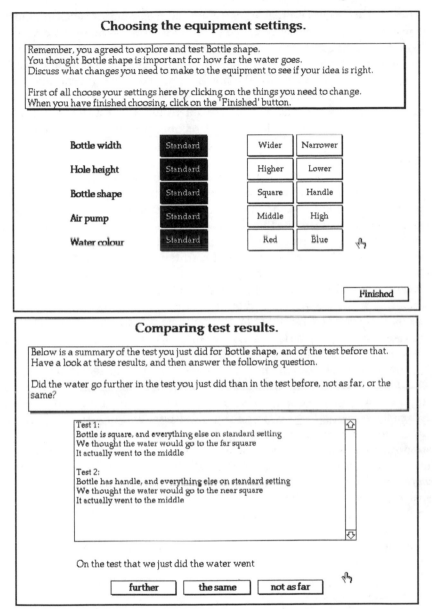

Figure 3.5 Sample screens directing hypothesis-testing activity for Study III

The on-screen responses were also used to guide the prompting which was the key difference between the supported and unsupported software. The prompting was inspired by Wood's (1989) notion of 'contingent control', and occurred whenever the supported groups departed from the hypothesis-testing ideal. This included failures to engage in valid testing (that is, failure to manipulate the variable being tested whilst holding all others constant), inconsistencies between predictions and initial ideas, inaccuracies in reports of test results, and erroneous conclusions. Two levels of prompt were used. The first level indicated that there was a problem, and asked the group to discuss their decision further. If after this responses were still inappropriate, a second-level prompt detailed the precise nature of the problem and again requested discussion (see Figure 3.6). If errors were repeated a third time, they were accepted and activity proceeded to the next stage. Correct decisions were met with positive feedback. A record was kept by the computer of the first and second level prompts issued, and the stage of activity at which they occurred.

About three weeks after the group sessions for Study III, and five weeks after for Study IV, group participants were post-tested using the same procedure as the pre-test, except that the second part focused on a different variable. Post-test responses to the second part were scored as before, and individual change on each of the six measures thus obtained was calculated by subtraction. These values were not on first sight encouraging. In Study III there was only significant pre- to post-test progress in comparisons and conclusions, and in neither case was the difference in change between the supported and unsupported conditions statistically significant. The picture was marginally better for Study IV, in that there was significant pre- to post-test advance on all measures, but again, except for comparisons, both conditions had equal impact on change.

However, closer examination of on-task activity and its relationship to change was again fruitful, revealing two important points. First, the supported software unquestionably made a difference to group performance, especially with regard to carrying out valid tests and drawing appropriate conclusions. For instance, in Study III the groups who worked with the supported software conducted thirty-three valid tests in total, as against three in the unsupported condition; in Study IV the corresponding figures were forty-four and nineteen. This was despite the fact that, on average, the supported groups conducted slightly *fewer* test cycles. Similarly, in both studies the supported groups drew between 40 and 50 per cent more appropriate conclusions than the unsupported, and this appeared to be a direct consequence of the greater number of valid tests, since the two were positively correlated (for Study III, $r = +0.45$, $df = 22$, $p < 0.05$; for Study IV, $r = +0.58$, $df = 26$, $p < 0.005$). The second point was that for those in the supported groups, carrying out valid tests apparently contributed directly to learning. In Study IV, change for these pupils on all measures except comparisons was positively and significantly associated with the number of valid tests carried out during the group sessions; and whilst the same strength of relationship was not apparent in Study III, in all instances the correlations remained positive.

Given this evidence, it was unclear why pupils in the supported conditions showed no greater pre- to post-test gain than pupils in the unsupported; and perhaps relatedly, why the benefits were in general weaker in Study III than

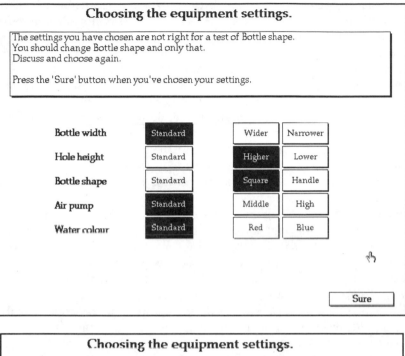

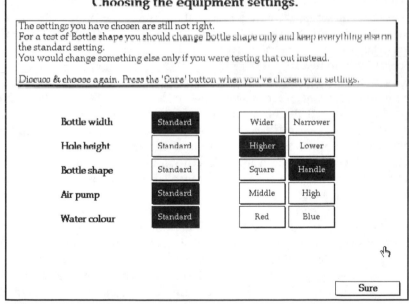

Figure 3.6 Examples of first- and second-level prompts for Study III

in Study IV. Further analysis of on-task activity suggested at least partial answers to both questions. The better performance of the supported groups with regard to conducting valid tests could only be attributable to the prompting provided by the software, since there was no other difference between the two conditions. However, it was clear that the prompts had not worked in a straightforward fashion. One indication of this was that they had a relatively low success rate: in Study III, less than a quarter of the prompts issued by the computer during the setting up of tests were followed by a valid test; in Study IV, the figure was slightly better, but it was still less than 30 per cent. What was more surprising, though, was that a considerable proportion of the valid tests that did occur took place without prompting, but on test cycles *after* prompts had been issued: in Study III, 36 per cent of valid tests occurred in this fashion; in Study IV, this rose to 52 per cent. From inspection of the videotapes, it became clear that the prompts had typically caused confusion when they were first issued. Up to this point, groups had often been happily discussing what their tests should look like, and coming up with joint formulations of how to proceed. The warning from the computer that they were on the wrong track tended to have an intrusive effect, breaking up the dialogue, and producing puzzled requests for alternative ideas and inappropriate suggestions. What appeared to put activity back on track was that on subsequent test cycles, perhaps after a number of prompts had been issued, one or other of the group members would suddenly have an insight into what was required (that is, that only the variable being tested should be manipulated), and they would take over direction of the group, if only temporarily, to show the others what to do. The discontinuation of prompting then served as a signal that this was the appropriate strategy, and activity would be carried forward more or less successfully from there.

One notable point about this pattern of activity was the resemblance it bore to what we had observed with the mixed pairs in Study I. What had apparently mattered for both group performance and individual learning was one person's actions, the computer feedback on that action, and the other group members' active observation of this sequence. Dialogue, which seemed in general to be at a lower level than in our previous group tasks, made no discernible positive contribution to either activity or learning. In a sense then, we had successfully established the potential of computer support for group learning by action, and yet plainly this potential was qualified. Prompting of action by the computer, at least in this form and this context, proved a double-edged sword, since its benefits were reliant on individual insight, which might not always occur (it did not for some younger groups), it failed to promote conceptual dialogue, which might be needed to consolidate this insight, and it provoked unproductive dialogue, which might actually get in the way. It was this implication that prompting could be a hindrance as well as a help that seemed to us to explain in part why the supported groups eventually did little better than the unsupported. One point in favour of this explanation was that it was entirely consistent with the weaker showing of those in the supported condition in Study III. This version of the software contained a number of sequences of prompted activity (for example with regard to initial plans about what variables ought to be manipulated) which were absent from the version used in Study IV. It would fit in with the broader picture if this greater profusion of prompting had tipped the balance more squarely in favour of its negative effects.

Conclusions

The studies reported above confirmed some of our hypotheses about group work, but also turned up a number of unexpected results. For instance, they helped us to isolate key elements of productive group interaction, and these were in many respects in line with what we had anticipated. The consistencies between Studies I and II and our earlier work suggest further that these findings have good generalisability, and that the main elements of productive interaction will often be the same in both computing and non-computing contexts. There was also some support for our intuition that the computer may facilitate productive interaction in a way that other media cannot, by dint of its capacity to maintain a clear task structure and to provide feedback. However, the studies also showed that in some contexts interaction may be of marginal significance, with shared action being crucial instead. It would appear that such contexts may be defined by a variety of factors, not all of which are readily controllable. Even here, though, the computer may still have a central role to play.

To enlarge on these points, Studies I and II both show that the single most important element of productive interaction is discussion of individual group members' conceptions of the material in hand. This fits neatly with our original studies and explains why greatest progress occurred when students with differing ideas worked together. It is also, as far as it goes, entirely consistent with the Piagetian theory that inspired those studies: conceptual growth would be expected to depend on the experience of conflicting ideas via discussion. Moreover, in Study I it appeared to be the *process* rather than the quality of discussion that mattered, as Piaget would anticipate. Amongst the female pairs for instance it was the frequency of reference to conceptual material that was associated with growth, consistent with the idea that lengthier discussion of differing ideas led to greater mental conflict, and eventually a more far-reaching conceptual reconciliation.

However, for the undergraduates in Study II discussion of conceptions was important only as a context for generating ideas; what mattered for learning was the co-ordination of these ideas and the application of the resulting product to the problems being dealt with. This pattern is more consistent with the model of Doise and Mugny (1984), which, following Piaget, emphasises conflicting individual conceptions, but predicates learning on the negotiation of superior conceptions which are then internalised, and not on the individual reconciliation of ideas. Taken together, the results from Studies I and II might indicate a progression from a

Piagetian pattern of productive interaction to one which is more in keeping with Doise and Mugny. After all, whilst the performance of the same-sex pairs in Study I was in line with Piaget, it contained some elements of the Study II pattern: the male pairs attempted to test whether negotiated ideas worked better, and the female pairs co-ordinated ideas across problems. However, it may not simply be age which brings about a shift in interactional pattern. The differences between the male and female pairs are consistent with broader gender differences in interactional style (Piliavin and Martin, 1978): faced with a difference of opinion, males tend to assert, elaborate and look for external evidence, whilst females tend to avoid contentious points and look for what they hold in common. These styles may not be rigidly gender-related, but this would still suggest that the undergraduates in Study II were mixing two basic patterns, and to do this they must have had sufficient exposure to both. In other words, which mode of productive interaction is adopted may depend on past interactional experience. The computer may have had an influence here too, however: the clear sequential structure it imposed on movement through the task, both within and between each problem, and the unambiguous feedback it provided on solutions may have made it substantially easier both to co-ordinate and test out different ideas, effectively promoting integration of different styles.

These lines of argument illustrate that even whilst focusing solely on interaction, research in the computing context has taken us beyond the Piagetian model with which we started. However, the emergent importance of shared action has taken us yet further afield. The effectiveness of the supported software in Studies III and IV appears consistent with a Vygotskian model, at least with regard to the impact of prompting on action. On the face of it, this is a classic instance of what Vygotsky (1978) termed the 'zone of proximal development'. Under the direction of a more knowledgeable other (in this case the computer) pupils' actions are taken beyond what they could achieve independently; individual learning occurs when pupils internalise this social direction, and become capable of reproducing it on their own. However, the mechanisms of reflection and insight which were apparently central to the effect of prompting are much less explicitly Vygotskian. Indeed, both this and the data relating to the mixed pairs in Study I seem to fit better with the neo-Vygotskian approach of authors such as Lave and Wenger (1991), which stresses observation and peripheral engagement in joint activity rather than the explicit shaping of action. As Lave and Wenger point out, in many learning contexts there is little observable teaching; instead the structure of work practices provides opportunities to develop views of what activities are about, and to become engaged with them. The important point about this perspective is that it suggests not only what the students were doing when they were involved in joint action, but what the *computer* was doing too, namely, creating the 'structure of work practices' which was both helping to shape student action and providing information about what was involved.

One conclusion to be drawn is that so far we have only managed to identify a *collection* of mechanisms involved in group work, not a unitary model. One future goal is to remedy this, and an important first step would be to establish which factors led to the different patterns reported here, in particular why interaction was focal in some contexts and shared action in others. In fact, our studies do suggest some leads. For instance, there were clear task differences between Studies I and II on the one hand, and Studies III and IV on the other. In the former, there were many cues to joint *interpretation* of the problem space, such as instructions to talk about why things turned out the way they did (see Figure 3.3). In Studies III and IV the focus was much more explicitly on the action of setting up and carrying out tests. However, even if task was an important factor, this can scarcely be the whole story, given the mixed pairs in Study I. Social unease occasioned by gender seemed important here, and there is other literature to support this notion. For example, research by Huguet and Monteil (1994) indicates that active effort on a task may vary according to the perceived abilities of co-performers, and that gender norms may have considerable impact on those perceptions (for instance, 'boys are good at science'). Similarly, in a survey of research on gender and classroom interaction, Howe (1996) notes extensive evidence that uncomfortable interactive experiences lead to compensatory learning strategies, but, as here, with no apparent detriment to learning. What is interesting about this is not only that it fits our observations, but that it suggests the *default* condition is learning from interaction.

By implication, a unified model of productive group work might need to establish how to promote shared action in a more positive fashion, and how to integrate it with interaction. However, no matter what that model turns out to look like, it is apparent from our studies that it will need to take into account both social or contextual factors *and* individual processes of cognition. Here, social exchange and joint action were crucial to group performance and individual learning, but at the same time individual perceptions, reflections and knowledge were key determinants of how interaction proceeded and what results it had. By concentrating on either group interaction or individual learning, much contemporary research tends to present these two types of factor as necessarily dichotomous, and representative of the opposing sides of a theoretical divide. We argue strongly that it is not only more informative to look at how group activity and individual cognition are related, but that in practice it is actually impossible to divorce the one from the other.

References

Bennett, N. (1985) 'Interaction and achievement in classroom groups', in N. Bennett and C. Desforges (eds) *Recent Advances in Classroom Research*, Edinburgh: Scottish Academic Press.

Champagne, A. B., Gunstone, R. and Klopfer, L. E. (1983) 'Effecting changes in cognitive structure amongst physics students', paper presented to *American Educational Research Association*, Montreal.

Doise, W. and Mugny, G. (1984) *The Social Development of the Intellect*, Oxford: Pergamon.

Driver, R. and Erickson, G. (1983) 'Theories in action: some theoretical and empirical issues in the study of students' conceptual frames in science', *Studies in Science Education* 10: 37–60.

Driver, R., Guesne, E. and Tiberghien, A. (1985) *Children's Ideas in Science*, Milton Keynes: Open University Press.

Gilbert, J. K. and Pope, M. L. (1986) 'Small group discussions about conceptions in science: a case study', *Research in Science and Technological Education* 4: 61–76.

Howe, C. J. (1996) 'Social interaction in primary and secondary classrooms: the gender dimension', report to Scottish Office Education and Industry Department.

Howe, C. J., Rodgers, C. and Tolmie, A. (1990) 'Physics in the primary school: peer interaction and the understanding of floating and sinking', *European Journal of Psychology of Education* 4: 459–475.

Howe, C. J., Tolmie, A., Anderson, A. and Mackenzie, M. (1992a) 'Conceptual knowledge in physics: the role of group interaction in computer-supported teaching', *Learning and Instruction* 2: 161–183.

Howe, C. J., Tolmie, A. and Rodgers, C. (1992b) 'The acquisition of conceptual knowledge in science by primary school children: group interaction and the understanding of motion down an incline', *British Journal of Developmental Psychology* 10: 113–130.

Howe, C. J., Tolmie, A. and Sofroniou, N. (1993) 'Hypothesis testing in nine- to fourteen-year-old children', paper presented at BPS Developmental Section Conference, Birmingham.

Howe, C. J., Tolmie, A. and Mackenzie, M. (1995) 'Computer support for the collaborative learning of physics concepts', in C. O'Malley (ed.) *Computer-Supported Collaborative Learning*, Berlin: Springer Verlag.

Huguet, P. and Monteil, J. M. (1994) 'Learning in co-acting groups: the role of social comparison and gender norms', in H. C. Foot, C. J. Howe, A. Anderson, A. Tolmie and D. Warden (eds) *Group and Interactive Learning*, Southampton, Boston: Computational Mechanics.

Jackson, A., Fletcher, B. C. and Messer, D. J. (1986) 'A survey of microcomputer use and provision in primary schools', *Journal of Computer Assisted Learning* 2: 45–55.

Lave, J. and Wenger, E. (1991) *Situated Learning: Legitimate Peripheral Participation*, Cambridge: Cambridge University Press.

McAteer, E. and Demissie, A. (1991) 'Writing competence across the curriculum', report to Scottish Office Education Department.

Nussbaum, J. and Novick, S. (1981) 'Brainstorming in the classroom to invent a model: a case study', *School Science Review* 62: 771–778.

Piaget, J. (1974) *Understanding Causality*, New York: W. W. Norton and Co.

—— (1985) *The Equilibration of Cognitive Structures*, Chicago: University of Chicago Press.

Piliavin, J. A. and Martin, R. R. (1978) 'The effects of the sex composition of groups on the style of social interaction', *Sex Roles* 4: 281–296.

Redish, E. F. and Risley, J. S. (1990) *Computers in Physics Education*, Redwood City: Addison-Wesley.

Siann, G. and McLeod, H. (1986) 'Computers and children of primary school age: issues and questions', *British Journal of Education Technology* 2: 133–144.

Tolmie, A. and Howe, C. J. (1993) 'Gender and dialogue in secondary school physics', *Gender and Education* 5: 191–209.

Tolmie, A., Howe, C. J., Mackenzie, M. and Greer, K. (1993) 'Task design as an influence on dialogue and learning: primary school group work with object flotation', *Social Development* 2: 183–201.

Underwood, G., McCaffrey, M. and Underwood, J. (1990) 'Gender differences in a cooperative computer-based language task', *Educational Research* 32: 44–49.

Vygotsky, L. S. (1978) *Mind in Society: The Development of Higher Psychological Processes*, Cambridge, MA: Harvard University Press.

Wood, D. (1989) 'Social interaction as tutoring', in M. H. Bornstein and J. S. Bruner (eds), *Interaction in Human Development*, Hillsdale, NJ: Lawrence Erlbaum.

4   Time-based analysis of students studying the Periodic Table

Kim Issroff

Introduction

I recently visited some colleagues at a university abroad. In collaboratively planning my trip with my colleagues, we communicated using e-mail. From a temporal perspective, our collaboration went through several phases. Initially, a large number of e-mails went backwards and forwards while we discussed the dates, transport, where I would stay and the talks that I would give. When these details had been finalised, our collaboration died down and little communication passed between us. As the date of my trip drew near, the number of e-mails increased, and their nature changed. They were more specific, about times and airports, even including precise details such as bus numbers. The collaboration had varied both qualitatively and quantitatively over time.

This chapter discusses ways in which we can investigate both qualitative and quantitative changes and highlights the significance of the temporal dimensions in the analysis of computer-supported collaborative learning interactions. There are now a variety of computer-based tools available for the analysis of videotapes, but these are seldom used to investigate the nature of collaborative interactions. This chapter provides a description of the use of a computer-based tool for the analysis of computer-supported collaborations and evaluates its use. It reports on an analysis of pairs of secondary school students completing a worksheet about the Periodic Table using a computer, focusing on the temporal features of the interactions. The original study (Issroff, 1995) was concerned with affective and cognitive factors as well as analysing the videotapes of the students' collaborations. The present chapter is concerned with the results of the videotape analysis and shows how features of collaborative interactions can be represented from a temporal perspective. The timelines and associated data show the changes that occur in both talk and behaviour over time.

My argument will be that a combination of quantitative data from the pre- and post-testing and the videotape analysis and qualitative data from observation and questionnaires provide in-depth descriptions of the nature of the collaborative interactions and the factors which impact on their efficacy.

This combination of analytic methods is essential in order to further our understanding of computer-supported collaborative learning and productive interactions.

The value of time-based analysis

Analysing the nature of collaborative interactions is a common way of investigating computer-supported collaborative learning. Researchers often videotape interactions and these videotapes are normally analysed using categories of behaviours or talk that are considered important. The number of occurrences of these categories are summed and differences between pairs and within pairs reported. These data are sometimes correlated with the cognitive results derived from the study and, for example, conclusions drawn about the behaviours of successful pairs or the ways in which different types of software or task affect the nature of collaborations.

However, this type of approach ignores the temporal aspects of the collaborations. As McGrath (1990) points out, 'Groups develop and exist in a temporal context. . . . Human behavior – at work and otherwise, alone and in groups – is temporally patterned in complex ways' (p.23). Several researchers have discussed developments which occur over the period of a collaboration. Salomon and Globerson (1989) discuss the development of interdependencies within a group over time and it is important that we understand the ways in which collaborations change as the collaborators develop ways in which to interact effectively. Crook (1994) discusses the development of shared understanding or socially shared cognition between participants over the course of a collaboration which he views as vital for a productive and effective interaction. Mercer (1994) discusses the historical and cumulative nature of talk and the way in which patterns of talk recur over time. He stresses the necessity to understand the ways in which this impacts on the nature and effectiveness of collaborations. However, none of these researchers has, so far, presented time-based representations of interactions. Neither have they shown, with empirical data, the ways in which these theoretical concepts develop over time.

The study presented in this chapter is concerned with charting the developments and changes in the ways in which groups or pairs of children interact over time. The time-based analyses of the interactions is achieved using software called Timelines[1] which facilitates the investigation of inter-pair, intra-pair and inter-individual differences as well as providing time-based views of interactions. Although there are now several software tools for analysing video data (for example, Ryan and Russell, 1994; Budenberg, 1994; Watts, 1994; Hoogland, 1994), these have not been used in the analysis of interactions. One exception is the work of Häkkinen (in press) who investigated the differences between students', teachers' and designers' interactions with different types of software using a neural network. However, the purpose of Häkkinen's study was to elucidate differences between students, teachers and designers, rather than to understand the nature of computer-supported collaborative learning.

Timelines

Timelines is a system for annotating or coding videotape data (for more information on Timelines, see Harrison and Chignell, 1994). It supports three different types of qualitative data: events, intervals and comments. Events are moments in time which are tagged with a category, which the user defines. Intervals represent time intervals on the videotape with a definite start and stop time. Like events, intervals are tagged with categories, defined by the user. Comments also represent a moment of time on the videotape, but these can be tagged with any text, defined by the user. The analysis in this study involved only the use of intervals. A set of finite categories was used which applied to the type of talk, the actions of either of the individuals and other external events. The videotapes were analysed using the software which produced two types of outputs: (i) a summary with the total number of entries, the number of categories and for each category, the total number, their total duration and their average duration, (ii) a timeline[2] display which shows the categories on the y-axis and time on the x-axis. The coding of the videotapes was validated by getting a second person to recode a section of videotape using the categories provided and comparing the coding. In 78 per cent of these instances, the codings of the categories were the same.

The study

This chapter presents the analysis of five pairs of students selected from the videotapes from a study involving fifty-five students in year 9, aged between 13 and 14 years. They were studied while using a commercially available software package called 'ChemAid'. This was described as 'a learning system that presents information on the elements in the Periodic Table'. It was designed to 'help students become familiar with each of the elements and their characteristics'.

Although there were several activities incorporated in the system, the students in this study used only one aspect of the program which allowed them to interrogate the database. They used a 'Query' option in which they specified which element name, symbol, classification, melting point, boiling point, thermal conductivity etc. was to be selected. They then chose a type of comparison (e.g. is equal to, is greater than) and then specified the criterion (e.g. the element name, a boiling point). They then clicked on a 'Go' button which instructed the computer to query the database. When this was completed they selected the 'Done' button and then went to a 'Data Screen Scan' menu item which allowed them to view the element/s that had been selected using the Query. This brought up a window with information about the selected element or elements.

The task was defined by a worksheet consisting of seventeen questions. Eleven of these questions simply asked for information from the computer (four of these asked for answers about more than one element) and two of the questions required the students to reason about the information they obtained from the computer. One of the questions was a prediction following from a previous question and three of the questions followed on from previous questions, the answers not being explicitly available from the computer.

There were three conditions in the empirical study to which the students were randomly assigned:

1   Individual – In this condition, a student was trained on his/her own and worked at the computer individually.
2   Non-cooperative task structure – In this condition, pairs of students were trained together with a training sheet each and then worked at the computer with a worksheet each.
3   Co-operative task structure – In this condition, pairs of students were trained together with one training sheet between them. They then worked at the computer sharing a worksheet. The pre- and post-tests were carried out individually.

The overall aim of the study was not only to compare individuals to pairs, but also to investigate how providing a co-operative task impacts on the nature of the students' interactions. The students were given pre- and post-tests about their knowledge of the Periodic Table and asked about their attitudes, using questionnaires, both before and after the interactions. More details are found in Issroff (1995).

Whilst the learning interaction was not part of a chemistry lesson, the study was conducted in the context of the classroom. Although this meant that the work was open to interruptions, it was felt that this would avoid anxiety and help to make the students feel at ease. The students were told that the research was concerned with the difference between students working at computers in pairs as opposed to individually. They were then told exactly what they would be required to do. It was explained that they would be taught how to use the computer and then asked some chemistry questions followed by some general questions about science, chemistry, working at the computer and working with their partners. They would then fill in a worksheet using the computer, without the researcher's help and answer similar questions at the end. The pairs were explicitly told that these would be individual tests.

After the students had been briefed, they were trained using the training sheet and then given the pre-tests. The pairs were reminded to work together and they were then left to complete the worksheet. Some of the sessions lasted more than one lesson, in which case the researcher would check that they still felt confident about using the software before they continued the worksheet.

Analysis of the videotapes of the five pairs

The five pairs of students whose interactions were analysed in depth were chosen to cover a range of criteria. One mixed-gender pair, two girl/girl pairs and two boy/boy pairs were chosen. Within this, two successful and two unsuccessful pairs in terms of pre- to post-test gains were chosen. This base-line information is summarised in Table 4.1. Additionally, the pairs selected vary in terms of the conditions under which they collaborated. Sue and Jane and Debbie and Kara had a co-operative task structure in that they shared a worksheet and training sheet. Two of these pairs, David and Andy and Debbie and Kara, spent two sessions completing the worksheet. David and Andy's second session was a week after the first and there was a two-week gap between Debbie and Kara's two sessions. The pairings were friendship pairs chosen by the teachers and the friendship ratings are averages of ratings of the friendship of each pair which were provided by randomly chosen children in the class. Details of the individual children's pre- to post-test change scores are also given.

From Table 4.1, it can be seen that those with high friendship ratings (Steve and Donna, David and Andy and Debbie and Kara) were more successful in terms of their pre- to post-test gain than those with low friend-ship ratings.

The analysis of the interactions aimed to investigate inter-individual, inter-pair and intra-pair differences. One aim of the coding was carried to look at the nature of the talk and any patterns within this. Additionally, the students' use of the mouse and typing behaviour were coded in order to investigate dominance of the hardware. Dominance has been found to be an important factor in successful performance (for example, Whitelock *et al.*, 1992).

In the next section, the results of the analysis are presented. The pairs are discussed in terms of time spent on task, time spent talking, the nature of

Table 4.1 Summary of the five pairs

Name	Task structure	Friendship rating	Pre- to post-test change
Steve	Non-	4	5.5
Donna	co-operative		-1.5
Nick	Non-	1.7	1
Mike	co-operative		0
Sue	Co-operative	2	-2
Jane			3.5
David	Non-	4.7	6
Andy	co-operative		8.5
Debbie	Co-operative	4.6	6
Kara			5

the talk, and their mouse and typing use. This is followed by selected time-lines and a discussion of the changes over two sessions seen in two of the pairs.

Results

Total time

Table 4.2 shows the total time spent using the computer to complete the worksheet for each pair. The average time spent on the worksheet was 41 minutes. David and Andy and Debbie and Kara spent longer completing the worksheet than the other pairs.

Table 4.2 The total time spent on the task by the five pairs

Pair	Total time spent using the computer to complete the worksheet (minutes)
Steve and Donna	31
Nick and Mike	31
Sue and Jane	36
David and Andy	61
Debbie and Kara	47

Figure 4.1 shows the total time and the total talk time for each pair. There are large variations in the amount of time spent talking. For example, Debbie and Kara spent 62 per cent of their time talking whereas Steve and Donna only spent 27 per cent of their time talking.

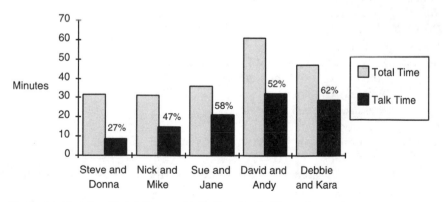

Figure 4.1 Graph of total time and talk time for the five pairs

Talk

Using the Timelines software, the talk was divided into four categories: *topic*, *next*, *control* and *other*. This analysis of talk is relatively high level, but still enables patterns of talk to be elucidated and it brings out distinct differences between the pairs.

Topic talk refers to any talk about the chemistry that the students were studying. For example Sue and Jane have just found out that their prediction for the electronic configuration is incorrect and have found the correct configuration:

Sue: Two, eight, four
Jane: Oh I know what that is. You know what it is? On the shells.
Sue: Oh yes.
Jane: *(Giggles)* It's confusing.
Sue: Oi, we nearly got it right. Two, eight.
Jane: *(Reading)* Is this the same as your prediction? If not why not? *(Laughter and mumbling)*
Jane: We got confused – well I did anyway.
Jane: *(Reading)* What does the atomic number of an element represent?
Jane: It's the . . . um . . .
Sue: . . . nucleus . . .
Both: . . . neutron . . . around the shells.

Next talk refers to any discussion about what to do next in terms of how to use the software. For example:

Kara: Less than 5.
Kara: Go to database.
Debbie: I am. I'm trying to get it . . .
Kara: Go to atomic number.
Debbie: Um . . . what have we got to do?
Kara: Less than . . . less than.
Debbie: Less than 5. . . . Should I just type 5 in?
Kara: No, 'cos it's not what you put in.
Debbie: Where do I go now?
Kara: Press go, delete, I mean done.
Debbie: *(Muttering)*
Kara: Datascreen scan, DATASCREEN SCAN.

Control talk refers to discussion of the control of the hardware, for example:

Steve: You can do this one.
Donna: OK, thanks.

Other talk refers to any talk that is not explicitly related to the task. For example:

Sue: I have to get another pair of *(inaudible)* I think my brother's taken it.
Jane: What? Do you think she might be *(inaudible)* . . . she should be . . . *(inaudible)*.
Sue: I haven't seen her have I?
Jane: No, I'm not going to see her either.

Figure 4.2 shows the percentages of the different types of talk that the pairs used during their interaction. As with the amount of talk overall, there was a large amount of variation between the pairs in the different types of talk which occurred. For three pairs, over half the talk was concerned with the topic. The girl/girl pairs spent more time than the other pairs discussing the interface and what to do next which may reflect their difficulties in understanding how the software worked. Nick and Mike spent over a quarter of their talk time discussing the interface and what to do next. However, this predominantly consisted of Mike asking Nick what he was doing and Nick telling (rather than explaining to) Mike what was happening. David and Andy spent nearly a quarter of their time talking about non-task related aspects and this is reflected in the length of time they spent completing their worksheets. The main finding from analysing the different types of talk is that the pairs who spent time talking about things that were off-task had greater pre- to post-test gain.

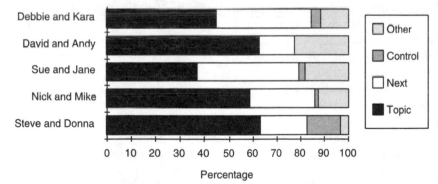

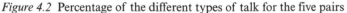

Figure 4.2 Percentage of the different types of talk for the five pairs

Mouse use and typing

Figure 4.3 shows the mouse and typing use of each individual within each of the pairs. The figure at the end of each bar shows the total number of occurrences of mouse and typing use. The girl/girl pairs are the only pairs in which there was no hardware dominance. Nick and Andy dominated their interactions and although Donna typed for a longer period than Steve, this

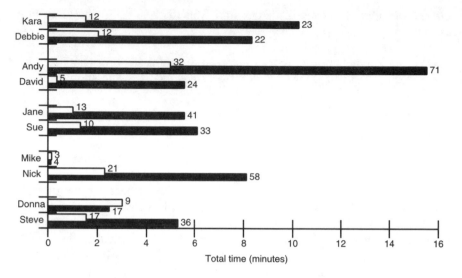

Figure 4.3 Mouse and typing use of the five pairs (typing use is represented by the white bars and mouse use by the black bars)

is a reflection of Donna's typing ability and Steve in fact dominated the typing, typing more often than Donna.

Timelines

This type of analysis produces a potentially very large number of timelines. The software allows the user to create timelines involving all the categories defined, or timelines with a selection of categories. The timelines presented below are a selection of those produced by the analysis, and were chosen to address specific points.

The three timelines in Figures 4.4, 4.5 and 4.6 show the hardware use and control talk of three of the pairs. From Sue and Jane's timeline (Figure 4.4) one can see a slightly uneven distribution of the hardware use, and that the control talk virtually always leads to Sue using the hardware. Steve and Donna's timeline (Figure 4.5) shows very clearly the uneven distribution of hardware control, and the control talk always leads to Donna using the hardware. Nick and Mike's timeline (Figure 4.6) also clearly shows the uneven distribution of control, with the one instance of control talk leading to Mike using the hardware.

Changes in patterns of interactions over sessions

There is evidence of changes in the way that the students interacted with each other over time. This is shown both in the distribution of the use of the hardware and writing and in the nature of the talk.

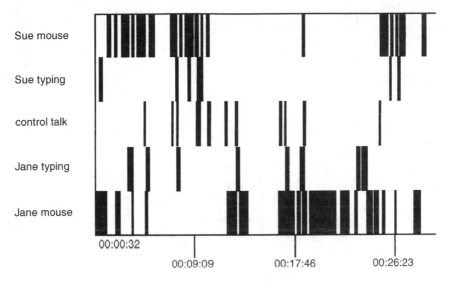

Figure 4.4 Sue and Jane's control talk and hardware timeline

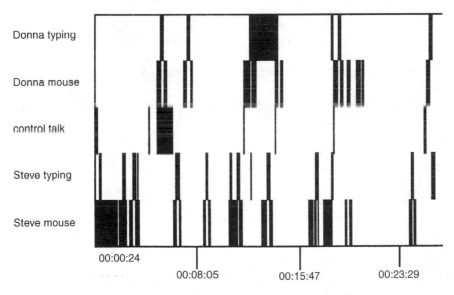

Figure 4.5 Steve and Donna's control talk and hardware timeline

The two pairs who spent more than one session using the computer showed changes in their patterns of interaction between their first and second session. For David and Andy, in their first session, the hardware use was evenly distributed between them, but during the second session, a week later, Andy dominated the hardware. This is shown in Table 4.3.

Changes over Debbie and Kara's two sessions can be seen in their use of

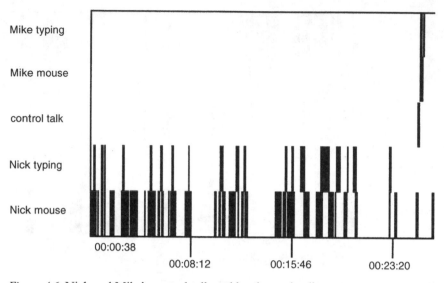

Figure 4.6 Nick and Mike's control talk and hardware timeline

the mouse and the amount of writing (Table 4.4). They physically fought over the use of the mouse and the typing. There were sixteen instances of this during the two sessions, but they were generally short lived, with Kara dominating the first session. Debbie used the mouse for the majority of the second session, which was two weeks later, and she insisted that Kara fill in the worksheet.

The density of the timelines in Figures 4.7 and 4.8 show how much talk occurred during some of the interactions. It is clear that Sue and Jane talked more than Steve and Donna. More importantly, they also show the distribution of the different types of talk which change over time. Steve and Donna's talk timeline (Figure 4.7) shows a decrease in talk about the interface (next talk) and an increase in the amount of topic talk over the session. In contrast, Sue and Jane's talk timeline (Figure 4.8) shows no decrease in next talk, with a slight increase in topic talk. This reflects the fact that they

Table 4.3 Mouse and typing use in David and Andy's two sessions

Session	First		Second	
	Mouse	Typing	Mouse	Typing
Andy	25	14	46	18
David	20	5	4	0

Table 4.4 Mouse and writing use in Debbie and Kara's two sessions

Session	First		Second	
	Writing	Mouse	Writing	Mouse
Debbie	20	9	0	13
Kara	2	21	11	2

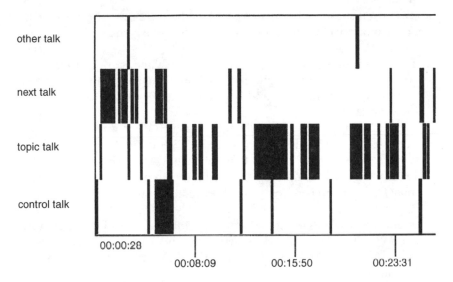

Figure 4.7 Steve and Donna's talk timeline

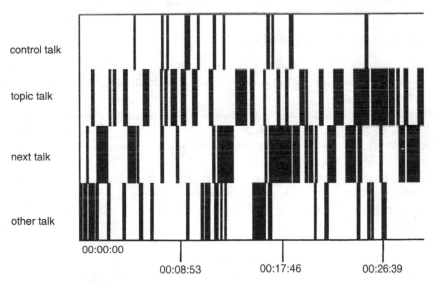

Figure 4.8 Sue and Jane's talk timeline

never fully mastered the use of the software. The timeline also shows the relatively large amount of other talk that occurred during their interaction.

Summary of results

Given the small sample of pairs, we cannot regard any of the observed patterns as statistically reliable. Nevertheless there are several features which seem to be indicative of pre-test to post-test cognitive gains.

- The pairs with high friendship ratings (Debbie and Kara and David and Andy) improved on their pre- to post-tests. The pairs with lower friendship ratings (Sue and Jane and Nick and Mike) were not as successful in these terms.
- The girl/girl pairs were the only pairs in which there was no dominance in the use of the hardware. This may be a gender difference, but it also may be a reflection of the fact that these students shared a worksheet.
- In the pairs where dominance did occur, the dominant member achieved more gain from the pre-test to the immediate post-test.
- The control of the hardware is often tacitly assumed. There is very little discussion of who is using the hardware. Only Steve and Donna discussed control of the hardware. However, Kara and Debbie physically fought over control of the hardware, although this is not apparent from the Timelines analysis.
- In the pairs that spent more than one session using the computer, changes in the ways that they interacted over the two sessions can be seen.

Evaluating the use of Timelines

The summaries that Timelines produces allow the analysis of inter-individual, inter-pair and intra-pair differences and from the timelines, patterns of behaviour and changes in behaviour over sessions can be seen. The fact that timelines of different intervals and using different categories can be created facilitates the analysis of the relations between different types of actions/talk. However, the meta-analysis of the data from the Timelines data also provides rich data for analysis.

This analysis of collaborative interactions has provided representations of a variety of features of the interactions. The qualitative data from the analysis reveals differences between and within the pairs. It has enabled a comparison of the amount of different types of talk within each collaboration, which provides one view of the nature of the interactions. It has also shown how the nature of the talk changes over time.

However, the timelines only partially represent the interactions. In order to have a more complete picture of the interactions, the timelines need to be considered in conjunction with qualitative information. The preceding analysis was supplemented with the data on pre- to post-test gains of the individuals involved. However, closer examinations of the interactions, together with information from the questionnaires, reveal interesting features of the collaborations. For example, although Nick and Mike's interaction was dominated both physically and cognitively by Nick, they spent a relatively short period of time using the computer and talked for about 45 per cent of the session. The majority of the talk was Nick explaining to

Mike either what he was doing, or some of the topic material. Mike would often joke about the subject matter which sometimes spurred Nick on. This can be seen in the following transcription of their dialogue:

Nick: The atomic number . . .

Mike: You're joking, huh.

Nick: The atomic number is the amount of . . .

Mike: The things in the . . . that make it up . . . into.

Nick: Yeah it would be wouldn't it. It would be the amount . . .

Mike: The amount of different sorts . . . of things that are bunged together to make one . . . one certain thing . . .

Nick: Yeah it would be the mass, it would be the mass I think. I think.

Mike: She said we didn't have to do all the questions.

Nick: Oh I know, it's the amount of protons.

Mike: The amount of different protons?

Nick: The amount of protons.

Thus Mike did have some influence on the interaction, although this was not necessarily topic related nor was it apparent from the timelines analysis. This piece of their dialogue also shows that, in a sense, Nick and Mike were speaking in a different language. Mike uses words like 'things' and 'bunged' while Nick's language involves scientific terms, like 'mass' and 'protons'. However, Mike did not improve his performance at all, possibly because he did not participate in the task from a cognitive perspective. Nick and Mike's lack of friendship may have contributed to this but, additionally, they were talking and operating on a completely different level. Thus it appears that the large differences in their abilities also contributed to the ineffectiveness of the interaction especially in terms of Nick's learning.

How do timelines help in the analysis of productive interactions? Traditionally, productive interactions have been viewed as those in which students exhibit pre- to post-test gain. This can be interpreted both in terms of each individual and in terms of the pair, or group of students. However, timelines enable an alternative interpretation of productive interactions. If a productive interaction is viewed as one in which the students discuss the topic, Steve and Donna's interaction was more productive than Sue and Jane's. The difference between the timelines showing the amount and type of talk show how Steve and Donna's interaction moved away from talking about how to use the software (next) with an increasing emphasis on talking about the chemistry (topic). In contrast, Sue and Jane's timeline shows that they continued to discuss the use of the software, with no change in the amount of discussion about the topic. Thus the timelines enabled a representation of the talk which occurred and which can be interpreted in terms of the productivity of the interactions. The fact that Steve and Donna learnt how to use the software, while Sue and Jane did not would be very important if the software was to be used several times in the classroom.

An alternative view of a productive interaction is one in which there was no dominance of the hardware. In this sample of the five pairs, the Timelines analysis shows that the two girl/girl pairs were the only pairs in which there was no dominance. However, this was not indicative of pre- to post-test gain for both pairs.

An important factor to consider in evaluating the use of Timelines for the videotape analysis is the amount of time spent. Videotape analysis is known to take a long time – some claim a ratio of 10:1 (10 hours of analysis to 1 hour of videotape). In this analysis, once the researcher had become familiar with the categories, the ratio was 2:1. This represents a significant saving in terms of time.

One of the major difficulties with using this type of tool is selecting the appropriate categories/events/intervals and the level of granularity for the analysis. For example, in this study, the behavioural categories were fine grained and enabled intra- and inter-pair differences to be represented. In contrast, the talk categories were at a higher level and, as the extract from Nick and Mike's dialogue shows, the Timelines analysis only provided a superficial analysis of the talk which occurred and its impact on the nature of the interaction. The higher-level talk categories did show features of the interactions but for more dialogue-focused analyses a finer level of granularity may be needed to explore the nature of the dialogues.

The collaborations presented in this chapter occurred over a relatively short period of time and the timelines produced show clear patterns. For collaborations which are longer, Timelines may not be a suitable tool for analysis as the resulting representations will be very dense and it may be impossible to distinguish any patterns. An alternative would be to use representations which are based on larger units of time. An example of this can be found in Issroff (1995) which used 'handmade' representations to show the patterns of interactions in a long-term collaboration.

In general though, this form of videotape analysis provides an efficient method of analysing interactions, while showing patterns in talk and behaviour which occur during the course of the collaborations. These enable alternative conceptions of productive interactions, but cannot provide a complete representation of all the features of collaborative interactions. The small sample presented in this chapter shows that temporal features of collaborative interactions are important, and by analysing interactions from a temporal perspective, differences between and within pairs are highlighted. One can hope that the emergence of Timelines and similar software packages will result in a new sensitivity amongst researchers to the temporal characteristics of productive interactions around computers and further our understanding of computer-based collaborations as well as the design of effective software to support collaboration.

Notes

1 Developed by Russell Owen, Ronald Baecker and Beverly Harrison at the University of Toronto for the Ontario Telepresence Project and the Institute for Robotics and Intelligent Systems.
2 When referring to the Timelines coding system, Timelines with a capital T is used. When referring to the output from the system, as here, lower case is used.

References

Budenberg, W. J. (1994) 'Video techniques for behavioural data collection', paper presented at *Computers in Psychology*, University of York.

Crook, C. (1994) *Computers and the Collaborative Experience of Learning*, London: Routledge.

Häkkinen, P. (in press) 'Neural network used to analyse multiple perspectives concerning computer-based learning environments', *Instructional Science*.

Harrison, B. L. and Chignell, M. H. (1994) 'Multimedia tools for social and interactional data collection and analysis', in P. Thomas, (ed.) *The Social and Interactional Dimensions of Human-Computer Interfaces*, Cambridge: Cambridge University Press.

Hoogland, A. J. (1994) 'CAMERA: a system for behavioral observation from video recordings', paper presented at *Computers in Psychology*, University of York.

Issroff, K. (1993) 'Methodology for research in computer-supported cooperative learning', in *PEG 93: AI Tools and the Classroom: Theory into Practice*, Moray House Institute of Education, Scotland.

—— (1995) 'Investigating computer-supported collaborative learning from an affective perspective', unpublished Ph.D. thesis, Institute of Educational Technology, The Open University, Milton Keynes.

McGrath, J. E. (1990) 'Time matters in groups', in J. Galegher, R. E. Kraut and C. Egido (eds) *Intellectual Teamwork: Social and Technological Foundations of Cooperative Work*, Hillsdale, NJ: Lawrence Erlbaum Associates.

Mercer, N. (1994) 'Personal communication', *Analysing Productive Peer-based Learning Environments* workshop, University of Southampton.

Ryan, C. C. and Russell, R. E. (1994) 'METAcoder for Windows: real-time and multi-pass event logging and analysis in the social and behavioural sciences', paper presented at *Computers in Psychology*, University of York.

Salomon G. and Globerson, R. (1989) 'When teams do not function the way they ought to', *International Journal of Educational Research* 13(1): 89–99.

Watts, L. A. (1994) 'ActionRecorder – integrating measurements of gaze with other indices of interaction processes', paper presented at *Computers in Psychology*, University of York.

Whitelock, D., O'Shea, T., Taylor, J., Scanlon, E., Clark, P., Sellman, R. and O'Malley, C. (1992) 'Investigating the role of socio-cognitive conflict in computer supported learning about elastic collisions', *CITE Report*, no. 169, Institute of Educational Technology, The Open University, Milton Keynes.

5 Collaborations in a primary classroom

Mediating science activities through new technology

Eileen Scanlon, Kim Issroff and Patricia Murphy

Introduction

Primary school science offers particularly interesting opportunities for considering ways in which collaboration may or may not support learning. It is well known that children develop prior conceptions which need to be changed in the direction of accepted science views, and conflict is often the mechanism for this. White and Frederiksen (1987) have suggested that revealing inconsistencies or conflicts in learners' different internal models of the topic under study can help their individual understanding in science. It is difficult with individual learners to generate situations in which the consequences of these different models become 'visible'. However, when a child works with another on a problem the difference in their views can produce conflict which forces each child to restructure their position. We believe, in the style of Cobb (1994), that science learning should be viewed both as a process of active individual construction (of knowledge), and a social process which involves significant others in this construction and a process of enculturation into the scientific practices of wider society.

This broad view of the influences on science learning has a number of consequences. First, consider the role of conflict, which is valued by constructivists as a learning mechanism. Some researchers have suggested that the cognitive conflict between collaborative learners, different views of the subject under study, should improve the performance of the group (e.g. Howe, 1992) and have presented data to support this view. However various factors combine to make the role of conflict in collaborative learning more problematic than this. Practitioners question it. For example, Harlen, an influential primary science educator (1992), rejects conflict as a technique to promote conceptual change among primary children, suggesting instead that teachers should build on the 'correct' conceptions which children display.

Second, consider the strong move towards investigative learning in science in recent years. Valuing investigative learning has links with the social constructivist notion that learning occurs through co-operative action and that concepts are progressively developed through action (Brown *et al.*,

1989). An investigative approach to learning is one which involves children in defining problems, developing strategies, collecting and interpreting data, evaluating actions and reporting conclusions. This interpretation of the value of investigative activity views both science concepts and procedures as essential elements of any solution, and investigative tasks as important vehicles or means of acquiring conceptual understanding. When looking at collaboration in primary science classrooms therefore children's procedural competency and how this mediates their conceptual development is highlighted (see Murphy, 1988).

Third, consider in more detail what these collaborative investigative science tasks involve and indeed what is the boundary placed round these tasks. Developmental psychologists such as Doise and Mugny (1984) have introduced the concept of group cognition as a necessary intermediary experience which leads to children's conceptually based, individual understanding. Bruner (1985) has elaborated on Vygotsky's view of the way that a child's potential for learning is revealed by working with others. In this view, the role of teachers is to help children to structure their activities and break down complex problems into smaller problems and thus provide them with models of how more experienced learners work. This social constructivist approach to understanding teaching and learning therefore leaves the role of conflict in the process problematic, and highlights the importance of the task which learners are engaged in and how they see it.

The focus on investigative learning in science in the curriculum would seem to prescribe the tasks which were of interest for us to study. Newman *et al.* (1984) illustrate how a difference in tasks is created by the task setting and stresses 'any time a task happens, one must ask how it has come to happen. How it was made to happen is not an incidental aspect of the task.' So our approach requires us to consider not only what the tasks set to the children were, but how children engaged in science learning involve themselves in the tasks set, and indeed how engaged they become with the tasks. Few researchers have explored the implication of how children become engaged with the tasks in learning science, even as opposed to the task of learning science, although research into gendered responses to science teaching is an honourable exception. We will illustrate below how individual students involve themselves in tasks and how their perception of the challenge the tasks offer have significant implications for the way particular examples of collaborative learning proceed.

Various accounts have been offered about the role that computers might play in supporting this science learning, especially the value of collaborative working on science simulations (e.g. Driver and Scanlon, 1988) or more controversially the value of child-produced computer games (e.g. Yarnall and Kafai, 1996). In this chapter we are focusing on tasks which involve the production of dynamic documents as examples of computer-supported writing about science. The children were working on investigative science activities and some of them used the computer to construct jointly an account of what they had learned in the form of a dynamic document. Two case studies are used to illustrate the issues which arise. One is taken from a series of studies of computer-based collaborations by learners whose ages ranged from 9 years to adult in a variety of settings (see Issroff, 1995). The other is from a series of studies of primary school children conducting science investigations, the Collaborative Learning and Primary Science (CLAPS) project (see Scanlon *et al.*, 1994). Examples of related work are the Computer Supported Intentional Learning Environments (CSILE) project (Scardamalia and Bereiter, 1992) where students contribute notes on their work to a communal database, Campione *et al.* (1992) who report on the collaborative working and document production by children in two schools who used e-mail and document sharing to compose scientific documents, and Galegher and Kraut (1990) who study adult collaborations on science writing.

Methodologies for studying computer-based collaboration

Issroff (1995) highlights a number of different measurement issues which arise in studying computer-based collaborative learning:

Time period

Many studies of computer-assisted co-operative learning are based on snap-shots of computer use over a relatively short time. For computer-based studies it is important to examine use over longer time periods for two reasons. First the relative novelty of computer use means that children need time to settle and familiarise themselves with the machine. Second, when working in a group it takes time to develop effective working relationships and patterns of task division (e.g. Salomon and Globerson, 1989; Kraut *et al.*, 1988).

Effects of collaboration

To assess the effects of co-operative learning it is necessary to do more than simply compare results on individuals' pre- and post-test cognitive performance. Some researchers have found that individual post-testing under-represents the learning gains made, and suggest that individual achievement tests are less informative than the examination of a group product (e.g. Forman, 1989; Webb, 1989). Others have found that administering delayed post-tests allows time for the effects of collaboration to appear (e.g. Scanlon *et al.*, 1993, 1996).

Structure of the learning situation, task and tool

Many studies investigate collaborative use of computers in artificial laboratory sessions, where neither the task nor the computer tools provided were designed to promote collaborative working. This has potential for confusing students as it can be unclear how they should interpret ambiguities in the structure of the learning situation, how strong the expectation is that they work together, or how they should most effectively use computer tools to facilitate their collaborative working.

Investigating social and psychological factors

Studies of computer-supported collaborative learning have often focused on cognitive factors and paid relatively little attention to non-cognitive factors. Studies such as Joiner *et al.* (1991) have demonstrated that post-test performance can be affected by the presence of other students, illustrating how social and psychological factors such as the anxiety-reducing effects of having others present or the motivational effects of working with others affect the nature of interactions. Recently researchers in motivation have asserted the importance of considering social goals (Urban and Maehr, 1995). Research on collaborative computer based learning requires attention to social and psychological factors as well as cognitive ones.

These methodological requirements make assumptions about what is interesting and productive in the interactions which take place during collaborative learning. Indeed, we contend that productive interactions during collaborative learning are to be recognised by both cognitive and socio-affective outcomes. We believe that naturalistic research is necessary to understand collaborative learning. Basing such research in the classroom allows the researcher to better address the influence of context on learning. More importantly, the complex phenomenon of collaboration we are trying to understand only occurs in the classroom and artificial contexts can only replicate aspects of this phenomenon divorced from the mediating influences of teachers' and children's agendas. Our approach was therefore to enter the context and to then discern through an evolutionary process what was salient. We describe the context below.

The context of the investigations: the water case study

The data collection

Our methodological review and review of the current perspectives on learning science led us to the conclusion that we should conduct long-term in-context observational research and that a number of data sources was necessary to allow us to track the children's experiences in terms of the progress of the interaction, and the variety of outcomes which might result, in terms of measuring cognitive or affective or social benefits. Issroff (1996) followed a group of three primary school children who were working together to produce a dynamic document on the water cycle. A dynamic document consists of a series of images with associated text and sound which are presented in sequence on a computer in a similar way to a slide show or an animation. In this chapter we draw on the data from Issroff's study, and also describe in some detail the work of another group of children who conducted an investigation on evaporation and also constructed a dynamic document together. These two case studies are taken from a large data archive of collaborative learning situations involving extended observations in two schools and more restricted observations in two further schools. The situations we can draw on range from a single group in one session, i.e. a snapshot of collaborative learning, to more extended observations of groups over a number of months.

Treating classroom realities as multi-layered, interactive, shared social experiences had significant consequences for the data collection in these projects. The data collection had a number of foci – the individual child, the individual child within a peer group, the teacher and the tasks. The research examined individual learning outcomes in relation to: children's perceptions of tasks, their level of engagement with them, their interaction with other children and their views of group work; and teachers' agendas and understandings, about the tasks and the children as groups and as individuals. The data collected about the teachers' and the children's views is extensive. First of all, the teachers were interviewed about their views of science learning and the role of investigations and group working. They were also interviewed about the purpose of the tasks they had selected for children. Questionnaires were administered to children about their views of science learning and their attitude to group working. Classroom data about children's understanding was also used. We used the sources of information from the teacher, together with information collected independently to elaborate the classroom-based sources of data. Children were interviewed before working on the task and, where appropriate, certain probes were used to assess their conceptual knowledge and procedural skill. These included a simple probe prior to the investigation involving a related activity which demonstrates the phenomenon. The children's explanations of the phenomenon were recorded and probed to see if they linked their initial understanding to this new context. Extended observations were undertaken and recorded on video to provide data about the children's performance of the tasks and to provide data about the children's interactions with each other and the task. The dialogue between children as they planned their investigation of the phenomenon and carried it out was an important source of information. The teachers' and children's accounts of the outcomes of the investigations were then collected. The teachers were simply interviewed again about how the sessions had worked. After the children had completed their investigation we probed, in recorded interviews, what their hypotheses were, what they found out and what they now understood about the concepts under study. At this point we also returned to the children's prior classroom work and questioned whether these now represented their thinking and discussed again the pre-experiment probes to see if their views had changed. The final data collection occurred several weeks after the completion of the work. In this delayed probe we looked in particular at whether children could apply their understanding in new contexts.

The tasks

The children reported in both case studies described had already experienced numerous activities as part of their topic on water. What do investigative science tasks require of a group of children? They usually involve a planning or design phase where the children have to agree on the selection of relevant variables and what they will do, an experimental or active phase where the children carry out the plan and a reporting phase where they produce an account in some form of what they have found out. Also, in primary science topics, groups of children typically work on the same concept of, say, evaporation but are given the freedom to decide *what* to investigate about the concept. They might, for example, focus on temperature effects or surface area effects. The children's choice of investigations provides them with very different learning opportunities. Consequently it is very common for teachers to draw together children's work in a whole-class setting so that all children can get access to each others' activities and thinking. A medium for doing this is a reporting back session which will typically involve communication in a variety of forms including writing. The purpose of the reporting back is crucial. It is a closure activity, i.e. an exposition of what has been found out and learnt. While it obviously provides opportunities for learning, teachers nevertheless do not explicitly require children to reconsider and review their ideas. Seeing such a task as an end point will again influence the potential for collaboration between children and the nature of it. The form of reporting back that we discuss here was the creation of a dynamic document using the KidPix software.

The children

Both studies were carried out in a Milton Keynes primary school and involved three children (aged between 9 and 10 years). Karen, Ellen and Ryan took part in the first study, and made a dynamic document collaboratively. The task occurred at the end of a seven-week period of work about water. The children had investigated their own use of water, where it comes from and the disposal of dirty water, including methods of filtering dirty water. They studied the significance of water in different religions and carried out a study of rainfall and river systems and looked at evaporation and condensation and then the water cycle. Two of the children had worked together on all of these activities whilst the third child had not. This third child was also a newcomer to the school, therefore was less aware than the other children of the particular classroom culture.

The teacher asked the three children as a final activity in the topic work to create a dynamic document of the water cycle. He asked them to do this in order to teach the rest of the class about the water cycle. The teacher chose these three children because it was a particularly difficult task, suitable only for the more able children. He did not give them any structure but checked on their progress throughout the interactions. The students first did their research from approximately ten books about water, then created a storyboard and implemented this on the computer. (Storyboards are used to plan this type of work and typically consist of hand-drawn pictures and text, which represent the future document.) The nature of the slide show was driven by the teacher's request that the children make it to teach the rest of the class. It largely consisted of a slide with a question, followed by the 'answer' to that question. In planning the storyboard, the children discussed what the 'stupidest' girl in the class would be able to answer before including things in the storyboard.

We will refer in detail to one other group who worked together on the evaporation investigation and also chose to produce a report using the KidPix software (and were allowed to do so by their teacher). This was a group of three children – this time two boys (Bill, Steve) and a girl (Rachel). This group had a different collaborative history to the children described in the first case study. They had worked together as a group on all the variety of tasks related to the topic of water which had been set over a period of seven weeks and as a result our data on the development of their collabora-tive learning is extensive. For part of this time, they had worked on an investigation which they had designed to establish what the influence of heat and moisture was on evaporation. The teacher offered this group a high level of support in the design of their investigation. Unlike the first group their KidPix document was a report for the class about what they had found in their particular investigation.

The outcomes of collaboration

Our approach provides a wealth of information by which the outcome of the collaboration can be assessed. As well as an investigation of the indi-vidual cognitive and affective benefits which resulted, as both groups of children were engaged in the production of a dynamic document, the docu-ment produced could itself be considered as an outcome.

The dynamic document produced by the first group (part of which is reproduced in Figure 5.1), was considered excellent by the teacher and the rest of the class when Karen, Ellen and Ryan presented it at a school assembly. When the final slide show was shown to researchers at a work-shop, it received applause and, from several perspectives, the product of the interaction was considered good. However, this does not offer an indication of the nature of the collaboration nor the children's knowledge and feelings after the collaboration. In interviews conducted after the slide show had been completed, the children were asked about the water cycle and how they felt about the collaboration. These showed that all the children had gaps in their understanding of the water cycle and the concepts involved. Karen's responses were often repetitions of the script from the slide show, although she did seem to understand some of the more difficult concepts. All three showed that they understood the process of water evaporating, forming clouds and raining again. Ryan showed an understanding of condensation but Ellen and Karen still had difficulties with the concept.

The nature of the dynamic document produced was determined by the children's perception of the activity that the teacher had given them. The document was considered excellent by the teacher and the other children in the class, although the collaboration, when investigated in detail, broke down. Although the product of the interaction (the KidPix document) was considered excellent, the process (how they worked together) was less than optimal (see next section) and the outcomes (cognitive or affective changes in the children) were mixed. Although the children seem to have made progress with their conceptual understanding, the affective and social outcomes were negative.

In the second case study the children were also pleased with the KidPix document they produced, and when it was used at the reporting back session it was greatly admired by the class. The group all made considerable conceptual progress as a result of designing, conducting an experiment and producing a dynamic document to report their findings. In collecting the

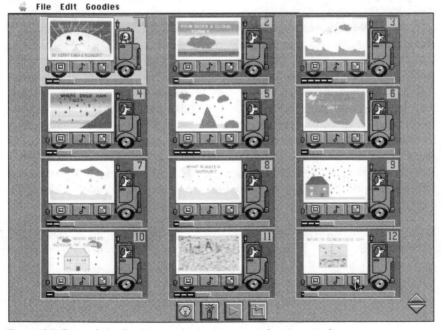

Figure 5.1 Part of the final dynamic document on the water cycle

data about children's understanding of the process of evaporation and how it was impacted by the experiment they did, we adopted a specific approach. First, we used classroom-based data – in this case children's annotated drawings (see Figure 5.2 for an example) and accompanying discussions of them, the dialogue between children as they planned their investigation of the phenomenon and carried it out, and teachers' and children's accounts of the outcomes of the investigations. Second, we used a simple probe prior to the investigation, involving a related activity which demonstrates the phenomenon, namely a wet hand print on a paper towel which the children were asked to observe over a period of time as the towel dried. The children's explanations of the phenomenon were recorded and probed to see if they linked their initial understanding of evaporation to this new context. After the children had completed their investigation we probed in recorded interviews what their hypotheses were, their view of what they found out and what they now understood about the process of evaporation. We also returned to the children's annotated diagrams and questioned whether these now represented their thinking and discussed again the 'hand print' phenomenon. Several weeks after the completion of the overall work on water, in the delayed probe we looked at whether the children could apply their understanding of evaporation to new contexts. We supplied them with wet washing and asked for explanations of how clothes dry and the factors that influence drying. After this we explicitly asked children to write and draw about evaporation again. We also used a series of photographs of everyday phenomena where evaporation is involved to probe further the children's thinking.

Using these data we were able to demonstrate progress for each child, and track this progress (Scanlon *et al.*, 1996). Although it is not possible to conclude that it was just the influence of the particular investigation performed by an individual child which changed their views on evaporation, because they will have heard accounts of other children's results of their investigations and hear and see things outside the classroom which they try to interpret in terms of their current conceptual framework, this caveat does not apply only to this style of observational research. In cognitive terms all members of the group made great progress.

However in affective terms at least one member of the group (Steve) who had made good progress in his own learning was quite unhappy about the experience due to social conflict within the group:

Interviewer: So in the end do you think working with them affected your work that day?

Steve: Well it certainly slowed down the work, it certainly made it tougher for me to handle so . . .

Interviewer: Do you think you have learned as much?

Steve: I learned twice as much, one that they don't get on and two, what we were trying to find out.

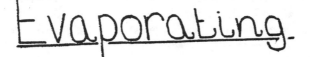

Evaporating.

I think the water is pulled up into the air/atmoshere, I think this is called "Evaporating". The water forms a cloud and this causes rain.

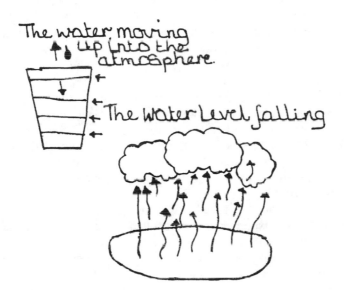

The water moving up into the atmosphere.

The water Level falling

Figure 5.2 Annotated drawing

The evolution of collaboration

It is clear that our approach results in a mass of data. Simply to track the progress of the collaborative interaction generates a wealth of videotape, which results in a large transcription task. Our approach is to construct a timeline of events for the interaction which deals with children's actions, and their conversations with each other and with the teacher. From this record, it becomes possible to track the emergence of ideas about how to proceed, whether with a plan for an experiment, its execution or its interpretation or the required form or content of a report of the event and its consequences. From these accounts certain interesting features of collaboration are exemplified. First, our data provide an extended observation of the process of collaboration and therefore offer us the opportunity of examining the way that collaboration develops over time. A good example of this is the way that ideas emerge but are not immediately followed up, can appear lost but then often resurface later. An idea about which variables to hold constant while planning an investigation, or selecting questions on which to base the construction of a dynamic document can appear to be dropped but can re-emerge when actions take place and yet again when results are being investigated. Sometimes these ideas come from their original source but occasionally they re-emerge from a different participant in the collaboration. This disappearance and re-emergence of ideas has been described as the 'dolphin' effect by Mercer (1994).

This evolution of collaboration over time is illustrated in the first case study. In terms of their behaviour at the computer, there was a very clear development in the way that the children collaborated. Initially all three of them sat together at the computer. By the end, each child was working on the computer individually, with the other two doing other work. This could be a result of Ryan going off when he was not given a chance to contribute or a result of Karen's need to get on with something. They all had to record the sound together, and although they were all sitting at the computer, the session was dominated by Karen. Both Ryan and Ellen showed that they could use the computer, but when Karen was there, she did not allow them to. From the children's perspectives, it could have been more effective and efficient for them to work individually on their own contribution to the production of the dynamic document, giving the other children time to carry out other work.

Another factor which contributed to the breakdown of collaboration was Karen's character and expertise. She controlled the entire interaction. She controlled the interaction in various ways, including determining the nature of the slide show, ignoring input from group members, persuading others to do things her way, allocating jobs, maintaining control of location of work, taking control rather than helping, or changing other group members' work. In this she often had the support of the teacher. On the rare occasions that Ryan and Ellen worked together, the situation was much more equitable. Ellen would help Ryan and guide him on tasks that he did not know how to achieve and Ryan would point out Ellen's errors. However, Karen would often interrupt this.

To capture the progress of the interaction we used graphical summaries of the ways in which the children collaborated (see Issroff, 1996). The collaboration was divided into ten-minute slots and these showed the activity of each child, who was working with whom and any teacher interventions. They clearly show how the collaboration broke down over the time period.

In the second case study there was no overt breakdown of the collaboration. Working on the KidPix report, this trio did not adopt the kind of task division we have described above. The threesome sat round the computer and contested the contents of each frame partly as a result of a degree of social conflict which continued throughout their interaction and had indeed continued throughout their interactions over a period of weeks. This conflict is described in a later section. In this particular interaction however there was an example of Mercer's dolphin effect. Their investigation had dealt with what happened when containers were put in hot and cold places. In the words of Rachel:

> We put a container into an incubator that was hot and one container of water into a fridge. . . . We thought the one on the fridge would evaporate the quickest but after we done the test and we were half way through it we thought oh no when puddles are out in the road and it's sunny they dry up and they evaporate quicker . . .

The children's accounts of their expectations of what would happen during their investigation differ slightly, but all mention the fact that originally they intended to study the effect of moisture on the rate of evaporation. The following extract from the conversation between the interviewer and Rachel shows that moisture played a role in her thinking about evaporation.

Interviewer: Can you remember your original ideas then about why the fridge would be quickest?

Rachel: Em because it had less moisture in there and there was more room for it to go up into.

This notion of the influence of moisture surfaces at different places in their discussions together while planning and working and in their discussion of results but they do not finally tie down the influence of moisture on their thinking. In Mercer's terms, the 'dolphin' may continue to be sighted in the future.

Building an account of collaboration by accreting data

In the accounts we have constructed of these group interactions, the detailed record of events is augmented by data from interviews with teachers and children on the variety of features we described above. We have experienced shifts in our interpretation of a particular interaction as we add to our account this data from another source. For example, in the first case study the children were asked about various aspects of the collaboration both by a questionnaire asking about their attitude to group working in general and by individual interview about this specific example of group working. Karen and Ellen said that they had enjoyed making the document but Ryan was not sure. He said that he did not enjoy working in groups (in contrast to his questionnaire) and when asked whether he enjoyed working with Karen and Ellen he said 'I don't know.' He also said that he wouldn't want to make another slide show with Karen and Ellen. This additional information showed that Ryan was obviously ambivalent in his attitudes to working, and perhaps it was the specific interactions with Karen and Ellen rather than group working in general he did not enjoy.

In the second case study data from another source also provide a fresh insight which allows us to interpret the interaction. The shared hypothesis which allowed the group to design their investigation was that heat would alter the rate of evaporation. However, interviews with each group showed they had different views about the effects of humidity (in summary, the boys felt low humidity would enable more water to evaporate, while the girl felt the opposite). In the post-investigation interviews Rachel remembered the outcome and her surprise at it, while Bill asserted that what had happened was what he expected. A simple record of the interaction would not have properly captured the more accurate but rather complicated account of what features of the hypothesis were truly shared by the group, and what the individual perspectives were.

The role of conflict in progressing collaboration

In the first case study, Karen's character and expertise dominated the interaction and contributed to the breakdown of the collaboration. It is particularly important to take into account the characters and expertise of the individuals involved in order to foster effective collaborations. There was conflict which was both social and conceptual but it had little impact on the outcome due to Karen's dominance. As she made the decisions about how to proceed the others became progressively less engaged in the task.

The interaction of the second group never broke down in the way that we have outlined that the first case study group did. It was, however, characterised by continuing conflicts about the design and execution of their investigation plan (Scanlon *et al.*, 1996). Working on the KidPix report, this trio did not adopt the kind of task division we have described in the first group. Their view of the experience of collaboration throughout the interaction was mixed. Most of the conflict occurred between Rachel and Billy, who were both quite dominant in their interactions with others. Steve acted as a mediator through much of the interaction. As we have described above, one of their conflicts was about what would be the outcome of their investigations. While sharing the hypothesis that heat would alter the rate of evaporation, they had differing views about effects of humidity (e.g. the boys felt low humidity would enable more water to evaporate, while the girl felt the opposite). They were able to design together an investigation to help them explore the issue, still sharing a common task even though they had developed individual views of it. The cognitive outcomes which resulted from this were positive. We have recorded interactions in this group at other times where the outcome of conflict was negative. We think the positive effect in this group was because the conflict resulted in increased task engagement for the whole group. In fact, in prior investigations, this group had experienced conflict on a number of occasions. They had experienced enormous difficulty due to differing perceptions of what the task set implied for the design of an activity (see Murphy *et al.*, 1994 for an account). As a consequence in this case, they argued through their individual views of the task and were continually attempting to make explicit their thinking.

This result stands in contrast to other groups we have observed which lack this engagement with the task. In this group the children had strong views which they argued through, and in fact the most marked progress was made between the post-probe and the delayed probe which suggests that the influence of task engagement continues.

Conclusion: the role of the computer in mediating interactions

This review of our own experience of studying collaboration in the particular context of the production of a dynamic document in a primary science classroom leads us to two types of conclusion. The first type is about the methodology which it is necessary to use to draw these conclusions about an example of collaborative working. The study must pay attention to collecting data which make sense of the context in which the children were working, what the teacher sees as the purpose of the task set and what the children perceived it to be. Also, in considering an example of collaboration, attention must be paid to the way such interaction develops. Those collaborating on a task will also have both a shared and a separate history of collaborative working. This is another requirement of our methodology, that data be collected on such aspects. These methodological requirements can only be met in long-term in-context studies of collaboration.

Our second methodological conclusion is that the affective perspective on collaboration needs to be considered. The interactions in the first case study were dominated by Karen, and Ryan was unhappy about the way the collaboration had progressed. Although some of the teacher's goals were met, and there was some collaborative working it is difficult to see this particular grouping as productive. Our second group was arguably more cognitively productive but there were similar concerns from one child at least about the way the collaboration progressed.

The main theoretical conclusion which comes from our analyses so far is that conflict plays a complex role in children's learning in groups. We have seen examples of conflict which produced positive outcomes, particularly where the conflict has engendered task engagement, and some where conflict may have impeded learning. In this chapter we have described examples of conceptual conflict where children disagree about what will happen in an investigation due to their different understandings, procedural conflict where children disagree about what to do and social conflict where children argue. We have referred to occasions where different interpretations of the task have led to conflict which hindered learning. We also see conflict having different effects at different times during the phases of collaborative activity on a particular task. An unexpressed or unresolved conflict at the planning stage can reappear later while an activity is in progress. It is unsurprising that the same contribution by a child might receive a different response by others in the group depending on the timing or that a child with a history of 'disagreeing' might have their contributions treated differently. The investigations we describe typically take more than one classroom session to complete, and may represent as much as ten hours of classroom time. In many cases the same children continue to work together on a series of investigations. Therefore the effect of such interventions and interactions is cumulative. So far we have observed several different types of conflict in our work-task, procedural and social and conceptual (see Murphy *et al*, 1995), and we are categorising these in terms of outcome and in terms of the phase of activity in which they appear.

In this chapter we have illustrated how our concerns with the methodological problems which have been observed in other research on collaborative learning led to a commitment to conduct long-term in-context studies of collaborative learning in science. We have drawn on two accounts of the construction of a dynamic document to illustrate our methods and themes in the study of collaboration which emerge. By locating this study in an extended period of authentic classroom activity we have illustrated how we had access to insights about the teacher's perceptions of the purpose of the activity, children's experience of collaboration and children's perceptions of how the collaboration influenced the progress of the activity. One particular area for further study which we have only begun to explore here is the role played by the construction of such dynamic documents as opposed to other forms of reporting of the results of science investigations in developing children's science understanding.

Acknowledgements

We are grateful to the teachers and children who have contributed to this research.

References

Brown, J. S., Collins, A. and Duguid, P. (1989) 'Situated cognition and the culture of learning', *Educational Researcher* 18(1): 32–42.

Bruner, J. (1985) 'Vygotsky: A historical and conceptual perspective', in J. V. Wertsch, (ed.) *Culture, Communication and Cognition: Vygotskian Perspectives*, Cambridge: Cambridge University Press.

Campione, J. C., Brown, A. L., and Jay, M. (1992) 'Computers in a community of learners', in E. De Corte *et al.* (eds) *Computer Based Learning Environments and Problem Solving*, Heidelberg: Springer Verlag.

Cobb, P. (1994) 'Where is the mind? Constructivist and sociocultural perspectives on mathematical development', *Educational Researcher* October: 13–19.

Doise, W. and Mugny, G. (1984) *The Social Development of the Intellect*, Oxford: Pergamon Press.

Driver, R. and Scanlon, E. (1988) 'Conceptual change in science', *Journal of Computer Assisted Learning* 5: 25–36.

Forman, E. (1989) 'The role of peer interaction in the social construction of mathematical knowledge', *International Journal of Educational Research* 13(1): 55–70.

Galegher, J. and Kraut, R. (1990) 'Computer mediated communication for intellectual teamwork: a field experiment in group writing', *Proceedings of Computer Supported Collaborative Work Conference*, Los Angeles.

Harlen, W. (1992) 'Research and the development of science in the primary school', *International Journal of Science Education* 14(5): 491–503.

Howe, C. (1992) 'Learning through peer interaction', presentation to the *British Association for the Advancement of Science*, Southampton.

Issroff, K. (1995) 'Investigating computer-supported collaborative learning from an affective perspective', unpublished Ph.D. thesis, Institute of Educational Technology, The Open University, Milton Keynes.

—— (1996) 'A case study of primary school children collaborating to create a multimedia document', paper presented at the *European Conference on Educational Research*, Seville.

Joiner, R., Littleton, K. and Riley, S. (1991) 'Peer presence and peer interaction in computer-based learning', paper presented at the *British Psychological Society Annual Conference: Developmental Psychology Section*, University of Cambridge.

Kraut, R. E., Galegher, J. and Egido, C. (1988) 'Relationships and tasks in scientific collaboration', *Human Computer Interaction* 3: 31–58.

Mercer, N. (1994) 'Personal communication', *Analysing Productive Peer-based Learning Environments* workshop, University of Southampton.

Murphy, P. (1988) 'Insights into pupils' responses to practical investigations from the APU', *Physics Education* 23: 330–336.

Murphy, P., Scanlon, E., Issroff, K., Hodgson, B. and Whitelegg, E. (1994) 'Developing investigative learning in science – the role of collaboration', paper presented at *ECUNET*, Holland.

Murphy, P., Scanlon, E., Issroff, K., with Hodgson, B. and Whitelegg, E. (1995) 'Case studies of conflict in primary science collaborations', paper presented at the *European Conference on Educational Research*, Bath.

Newman, D., Griffin, P. and Cole, M. (1984) 'Social constraints in laboratory and classroom tasks', in B. Rogoff and J. Lave (eds) *Everyday Cognition: Its Development in Social Context*, Cambridge, MA: Harvard University Press.

Salomon, G. and Globerson, R. (1989) 'When teams do not function the way they ought to', *International Journal of Educational Research* 13(1): 89–99.

Scanlon, E., Murphy, P., Hodgson, B. and Whitelegg, E. (1994) 'A case study approach to studying collaboration in primary science classrooms', in H. Foot *et al.* (eds) *Group and Interactive Learning*, Southampton, Boston: Computational Mechanics.

Scanlon, E., Murphy, P., Issroff, K., Hodgson, B. and Whitelegg, E. (1996) 'Collaboration in primary science classrooms: learning about evaporation', proceedings of the *19th Cognitive Science Conference*, San Diego, California.

Scanlon, E., O'Shea, T., Byard, M., Draper, S., Driver, R., Hennessy, S., Hartley, J. R., O'Malley, C., Mallen, C., Mohamed, G., Twigger, D. (1993) 'Promoting conceptual change in children learning mechanics', proceedings of the *15th Cognitive Science Conference*, Boulder, Colorado.

Scardamalia, M. and Bereiter, C. (1992) 'An architecture for collaborative knowledge building', in E. De Corte *et al.* (eds) *Computer Based Learning Environments and Problem Solving*, Heidelberg: Springer Verlag.

Urban, T. and Maehr, M. (1995) 'Beyond a two-goal theory of motivation and achievement: a case for social goals', *Review of Educational Research* 65(3): 213–244.

Webb, N. (1989) 'Peer interaction and learning in small groups', *International Journal of Educational Research* 13(1): 21–39.

White, B. and Frederiksen, J. (1987) 'Causal model progressions as a foundation of intelligent learning environments', report no. 6686, BBN laboratories, Cambridge, MA.

Yarnall, L. and Kafai, Y. (1996) 'Issues in project-based science activities: children's constructions of ocean software games', paper presented at American *Educational Research Association Annual Meeting*, New York.

6 Is 'exploratory talk' productive talk?

Neil Mercer and Rupert Wegerif

Introduction

This chapter is about the effective use of talk by children as a social mode of thinking and as a medium for their education. It also deals with the role of the classroom teacher and the use of computer-based activities in school. We put forward a characterisation of an educationally productive kind of talk, derived mainly from observational research on children working together at the computer in classrooms. This characterisation involves the concept of *exploratory talk*, a concept which we will explain in due course. We also deal with some issues of methodology, suggesting that new tools are needed for the investigation of the role of spoken language and joint activity in collaborative learning: tools which address the ways that intersubjectivity is pursued through dialogue, and which allow applied educational researchers to evaluate the quality of collaborative activity. The results of a recent classroom-based study are used to illustrate the utility of our conception of exploratory talk as educationally productive talk, and to demonstrate how qualitative and quantitative methods of analysis can complement one another in this field of investigation.

Sociocultural theory and intellectual development

Our theoretical approach has roots in the work of Vygotsky. But although he is celebrated as the founding father of a psychology of learning and cognitive development based on intersubjectivity rather than individuality, Van der Veer and Valsiner (1991) and others have suggested that the extent of Vygotsky's theoretical divergence from the individualistic developmental perspective of Piaget may have been overstated. Vygotsky saw what he called 'higher order thought' as an individual property (Wertsch, 1985, p. 201), at best 'quasi-social' (Vygotsky, 1991, p. 41), and produced through the individual's 'internalisation' of language use. His focus on the individual, albeit the individual in social and historical context, is reflected in his explanation of key Vygotskian concepts such as the zone of proximal development in terms of the supportive intervention of adults in the learning of *individual* children. Vygotsky reported no research carried out in normal classrooms, and most of the neo-Vygotskian developmental psychology which has followed in his footsteps has avoided or ignored – both theoretically and methodologically – the social and cultural realities of classrooms, places where one adult is responsible for the learning of many children, in which specific educational goals are being pursued, and in which children may often (as in British primary schools) work in pairs or groups. It therefore seemed to us that in order to research the educational role of talk between children working together in classrooms we needed to go beyond Vygotsky and the neo-Vygotskians both theoretically and methodologically, to develop analytic tools which treat discourse and joint activity as intrinsic features of the educational process (not merely as factors in some stages of individual learning).

Some current psychological perspectives on language and social action show the influence of ideas which have emerged since Vygotsky's death, such as the pragmatics of Austin (1962) and Grice (1975), ethnomethodology (e.g. Garfinkel, 1967) and the related recent development of conversation analysis (e.g. Drew and Heritage, 1992). Thus some 'discursive psychologists' now propose that participation in social interactions is not distinct from the internalisation of social interactions (Harré and Gillet, 1994; Edwards and Potter, 1992; Forrester, 1992). A similar paradigm shift can be seen in Lave's suggestion that we conceptualise what Vygotsky called 'internalisation' in terms of the 'process of becoming a member of a sustained community of practice' (Lave, 1991, p. 65). These ideas resonate with recent social anthropological research which describes culturally based language practices in schools and other cultural settings (Heath, 1983; Street, 1993; Maybin, 1994), and with the work of Swales (e.g. 1990) and other linguists working with the concepts of 'genre' and 'community of discourse' to explain the functional variety of language in use.

The various lines of research described above provide resources for the development of a sociocultural perspective on learning, cognitive development and educational practice (as discussed in more detail by Mercer, 1995). The application of such a sociocultural perspective to the study of children's joint activity requires an appropriate methodology, and here other traditions of research, especially those of educational researchers expressly concerned with the quality of children's educational experience, have a great deal to offer. The sort of analytical tools we have been seeking must deal with the diversity of social contexts of formal education in which groups of children work together in classrooms, around computers or otherwise, and yet also have sufficient general applicability that they can be used to draw general comparisons between different educational events, programmes and activities. But before we put our own toolbox on display, we will briefly outline some of the methodological issues and problems which shaped its contents.

Methodological issues in the study of collaborative learning

There has been a great deal of research interest in collaborative learning in recent years. It has been investigated in various ways, of which most can be crudely categorised as either (a) experimental studies in which subjects carry out specially designed problem-solving tasks, their interactions are analysed using some sort of coding scheme yielding quantitative data, and this analysis is related to outcome measures of subjects' success with the set task; and (b) observational studies of the talk and interactions of children working together in their usual curriculum-based classroom activities, in which researchers use qualitative, interpretative methods to describe and explain the processes observed, with little attention usually being given to outcomes. We will briefly review some of the methodological benefits and problems which these very different kinds of enquiry have generated, as they are relevant to our interests here.

Experimental methods based upon coding

There are methods for analysing talk and interaction in which talk data is reduced to coded categories which are then statistically compared. (There is in fact a well-established methodological tradition, commonly called 'systematic observation', of studying the classroom talk of teachers and children in this way: see for example Croll, 1986.) The particular set of categories employed varies according to the focus of the research study. Teasley (1995) offers a recent example of this type of method, applied to the study of collaborative learning. In Teasley's study the talk of children working in pairs on a problem-solving task was transcribed and each utterance attributed to one of fourteen mutually exclusive categories. These categories included such functions as 'prediction' and 'hypothesis'. Transcripts were coded independently by two coders and the level of agreement measured to ensure reliability. A count of categories of talk in different groups was correlated with outcome measures on the problem-solving activity in order to draw conclusions about the kinds of utterances which promote effective collaborative learning. There have been many other studies of collaborative learning which have used some version of this coding approach to analysing talk. King (1989), for example, used measures such as length of utterance as well as pragmatic functional categories to investigate variables affecting the success of collaborations. Kruger (1993) counted utterances considered indicative of 'transactive reasoning' and correlated their incidence with measures of the success of children's problem solving. Barbieri and Light (1992) similarly measured the incidence of plans and explanations expressed in talk, while Azmitia and Montgomery (1993) looked for talk features indicative of scientific reasoning. And, drawing on the neo-Piagetian concept of 'sociocognitive conflict' (Doise and Mugny, 1984; Perret-Clermont, 1980), Joiner (1993) counted the number and type of disagreements in interactions and related these to problem-solving outcome measures.

These and other studies using similar coding methods have produced interesting and valuable results. Their strength, as opposed to the qualitative methods discussed below, lies in their capacity to handle large corpora of data, to offer explicit criteria for comprehensively categorising the whole of a data set, to offer a basis for making systematic comparisons between the communicative behaviour of groups of children and to enable researchers to relate this behaviour to measures of the outcomes of collaborative activity. However, the use of coding methods in studies of talk and joint activity has encountered serious criticisms. Edwards and Mercer (1987, p. 11) note that in reports of such studies the coded analysis is often presented as a *fait accompli*, so that the original observational data is lost and the coded information appears as if it were the data; the prior interpretative analysis that generated the codes from the data is commonly obscured or forgotten. Focusing on the analysis itself, Draper and Anderson (1991) identify four specific kinds of problem that coding methods must encounter in dealing with language in use:

1   Utterances are often ambiguous in meaning, making coding difficult or arbitrary.
2   Utterances may have – indeed often have – multiple simultaneous functions, which is not recognised by most coding schemes which normally involve the assignment of utterances to mutually exclusive categories.
3   The phenomena of interest to the investigator may be spread over several utterances, and so any scheme based on single utterances as the unit of analysis may not capture such phenomena.
4   Meanings change and are renegotiated during the course of the ongoing conversation.

It might be thought that using two or more independent coders and measuring their level of agreement overcomes the first problem. Indeed, coding schemes are often used in preference to other discourse analysis methods because they appear to offer a more 'objective' basis for validity claims. But, as Potter and Wetherell (1994) point out, this widely held belief confuses the reliability of a measure with its validity. That two or more coders can consistently agree on how to code different classes of ambiguous utterances tells us only that they have a shared way of interpreting utterances – it tells us little if anything about the validity of their way of interpreting utterances. If, as Edwards and Mercer (1987) suggest, such researchers frequently offer no examples of the utterances they have coded in their original discursive contexts, readers of their research reports have to take the validity of any interpretations entirely on trust. Moreover, Potter and Wetherell argue that talk is inevitably and necessarily ambiguous in its meanings because it is a means by which shared meaning is negotiated.

Crook (1994) suggests that coding methods encounter particularly serious problems when applied to the study of collaborative learning, because the process under study is one of the development of shared knowledge, through language use and joint activity, over time. Because coding schemes for talk fail to capture this crucial temporal dimension of co-operative activity, and tend to reduce collaborations into atemporal 'inventories of utterances' (*ibid.*, p. 150), their value for such research is necessarily limited.

As mentioned above, coding schemes are often used to search for correlations between the incidence of some kinds of talk and particular outcomes of joint activity (for example, success or failure in solving problems). But while coding methods can show a statistical relationship between two events in time, i.e. that event B generally follows event A, they are not good at demonstrating causal relations between two events, i.e. how and why event A led to event B. For example, King's (1989) finding that there is a statistical correlation between the incidence of task-focused questions and group success in problem solving is interesting, and suggestive of a causal link; but that kind of analysis does not in itself explain how such a link is achieved. To explain such a relationship, a researcher would have to show exactly how asking questions helped the groups of learners to solve the problems.

Interpretative approaches to the analysis of talk and collaborative activity in classrooms

Douglas Barnes (Barnes, 1976; Barnes and Todd, 1978, 1995) was amongst the first researchers to devise an analytic method for studying collaborative learning in classrooms which was sensitive to context and to the temporal development of shared meanings. In contrast to the coding approaches described above, Barnes has used detailed classroom observation and the interpretation of transcribed talk of children engaged in normal classroom tasks to explore the processes through which knowledge is shared and constructed. His approach is allied to ethnography in that it incorporates intuitive understanding gained through discussions with teachers and children and participation in the contexts described. His usual method of reporting his research is to demonstrate and illustrate his analysis by including transcribed extracts of talk, on each of which he provides a commentary. Since Barnes's pioneering work, many other educational researchers have developed similar methods of discourse analysis, and some have applied them to the study of children's talk and joint activity (e.g. Lyle, 1993; Maybin, 1994; Mercer, 1995).

In their comprehensive review of methods for researching talk in classrooms, Edwards and Westgate (1994, p. 58) argue that the strength of Barnes's early work lay in making 'visible' aspects of classroom life which are easily taken for granted and so making them available for reflection and that the value of this can be seen in the recognition his insights gained immediately from many teachers. However, they also quote many critics of such 'insightful observation' methods (*ibid.*, p. 108). It is easy, they write, to pull transcript evidence out of context in order to illustrate a case already made and so to offer 'only the illusion of proof'. Stubbs (1994) similarly argues that while studies based on the presentation of fragments of recorded talk can be insightful and plausible they raise 'problems of evidence and generalisation'; it is often not clear how such studies could be replicated and results compared. While we are not convinced that Stubbs's own methods of sociolinguistic analysis are appropriate for the investigation of collaboration and the development of shared understanding, his criticisms of fragment-based discourse analysis are particularly relevant to our concerns here – and all the more so because they lead him to advocate the use of computer-based text analysis.

Qualitative discourse analysis in the tradition of Barnes must rely on presenting short selected texts. Yet educational research often seeks generalisations, and evaluative comparisons, which cannot rest only on these samples. This is why, as Hammersley (1992) has argued, qualitative analysis can be effective for generating theories but not so effective for rigorously testing them. In contrast, the quasi-experimental research designs which are often associated with the use of coding schemes and other quantitative measures can offer explicit tests of hypotheses and systematic comparisons between the communicative behaviour and outcomes of 'target' and 'control' groups.

Because quantitative and qualitative methods have such different strengths and weaknesses, they might well seem to offer complementary approaches to the study of collaborative activity, approaches which could be combined in one research design. However, as Snyder (1995) points out in her discussion of integrating multiple perspectives in classroom research, different methodologies embody different views of the nature of meaning. To engage in the act of coding a text into a limited number of discrete categories, for example, would seem to imply that researchers view the meaning of utterances as relatively unambiguous, and that 'types' of utterance (as identified by their surface features) will always fulfil the same pragmatic functions independent of context. But, as noted above, many language researchers insist otherwise, arguing instead that the meaning and function of any utterance depends upon the way it is interpreted by participants in the collaboration and so is not only highly sensitive to historical and contemporaneous context but also necessarily always ambiguous (Potter and Wetherell, 1994; Graddol *et al.*, 1994; Mercer, 1995).

All these considerations suggest that any successful combination of such different kinds of method needs to be underpinned by a practical theory of discourse and the construction of knowledge, one which can enable researchers to transcend such positions and make a systematic, selective, complementary use of particular methods. It must enable researchers to move between the de-contextualised units measured by coding schemes and the highly context-sensitive descriptive accounts of the more qualitative approaches. It must deal with both processes and outcomes, allowing researchers to explore the development of intersubjectivity over time through actual classroom events, while also enabling them to make some useful generalisations about the process of collaborative activity in classrooms and its observable consequences.

Three types of talk

In this section of the chapter we will describe some findings of our continuing study of children's talk and joint activity. We will focus on the conventions, or 'ground rules', operating in talk in classrooms and consider how these ground rules affect children's use of language as a way of thinking together – language as a social mode of thinking (Mercer, 1995). Drawing on the various theoretical approaches and research traditions mentioned earlier in the chapter, we are attempting to provide an explanation of how children learn to reason in terms of their induction into genres of language use.

The work described emerged mainly from the SLANT project (Fisher, 1992; Dawes *et al.*, 1992; Mercer 1994) in which many hours of videotape of children talking together at computer-based tasks in British primary school classrooms were taken and analysed in search of patterns in the talk. In analysing this wealth of data, the SLANT team found it useful to typify three distinct types of talk. These (as presented by Mercer, 1995, p. 104) were as follows:

- Disputational talk, which is characterised by disagreement and individualised decision making. There are few attempts to pool resources, or to offer constructive criticism of suggestions. Disputational talk also has some characteristic discourse features – short exchanges consisting of assertions and challenges or counter-assertions.
- Cumulative talk, in which speakers build positively but uncritically on what the other has said. Partners use talk to construct a 'common knowledge' by accumulation. Cumulative discourse is characterised by repetitions, confirmations and elaborations.
- Exploratory talk, in which partners engage critically but constructively with each other's ideas. Statements and suggestions are offered for joint consideration. These may be challenged and counter-challenged, but challenges are justified and alternative hypotheses are offered. Compared with the other two types, in exploratory talk *knowledge is made more publicly accountable and reasoning is more visible in the talk*.

'Disputational', 'cumulative' and 'exploratory' are not meant to be descriptive categories into which all observed speech can be neatly and separately coded. They are nevertheless analytic categories because they typify ways that children observed in the SLANT project talked together in collaborative activities. We continue to find this typology a useful frame of reference for understanding how talk (which is inevitably resistant to neat categorisation) is used by children to 'think together' in class. The following three short sequences of talk, taken from SLANT data, illustrate something of the kind of variation with which we are concerned. All three sequences come from activities in which pairs or groups of girls (aged 10–11 years) were working together at the computer, writing dialogues between fictional characters. (Note: the fictional dialogue they generate is presented in inverted commas; any talk which was unclear is in brackets and additional contextual information is in brackets and is italicised. The transcripts have been punctuated to make the talk more intelligible to a reader.)

Sequence 1 shows talk which has some obvious 'disputational' features:

Sequence 1

Carol: Just write in the next letter. 'Did you have a nice English lesson'. (*Jo typing on computer*)

Jo: You've got to get it on there. Yes that's you. Let's just have a look at that. 'Hi, Alan did you have a nice English lesson. Yes thank you, Yeah. Yes thank you it was fine.'

Carol: You've got to let me get some in sometimes.

Jo: You're typing.

Carol: Well you can do some, go on.

Jo: 'Yes thank you'

Carol: (*Mumbles*)

Jo: You're typing. 'Yes thank you' 'I did, yeah, yes, thank you I did.'

Carol: You can spell that.

Jo: Why don't you do it?

Carol: No, because (you should).

In the next sequence, where two other girls are involved in this joint writing task, a more 'cumulative' style of talk is apparent:

Sequence 2

Sally: Yeah. What if she says erm erm 'All right, yeah.' No, just put 'Yeah all right.' No, no.

Emma: (*Laughs*) No. 'Well I suppose I could . . .

Sally: ' . . . spare 15p.' Yeah?

Emma: Yeah.

Sally: 'I suppose . . . '

Emma: 'I suppose I could spare 50p.'

Sally: '50?'

Emma: Yeah. 'Spare 50 pence.'

Sally: '50 pence.'

Emma: '50 pence.' And Angela says 'That isn't enough I want to buy some-
thing else.'
Sally: Yeah, no no. 'I want a drink as well you know I want some coke as
well'.
Emma: 'That isn't enough for bubble gum and some coke.'
Sally: Yeah, yeah.

In the third sequence, three girls are working together. One of their fictional
characters is a teenage girl, who has to explain to her angry father why she
has stayed out so late. Here we can see talk which is more 'exploratory':
ideas are explicitly debated, requests for ideas and justifications for challenges are made, and alternative suggestions are offered.

Sequence 3

Kris: 'I was only at the disco with Gemma.'
Fiona: No.
Helen: No.
Kris: That's too nice.
Helen: That's too um. . .
Fiona: Outrageous! *(laughs)*
Helen: Yeah.
Kris: It's got to be really silly.

(*Brief interruption from some other children outside the group: the girls then
resume.*)

Fiona: What can we say?
Helen: Um, what is a totally innocent place?
Fiona: The park?
Helen: No, it's late, remember?
Fiona: Oh yeah.
Kris: Yes, exactly.
Helen: It's dark.
Kris: Oh no, she's not the brainiest of people, is she?
Fiona: Where, where can it be? Um, um, no, she could be staying at school.

The intellectual and educational significance of exploratory talk

Our conceptualisation of the different types of talk is generated by a theory
of language and cognition which is essentially sociocultural, and which iden-
tifies a developed capacity for the joint creation of knowledge between
contemporaries and across generations as a crucial and distinctive psychological characteristic of our species (Mercer, 1995). This theory incorporates
a strong interpretation of the significance of *context*, which here means that

we believe that talk which resembles any one of the three types – disputational, cumulative, and exploratory – may be socially appropriate and effective in some specific social contexts. But the theory also suggests that the kind of talk which (following Barnes and Todd, 1978, 1995) we call 'exploratory' represents a *distinctive social mode of thinking* – a way of using language which is not only the embodiment of critical thinking, but which is also essential for successful participation in 'educated' communities of discourse (such as those associated with the practice of law, science, technology, the arts, business administration and politics). Of course, there is much more involved in participating in an educated discourse than using talk in an 'exploratory' way: the accumulated knowledge, the specialised vocabulary and other linguistic conventions of any particular discourse community have to be learned, and account has to be taken of members' relative status and power. And such language is essentially situated and context-sensitive, not 'context-free' or 'de-contextualised' as some (e.g. Donaldson, 1978, 1992; Wells, 1986) have suggested. There are limits on how explicit members of a discourse community need to be to make meanings clear: they can share new ideas effectively enough by implicitly invoking the community's shared knowledge and understanding. The key judgement made by effective communicators within a discourse is about what needs to be made explicit to any particular audience on any particular occasion. Our conception of exploratory talk embodies qualities that are a vital, basic part of many such educated discourses. Encouraging an awareness and use of that kind of talk may help learners develop intellectual habits that will serve them well across a range of different situations.

Exploratory talk and effective collaboration in the classroom

'Exploratory talk', then, in the sense we use the term, is a communicative process for reasoning through talk in the context of some specific joint activity. Participants in exploratory talk offer reasons for assertions and expect reasons from others as they pursue some common goal. The ground rules for exploratory talk as a language practice facilitate the production and the critical examination of varied ideas in such a way that the proposal best supported by reasons will be accepted by all. Participants must therefore recognise each others' rights to participate and respect the potential validity of each others' contributions, and so there are implications for the social order of a collaborative pair or group. This requirement can be related to the results of studies of collaborative activity which have found that socially symmetrical pairs or groups reason together better and produce a better learning outcome than asymmetrical groups (Light and Littleton, 1994), and that friendship is an important factor in supporting explicit reasoning (Azmitia and Montgomery, 1993).

The cumulative educational implication of all these ideas is that pupils should be encouraged and enabled to practise exploratory talk in the classroom. There are, however, some difficult problems to be faced in transforming this proposal into educational practice. Barnes's early advocacy of the educational importance of talk of an 'exploratory' kind (Barnes, 1976; Barnes and Todd, 1978) found official endorsement in British education, in *The Bullock Report* (DES, 1975), through the National Oracy Project (Open University, 1991; Norman, 1992) and eventually in the orders for the National Curriculum (DFE, 1995). But recent studies of British primary classrooms indicate that children still have very little opportunity to engage in open and questioning enquiry through talk (Bennett and Dunne, 1990; Galton and Williamson, 1992). One reason for this could be the dilemma that teachers face in combining free and open discussions with their professional responsibility to teach a set curriculum. The role of the teacher in guiding students into explicitly rational discussions is a difficult one. The teacher–student relationship is, by definition, asymmetrical. Research has shown that teachers' questions commonly constrain pupils' contributions and discourage extended responses (Dillon, 1990; Wood, 1992). And as Douglas Barnes noted:

> the very presence of a teacher alters the way in which pupils use language, so that they are more likely to be aiming at 'answers' which will gain approval than using language to reshape knowledge. Only the most skilful teaching can avoid this.
>
> (Barnes, 1976, p. 78)

In modelling and coaching exploratory talk teachers have to simulate a situation of symmetry. How can this be done? The teaching of 'exploratory talk' in schools may also face a second problem. This is the issue of how well children can adapt and apply ways of talking or thinking that they have learned to the demands of subject-specific areas of the curriculum. We believe that the computer can help with both these problems.

The role of the computer

In their classic discourse analysis research, Sinclair and Coulthard (1975) proposed that the basic exchange structure for classroom discourse had the following form:

- Initiation (by the teacher)
- Response (by the pupil)
- Feedback (by the teacher)

It is generally accepted that the IRF exchange is a fundamental feature of teacher-centred education, and one associated with teachers' power to direct, shape and control the learning of students (see e.g. Mehan, 1979; Edwards and Westgate, 1994; Edwards and Mercer, 1987; Mercer, 1995).

Fisher's (1992) analysis of SLANT project data suggested that some types of exchanges occurring between students and computers also have an IRF structure (see also Crook, 1994, p. 11). She argued that this exchange type occurred where the computer–user dialogue structure was relatively 'closed' and directive. That is, the computer programme initiated exchanges (I) and acknowledged responses (F). Pupils' responses (R), according to Fisher, could be assigned to one of the following three categories:

1   a key press
2   a key press accompanied by an oral description of what is being done by the operator
3   some discussion of what should be done followed by a key press

This observation is valuable, and can be developed to serve our current interests. We wish to distinguish exchanges in which some discussion between children takes place from those in which computer initiations are merely followed by key presses or some other 'action-response'. We therefore find it useful to identify an exchange structure IDRF, as follows:

- I – Initiation (by the computer)
- D – Discussion (between the children)
- R – Response (by the children acting together)
- F – Follow-up (by the computer)

The IDRF structure combines two very different kinds of interaction: the IRF interaction between computer and users, and the D which is discussion between the users. The IDRF exchange structure also potentially combines two very different educational genres. In terms of the basic IRF sequence, users are passive and the computer plays a role similar to that of a teacher who directs and evaluates the responses of learners. But the computer does not have the same social role and authority status as a teacher: children are much less inhibited in their discussions by its presence (Dawes *et al.*, 1992; Mercer, 1995). The computer–user interaction frames their discussion and can direct it towards specific areas and outcomes (Wegerif, 1996a, 1996b). In discussion mode, on the other hand, users are potentially active, deciding together what answers they will test out on the computer and so pushing the computer into the passive role of a learning environment.

To maximise the educational potential of group work around computers, children must talk together effectively before responding to computer prompts. For educationally valuable talk to occur there must be a switch in mode after the computer's 'initiation', putting active engagement with the software on hold while pupils reflect on their current situation and what their next move should be.

Applying the concept of exploratory talk

The SLANT project analysis suggested that the quality of children's discussion could be influenced by both the design of the software factors and the input of teachers. The largest amount of exploratory talk between children was observed when off-computer teaching of effective ways of talking together in groups was combined with the use of software which encouraged discussion (Mercer, 1994; Wegerif, 1996a). Other research (for example, that discussed by Crook, 1994 and Light and Littleton, 1994) supports the view that one of the most effective ways of using computers for teaching and learning in school is through classroom activities which integrate (a) the instructional and supportive involvement of a teacher with (b) software expressly designed to elicit discussion and (c) opportunities for pupils to work together without constant teacher supervision. In the next part of the chapter, we describe how these observations were used to design, implement and evaluate a small-scale experimental teaching programme with both off-computer and on-computer components. We will use this account to illustrate the points we have made about the need for concepts which can be used with rigorous 'objective' comparisons and generalisations while remaining sensitive to the cumulative and temporal nature of the development of shared knowledge in productive talk.

The intervention programme

The intervention programme consisted of a series of lessons focusing on exploratory talk (further information on this is given in Dawes, 1995; Wegerif and Mercer, 1996). A central feature of this programme was the promotion of a set of ground rules for exploratory talk which could be accepted by the children and then taught through modelling and learned through practice. The specific ground rules which the children and a teacher agreed upon were as follows:

Ground rules for talk

1   Everyone should have a chance to talk
2   Everyone's ideas should be carefully considered
3   Each member of the group should be asked: what do you think? and why do you think that?
4   Look and listen to the person talking
5   After discussion, the group should agree on a group idea.

This list was displayed prominently on the wall and referred to throughout the programme. The programme also included software designed to support exploratory talk within curriculum areas. (More detail on the design of this software and the principles behind it can be found in Wegerif, 1995, 1996b.)

The evaluation

The evaluation of this intervention programme also applied the concept of exploratory talk in a way that combined classroom observation and detailed discourse analysis with the use of a pre- and post-intervention comparison. The pre- to post-intervention comparison used scores from a group reasoning test and pre- to post-intervention comparisons of the recording talk of videotaped groups of children doing this reasoning test. A control class of same-age children in a neighbouring school were also given the group reasoning test both before and after the intervention. The use of video made it possible to relate the talk to the answers given to particular problems in the test. With this research design it was possible to relate changes in test score measures to changes in linguistic features, in a similar way to many coding and counting studies; but it was also possible to relate the talk of groups to their work on specific problems, as is normally done in the qualitative discourse analysis tradition.

Assessing the 'educational productivity' of talk

Using problems from an established test of reasoning, Raven's Standard Progressive Matrices (performance on which correlates well with educational achievement), we devised a simple way of investigating the productivity of the children's talk. Graphical problems from the Raven's test were given to the children who were asked to work together in groups of three coming to joint answers. The same test was given to the target class (who had received the training) and to the control class (who had not). Children in both classes were in the same school year, and were 9 –10 years old. Each class was divided up into groups of three, and each group in each class was tested at the beginning of the intervention programme and again at the end.

All the group scores in both target and control classes increased over the period of the intervention programme. As illustrated in Figure 6.1, the target class group scores increased by 32 per cent while the control class group scores increased by 15 per cent. The differences between the pre- and post-intervention test scores for all groups in the target class were compared to the differences between the pre- and post-intervention test scores for all groups in the control class and it was found that this difference was significant ($Z = -1.87$ p $= 0.031$. One-tailed Mann-Whitney test, corrected for ties).

An analysis of the quality of children's talk during the reasoning test

The test results show that the groups of children in the target class became more effective in solving problems together. However, these results do not in themselves provide evidence of the intervention programme leading to the increased use of exploratory talk by children. To find out if this indeed was

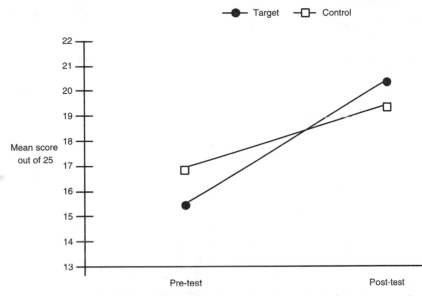

Figure 6.1 Pre- to post-intervention change in the mean scores of the target and
control classes on the group reasoning test

the case, we analysed videotapes of groups in the target class working
together on the same reasoning problems during the initial pre-intervention
test and during the post-intervention test. From these it was possible to
isolate and compare the talk of groups successfully solving problems on the
later occasion with their talk on the earlier occasion when they had failed to
solve exactly the same kinds of problem.

It was generally found that problems which had not been solved in the
pre-intervention task and were then solved in the post-intervention task
(leading to the marked increase in group scores) were solved as a result of
group interaction strategies associated with exploratory talk and coached in
the intervention programme. The following two transcribed sequences
(taken from the activity of one group) illustrate the findings of this
discourse analysis. The problem they are facing is shown in Figure 6.2.

Group 1: pre-intervention talk in the reasoning test

John: *(Rude noise)*
Elaine: How do you do that?
Graham: That one look.
All: It's that. *(Elaine rings 1 as answer for A9)*
Elaine: No, because it will come along like that. *(Elaine rings 5 as answer
           for A11)*
John: Look it's that one. *(Elaine rings 2 as answer for B1)*

Group 1: post-intervention talk in the reasoning test

John: Number 5.
Graham: I think it's number 2.
John: No, it's out, that goes out, look.
Graham: Yeh, but as it comes in it goes this.
Elaine: Now we're talking about this bit, so it can't be number 2 it's that one.
Elaine: It's that one, it's that one.
Graham: Yeh 'cos look.
Elaine: 4.
Graham: I agree with 4. *(Elaine rings 4 as answer for A11)*

A 11

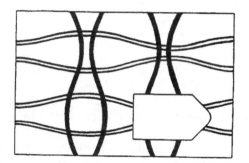

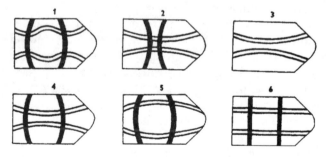

Figure 6.2 Problem A11 of the Raven's Progressive Matrices Test

Commentary

In the pre-intervention task question A11 was answered wrongly in the context of a series of several problems which were moved through very rapidly. The other problems in this short series were answered correctly. Elaine's second utterance 'No, because it will come along like that' implies that one of the other two group members had just pointed to a different answer on the page. She gives a reason to support her view and this is not challenged. There is no evidence that agreement is reached before the answer is given. The group move on to the next problem. An examination of the full transcript suggests that the children do not take the task set very seriously and much of their talk is off-task.

In the post-intervention task episode much more time is spent by the group on A11. Two alternatives are considered and rejected before the right answer is found and agreed on. This is crucial. In the pre-intervention task example only one alternative was considered and rejected before a decision was reached. The structure of the problem is such that, to be sure of a right answer it is necessary to consider at least two aspects of the pattern. John first spots the pattern of the dark vertical lines moving outwards and so suggests answer 5. Graham then spots the pattern of the lighter horizontal lines moving inwards and so contradicts John saying the answer must be 2. Just as Graham's reason means number 5 is wrong so John's reason means that number 2 is wrong. Elaine apparently sees this and so turns to number 4. Graham sees that she is right and points to confirming evidence on the page. In the context of John's vocal objections to previous assertions made by his two partners his silence at this point implies a tacit acceptance of their decision. Both episodes contain talk of an 'exploratory' kind: challenges are offered, reasons are given and the group appear to be working together. However, the second episode includes a much longer sustained sequence of exploratory talk about the same shared focus.

We had also wanted to know if computers could be used effectively to enable children to apply, develop and practise exploratory talk in curriculum-related activities. The effectiveness of the intervention in achieving this was assessed by analysing the talk of children doing the specially designed computer-based tasks on science and citizenship. This analysis (reported in more detail in Wegerif, 1995, 1996b) showed that children in the target class were able to apply exploratory talk effectively in dealing with these tasks. Moreover, we were able to make systematic comparisons between the talk of children in the target class (who had taken part in the off-computer component of the programme) and the talk of children in the control class (who had not) working at the computer, and between the talk of children working at the computer and those working on off-computer tasks. The evidence of this analysis supports the view that when children experience the off-computer teaching about talk combined with the use of the specially designed computer tasks of the programme, this is especially effective in both expanding the amount of discussion which takes place at the computer (the D of the IDRF exchange) and encouraging more exploratory talk.

Changes in word usage studied through the use of computer-based text analysis

The brief analysis of episodes of talk above illustrates how the concept of exploratory talk applied to educational practice through our intervention programme generated productive talk. This sort of analysis can show how, through applying the ground rules of exploratory talk which they have been taught, children find solutions to problems and construct knowledge together over time. But by being based on very short extracts of transcript, they face the criticism commonly made of ethnographic and similar interpretative studies, that it is difficult to draw general or comparative conclusions from them. One way to overcome this is to supplement interpretative studies with the use of computer-based text analysis programmes. Devised mainly for lexicographical work and literary analysis, such programmes allow researchers to investigate (amongst other things) the relative occurrence and co-occurrence (or 'concordance') of selected linguistic features through and across texts. One such programme has been designed by our Open University colleague David Graddol to serve the particular needs of discourse analysts; it is called !KwicTex (Graddol, in preparation).The use of this programme brings with it some of the advantages of coding schemes in terms of a capacity to deal with large amounts of transcribed talk data, to generate quantitative results and do so with rigour and 'objectivity', and yet it does so without the disadvantage of losing the contexts of the actual words spoken.

Used in conjunction with our characterisation of types of talk and with more detailed interpretative studies, a text analysis of linguistic features can show changes in the kind of talk being used over time and between conditions. For example, we used our qualitative analysis to identify a number of linguistic features which appeared to be indicative of exploratory talk. We then used !KwicTex to determine the relative occurrence of these throughout the data, and check whether or not their relative incidence was indeed associated with the use of talk of an 'exploratory' kind. We then compared their relative occurrence in the talk of the target class groups doing the reasoning test before and after the teaching programme. We found that the incidence of some of these features – children's use of questions, and their use of 'because' and 'if' – increased dramatically after the teaching programme (see Table 6.1).

The same sort of results were obtained for counts of word usage in talk around the software. It must be stressed that, unlike coding schemes, this kind of text analysis works with the actual words spoken and reveals their occurrence in their linguistic context. By looking at key words in their linguistic context, it is possible also to explore differences and changes in the ways in which particular words are being used. For instance, in the talk of one group the use of 'because/'cos' shifted from primarily co-occurring with 'look' (as an appeal to, say, information on a computer screen) to being found more in passages of elaborated verbal reasoning.

Table 6.1 The relative occurrence of linguistic features associated with exploratory talk in the pre- and post-test talk of the three target-class groups

Linguistic features	Pre-test				Post-test			
	Gp1	Gp2	Gp3	Total	Gp1	Gp2	Gp3	Total
Questions	2	8	7	17	9	33	44	86
Because/'cos	12	18	9	39	21	34	40	95
So	6	3	1	10	6	5	7	18
If	1	1	0	2	13	8	14	35
Total words	1460	1309	715	3484	2166	1575	2120	5761

Exploratory talk revisited

The findings of the study we have described lead us to conclude that the combination of specially designed software and intervention programme succeeded in both expanding the amount of discussion and enhancing its quality; there was more talk, and more of it was 'exploratory'. Moreover, it seems reasonable to infer that increased use of exploratory talk was a key factor in improving the problem-solving performance of groups of children. These findings therefore provide some support for a sociocultural theory of language and cognition because they show that exploratory talk is indeed productive talk, in terms of children's capacity to solve reasoning problems.

However, the concept of exploratory talk and the three-part typology from which it emerged should not be judged as finished products. Rather, they are provisional and tentative attempts to provide the kind of concepts that are needed if we are to understand the ways that pupils' talk in classrooms functions as a social mode of thinking. Our intention is to relate talk to cultural practices, or genres, based on cultural conventions or ground rules. In this way we attempt to overcome the weaknesses of more usual qualitative approaches by providing a framework for comparison and evaluation. Nevertheless, we know that actual talk is not reducible to such typifications, and requires contextualised interpretation by some method of qualitative discourse analysis. We have therefore described how such a qualitative analysis can be combined with the use of computer-based concordancers or text analysis programmes to explore the way patterns of language use emerge and re-emerge in different contexts and at different times. It is worth noting that we have only provided a glimpse of what such text analysis programmes offer the discourse analyst.

Summary and conclusions

This chapter has described our attempt to develop theoretical and methodological tools for the investigation of collaborative talk, and in so doing we have elaborated the concept of a particular way of using language as a social mode of thinking, called *exploratory talk*. We have suggested that this concept, when embedded in a sociocultural theory of language and cognition, is particularly useful for the study of collaborative activity in educational settings. We described a role the computer might play in prompting and sustaining children's use of exploratory talk, and of doing so in a way that integrated the role of a teacher as a crucial mentor for children's initiation into culturally based discourse practices, and which also took account of curriculum constraints and imperatives. By combining selected qualitative and quantitative methods, we were able to evaluate the success of an experimental programme for encouraging exploratory talk. We find the results of our small-scale classroom-based research encouraging, not only because of the support provided for our developing theory and methodology, but also because the research indicates how classroom activities could be designed to deal more directly with the development of children's capacities for collaborating and using language to reason. At the time of writing, we are embarking on a new school-based project which will allow us to pursue this work on a much larger scale.

References

Austin, J. (1962) *How to Do Things with Words*, Oxford: Oxford University Press.

Azmitia, M, and Montgomery, R. (1993) 'Friendship, transactive dialogues, and the development of scientific reasoning', *Social Development* 2(3): 202–221.

Barbieri, M. and Light, P. (1992) 'Interaction, gender and performance on a computer-based task', *Learning and Instruction* 2: 199–213.

Barnes, D. (1976) *From Communication to Curriculum*, Harmondsworth: Penguin Books.

—— (1992) 'The role of talk in learning', in K. Norman (ed.), *Thinking Voices*, London: Hodder and Stoughton.

Barnes, D. and Todd, F. (1978) *Communication and Learning in Small Groups*, London: Routledge and Kegan Paul.

—— (1995) *Communication and Learning Revisited*, Portsmouth, NH: Boynton/Cook Heinemann.

Bennett, N. and Dunne, E. (1990) *Talk and Learning in Groups*, London: Macmillan.

Croll, P. (1986) *Systematic Classroom Observation*, Lewes, Sussex: The Falmer Press.

Crook, C. (1994) *Computers and the Collaborative Experience of Learning*, London and New York: Routledge.

Dawes, L. (1995) 'Team talk', *Junior Education* March: 26–27.

Dawes, L., Fisher, E. and Mercer, N. (1992) 'The quality of talk at the computer', *Language and Learning*, October: 22–25.

DES (Department of Education and Science) (1975) *The Bullock Report*, London: HMSO.
—— (1990) *Curriculum Guidance, 8*, London: HMSO.
DFE (Department For Education) (1995) *The Orders of the National Curriculum*, London: HMSO.
Dillon, J. T. (1990) *The Practice of Questioning*, London: Routledge.
Doise, W. and Mugny, G. (1984) *The Social Development of the Intellect*, Oxford: Pergamon Press.
Donaldson, M. (1978) *Children's Minds*, London: Fontana.
—— (1992) *Human Minds*, London: Allen Lane.
Draper, S. and Anderson, A. (1991) 'The significance of dialogue in learning and observing learning', *Computers and Education* 17(1): 93–107.
Drew, P. and Heritage, P. (eds) (1992) *Talk at Work: Interaction in Institutional Settings*, Cambridge: Cambridge University Press.
Edwards, A. D. and Westgate, D. (1994) *Investigating Classroom Talk* (second edn), London: The Falmer Press.
Edwards, D. and Mercer, N. (1987) *Common Knowledge*, London: Methuen/Routledge.
Edwards, D. and Potter, J. (1992) *Discursive Psychology*, London: Sage.
Fisher, E. (1992) 'Characteristics of children's talk at the computer and its relationship to the computer software', *Language and Education* 7(2): 187–215.
—— (1993) 'Distinctive features of pupil–pupil talk and their relationship to learning', *Language and Education* 7(4): 239–258.
Forrester, M. A. (1992) *The Development of Young Children's Social-Cognitive Skills*, New Jersey: Lawrence Erlbaum Associates.
Galton, M. and Williamson, J. (1992) *Group Work in the Primary Classroom*, London: Routledge.
Garfinkel, H. (1967) *Studies in Ethnomethodology*, Englewood Cliff, NJ: Prentice Hall.
Graddol, D. (in preparation) '!KwicTex – a computer-based tool for discourse analysis', *CLAC Occasional Papers in Language and Communications*, Centre for Language and Communication, The Open University.
Graddol, D., Maybin, J. and Stierer, B. (1994) *Researching Language and Literacy in Social Context*, Clevedon: Multilingual Matters.
Grice, H. (1975) 'Logic and conversation', in P. Cole and J. Morgan (eds) *Syntax and Semantics 3: Speech Acts*, New York: Academic Press.
Hammersley, M. (1992) *What's Wrong with Ethnography*, London: Routledge.
Harré, R. and Gillet, G. (1994) *The Discursive Mind*, London: Sage.
Heath, S. B. (1983) *Ways with Words: Language, Life and Work in Communities and Classrooms*, Cambridge: Cambridge University Press.
Joiner, R. (1993) 'A dialogue model of the resolution of inter-individual conflicts: implications for computer-based collaborative learning', unpublished Ph.D. thesis, IET, Open University, Milton Keynes.
King, A. (1989) 'Verbal interaction and problem solving within computer aided learning groups', *Journal of Educational Computing Research* 5: 1–15.
Kruger, A. (1993) 'Peer collaboration: conflict, cooperation or both?', *Social Development* 2(3): 165–182.
Lave, J. (1991) 'Situated learning in communities of practice', in L. Resnick, J. Levine

and S. Teasley (eds) *Perspectives on Socially Shared Cognition*, Washington, DC: American Psychological Association.

Light, P. and Littleton, K. (1994) 'Cognitive approaches to group work', in P. Kutnick and C. Rogers (eds) *Groups in Schools*, London: Cassell.

Lyle, S. (1993) 'An investigation into ways in which children "talk themselves into meaning"', *Language and Education*, 7(3): 181–197.

Maybin, J. (1994) 'Children's voices: talk, knowledge and identity', in D. Graddol, J. Maybin and B. Stierer (eds) *Researching Language and Literacy in Social Context*, Clevedon: Multilingual Matters.

Mehan, H. (1979) *Learning Lessons: Social Organisation in the Classroom*, Cambridge, MA: Harvard University Press.

Mercer, N. (1994) 'The quality of talk in children's joint activity at the computer', *Journal of Computer Assisted Learning* 10: 24–32.

—— (1995) *The Guided Construction of Knowledge: Talk Amongst Teachers and Learners*, Clevedon: Multilingual Matters.

Norman, K. (ed.) (1992) *Thinking Voices: The Work of the National Oracy Project*, London: Hodder and Stoughton.

Perret-Clermont, A-N. (1980) *Social Interaction and Cognitive Development in Children*, London: Academic Press.

Potter J. and Wetherell, M. (1994) *Discourse Analysis and Social Psychology*, London: Sage.

Sinclair, J. M. and Coulthard, R. M. (1975) *Towards an Analysis of Discourse*, Oxford: Oxford University Press.

Snyder, I. (1995) 'Multiple perspectives in literacy research: integrating the quantitative and qualitative', *Language and Education* 9(11).

Street, B. (ed.) (1993) *Cross-Cultural Approaches to Literacy*, Cambridge: Cambridge University Press.

Stubbs, M. (1994) 'Grammar, text and ideology: computer-assisted methods in the linguistics of representation', *Applied Linguistics* 15(2): 202–223.

Swales, J. (1990) *Genre Analysis: English in Academic and Research Settings*, Cambridge: Cambridge University Press.

Teasley, S. (1995) 'The role of talk in children's peer collaborations', *Developmental Psychology* 31(2): 207–220.

The Open University (1991) *Talk and Learning 5–16: An In-Service Pack on Oracy for Teachers*, Milton Keynes: The Open University.

Van der Veer, R. and Valsiner, J. (1991) *Understanding Vygotsky: A Quest for Synthesis*, Oxford: Blackwells.

Vygotsky, L. (1991) 'The Genesis of Higher Mental functions', in P. Light, S. Sheldon and M. Woodhead (eds) *Learning to Think*, London: Routledge.

Wegerif, R. (1995) 'Computers, talk and learning: using computers to support reasoning through talk across the curriculum', unpublished Ph.D. thesis, Open University, Milton Keynes.

—— (1996a) 'Collaborative learning and directive software', *Journal of Computer Assisted Learning* 12(1): 22–32.

—— (1996b) 'Using computers to help coach exploratory talk across the curriculum', *Computers and Education* 26(1–3): 51–60.

Wegerif, R. and Mercer, N. (1996) 'Computers and reasoning through talk in the classroom', *Language and Education* 10(1): 47–64.

Wells, G. (1986) *The Meaning Makers*, London: Hodder and Stoughton.

Wertsch, J. V. (1985) *Vygotsky and the Social Formation of Mind*, Cambridge, MA: Harvard University Press.
Wood, D. (1992) 'Teaching talk', in K. Norman (ed.) *Thinking Voices: the Work of the National Oracy Project*, London: Hodder and Stoughton.

7 Computers in the community of classrooms

Charles Crook

Introduction

It is a familiar idea that scientists should be engaged in revealing things about nature. Scientists are expected to confront us with their discoveries. In these terms, it is less obvious what we should expect from psychologists. Much of what we wish to understand in their domain is already visible to us. This is certainly the case for social behaviour; the understanding of which does not seem to hinge on any paraphernalia of microscopes, telescopes or equivalent instrumentation for making hidden events visible. So, it is unlikely that progress in social or educational psychology depends quite so much on innovation of method – in the sense of new technologies for exposing what is concealed. Instead, progress arises from new ways of *systematising* that with which we are already familiar. Certainly, this entails the application of scientific method – whether natural history or experimentation – but what holds us back is not usually the need for some method, tool or trick. What is usually needed is observation or experiment guided by a better conceptual analysis of the domain being examined. Empirical studies of social action must be driven by the difficult prior work of useful theorising. Effective social psychological research pursues phenomena that first have been framed with some vocabulary of concepts that is coherent and comprehensive.

So it is with the study of social behaviour in classrooms. We may feel that varying circumstances for learning render classroom interactions more or less 'productive' for pupils. This feeling makes us want to understand better how some intervention – such as new technology – has particular effects of this kind. If understanding the effects then turns out to be difficult, it is tempting to bemoan the lack of a powerful enough 'method' for tackling a slippery topic. Yet the way forward may not depend upon finding some new research instrument. It may depend instead upon us doing more conceptual work: such as unpacking what is understood by the 'productivity' of classroom experiences, or characterising more carefully the interpersonal framework within which pupils organise joint activity.

In the present chapter I do wish to converge upon some suggestions about method, but I shall not be revealing any valuable new tools or techniques for capturing and explaining 'productive interactions'. Any implications here for the mechanics of research will not be radical: the research mentioned below continues to comprise familiar procedures for watching, asking and comparing. I am more interested in defining the events over which this research net should be cast: arguing that such considerations will help us with ambitions for analysis and intervention. There are three sections to this chapter. In the first, I argue that the study of social processes in relation to computers has been too narrowly pursued. This entails a critique of such research in terms of the circumscribed nature of the social exchanges which get studied. It also entails a consideration of limitations in the way collaborative talk has been conceptualised by psychologists. These arguments lead to a claim that more attention must be given to classrooms as communities. In the second section, I describe a classroom computer application designed to support community structure. In the third section, I consider a research strategy that might help evaluate this intervention – bringing into sharper focus some of the conceptual issues raised in the first section.

The territory of collaborative interaction

One of the spin-off effects of computers in early education has been the growth of interest among developmental psychologists in collaborative learning. As many commentators note, the scarcity of computers in schools almost demanded that children were organised to work at them in small groups. However, it is not that this new educational technology thereby *created* collaborative learning practices: classrooms were already 'bustling places' in this sense. Rather, computers made pupil interaction *visible* to researchers and, perhaps, suggested an attractively bounded situation in which students of cognitive development might study the topic of productive peer interaction. Thus, ways of using new educational technology brought a social psychological phenomenon into focus.

Most researchers in schools have the status of 'visitors'. This is understandable. The pressure of their own disciplinary practices demands that field projects are turned around fairly quickly. Moreover, often academics may have other responsibilities of teaching, research or administration to distract them from spending too much time at any particular site. Thus, if children-at-computers defined a conveniently bounded and visible *physical* setting for studying peer interaction, so the same occasion was (usually) found to be conveniently bounded in *time* – pupils tackling tasks of limited duration that defined attractively self-contained 'sessions'.

It is quite appropriate for students of learning and cognitive development to exploit these conveniences. Certainly, much recent research into peer interaction at computers proves interesting and provocative – despite the circumscribed format of the situations studied. However, we should be aware of possible limitations in the reach of this work. One limitation might

be how readily any observation of peer interaction effects can be generalised. Where such research includes evaluation of interaction outcomes, we
need to be sure that the setting for peer-supported learning and the pupils'
experience of participating in it does correspond to circumstances that
might be constructed in the normal classroom by teachers working to
routine. As it happens, the educational application of computers often has a
bolted-on character that is similar to their status in research projects. So, in
discussing the outcomes of interacting at a computer, this parallel may
authenticate the link from research to classroom practice. But it may still
undermine making a confident link between what is learned from such interactions at *computers* and what happens in peer-based learning interactions
more generally.

The tradition of observing self-contained collaborations at classroom
computers has another limitation. Such interactions are typically not
considered to have any history. What gets transcribed for analysis is the
interaction that occurred during the 'session(s)'. The exchanges thus docu-
mented are not usually understood with any reference to the broader social
context within which they are located: this context might include previous
experiences of shared activity that the participants bring to the task being
studied. The point being developed here is that the psychologically interesting 'territory' of collaborative learning extends beyond the arrangements
typical of circumscribed problem-solving sessions (such as might be organised at computers). Any productivity of interactions within such sessions
arises from circumstances that have been previously established outside of
them – circumstances that comprise a broader social context in which they
are located. In order to establish that there is a such a context (and that it is
useful to explore it), first I need to review what is on offer from the more
limited agenda of traditional analyses in this area. This involves considering
the terms in which psychologists have traditionally made sense of pupils'
collaborative exchanges – understood as brief, localised sessions of joint
classroom activity. It will not be a matter of questioning this analysis: more
a matter of recognising the need to go beyond it to make full sense of what
happens when learners engage in joint problem solving.

When pupils work together at some classroom task, researchers typically
will judge the value of their activity in terms of conversational features.
Different theorists stress different features as being important for learning or
cognitive change. For example, the existence of conflict and argument might
be important for some (Doise, 1985). For others, the opportunity to articulate thinking publicly may be what matters (Hoyles and Sutherland, 1989).
Still others may attach importance to the exercise and exploration of distinct
rhetorical devices: pupils encountering pressure to practise particular forms
of reasoning-in-talk. In this case, researchers may catalogue speech acts of
pre-defined kinds – hypothesising, predicting, negotiating, confirming, challenging and so on (Webb, 1986). Whichever theoretical gloss is placed on the
interactions observed, it is rare that any such features of pupils' talk are

novel to the problem-solving activities within which they occur. These are not ways of interacting that are uniquely elicited and nurtured by the classroom tasks that teachers or researchers come up with. Jointly working at a computer (for example) does not *create* such discursive capabilities among learners. In their domestic or playful lives pupils may frequently engage in talk where conflict must be managed; they may also come under pressure to articulate the basis of their everyday actions or opinions; and out of class they are likely routinely to use talk for hypothesising, predicting, negotiating and so forth (Dunn, 1993; Tizard and Hughes, 1984). Therefore, what is potent about the occurrence of such interactions around a classroom problem is that an *existing* repertoire of discursive capabilities is getting successfully mobilised for *schooled* purposes.

If it is an aim of education to help children solve problems collaboratively, then the above analysis suggests what might comprise a successful programme. It might comprise at least the following three ingredients: (a) a directing of children's discursive resources towards the content of particular academic domains (geography, mathematics or whatever) – incidentally appropriating into pupils' social reasoning the particular vocabularies of the relevant disciplines that we confront them with (mathematical symbolism, for example); (b) an encouragement to mobilise such resources in order to talk about and solve problems that are often arbitrary and summoned up for purposes of pure exercise   an attitude of controlled problem solving, prompted to order and (c) goals and incentives for maintaining pupils' joint focus on these problems – concentrating and sustaining a systematic explo ration of a certain kind of academic material. The form of these achievements indicates why modern educational commentators discuss educational practice in terms of the *socialisation* of modes of thought (Bruner, 1996).

Such an analysis of the status quo encourages a useful move: namely, to foreground the idea of (teacher-managed) *appropriation*. What is made possible by the collaborative tasks we conjure up for pupils is an appropriation of their socially grounded modes of thinking and communicating into domains of knowledge that we value. This theoretical perspective then defines a distinctive research agenda for any psychology of productive interaction. A central challenge for educational practice becomes the successful creation of continuities between pupils' existing concerns and new ones that we are asking them to reason about together in classrooms. More generally, this perspective makes us more interested in what can *motivate* pupils into collaborative forms of engagement with the new species of problem that schools define for them. Once we start from accepting that the learner already has available a repertoire of discursive resources, our attention can become focused on how to bridge that gap between the playful and the schooled deployment of those resources. This process of appropriation into schooled purposes must be carefully orchestrated by those who teach. It depends upon care in the design and introduction of classroom tasks, such that the possibilities of continuities in learners' experience can be exploited.

What needs to happen in the end is a redirection of the energy that accompanies playful collaboration into the collaborations that arise in school settings. Often it may be difficult to judge whether this has been successfully achieved. In describing children writing stories together, I have suggested that there are differences among pairings that arise from a motivational dimension of this social situation (Crook, 1994a); all individual participants may voice suitable public contributions to some degree, but only some pairings may display a vigorous concern to do so *collaboratively*. What is entailed in making such a contrast?

The claim is that some exchanges will be more vigorous because of a greater commitment among the partners to a process of cognitive co-ordination. The typical psychological analysis of children's collaborative talk into taxonomies of speech acts causes us to miss the central feature of this kind of discourse. It is about creating joint reference, and doing so in the interests of constructing (and exploiting) a shared understanding of some problem. If such a feature of talk is to be detected, it can only be detected from an analysis of narrative structure – not from frequency analyses of the participants' individual contributions. In pursuing this, we might then be able to say that some partnerships display a greater 'joint engagement' with a task. Or that they adopt a more 'collaborative attitude' towards it. In such cases, the individuals may admit to us that they are actively aiming to negotiate a mutual view on their problem. Of course this is not the same as saying they must *agree* in what they say about it; the mutuality does not arise from simple consensus. It arises from the investment in determining what a partner understands and publicly bringing that into balance with one's own understanding – thereby fashioning a common object of inquiry. Although, as it happens, the possibility of resolving any *disagreement* of analysis probably will depend on the scope and depth of the investment in constructing such an abstraction.

Note that traditional reluctance to theorise joint activity in this way prevents us from illuminating situations in which (on a quite acceptable common-sense basis) we suppose there is *failure* to collaborate. This will happen if analysis is only directed at enumerating categories of speech act. For it may transpire that a 'failing' collaboration is quite rich in utterances of conflict, predicting, questioning or whatever and that, therefore, we might count high numbers of them. What such measures will miss, however, is the fact that the corpus of talk does not get mobilised towards the particular goal of creating a common knowledge – that is, knowledge that is *understood* to be held in common and valued for this status.

The point reached in the present argument suggests themes that have been more fully developed by students of routine conversation (Clark, 1985). In their research literature, one finds description of those conversational devices that manage the creation of common understanding (Clark and Schaefer, 1989). For conversational analysts, the processes whereby mutual beliefs are attained is discussed as a process of 'grounding' (Clark and Brennan, 1991). Thus, there is nothing new in drawing attention to mutual knowledge as a central feature of communicative practices. Any novelty in the present analysis arises from two concerns that attempt to take us forward from recognising this. First, how is the routine 'grounding' process of conversational management to be conceptualised in relation to those conversations that are said to be *'collaborative'*? Second, what events define the full set of resources needed for management of the grounding process – say as it might be carried out for some collaborative conversation in a classroom?

One response to the first of these concerns is to suggest that the state of 'collaboration' becomes defined as an interaction in which the participants have a particularly focused intent on co-ordinating shared meaning. So, a partnership organised for collaborative learning should provoke exchanges in which the need to create a rich structure of mutuality is strongly apparent and self-consciously pursued. Such pursuit is relatively prominent in the participants' orientation. Perhaps it is made so by the task-directed nature of typical collaborative encounters. This definition of collaboration encourages research into the way language is used on these special conversational occasions – in order that we may expose the techniques deployed when this explicit orientation to common knowledge is active.

However, my second concern proposed above encourages a different but complementary research agenda. I noted that taking forward the 'grounding' of common knowledge as an analytic notion involves consideration of how much more widely that grounding process should be defined – how it might go beyond attending to details of an interaction while it is in progress. I wish to suggest here that it is useful to study more than just those conversational devices comprising talk at the time of the collaborative event itself. While analysing the structure of transcribed talk will be central to understanding how collaborations are achieved, there will be more that we need to study.

Consider the case of pupils working jointly at a computer task. First, I have argued above that research observers of this situation need to do more than simply classify and enumerate individual utterances of the participants. Going further than this entails examination of how an unfolding conversation reveals more or less of a concern for establishing strong mutual understanding – for constructing a joint 'object' of collaborative interest. Close attention to the talk-in-progress will be a significant part of any research account of what the collaborating pupils are doing. However, second, I argue that the productivity of such joint activities in classrooms (or elsewhere) may also be dependent on events and experiences prior to the occasions themselves. Collaborating pupils bring to an interaction a history of other experiences that are potentially shared and potentially known to be shared. Sometimes, the value of these experiences may be obvious: they are about circumstances that are very closely related to the intellectual demands of some task that collaborators are currently engaged with. In this case their relevance arises because such shared history is available for reference and, thereby, for constructing an ever-richer object of joint attention. As research observers, we may identify how and where this shared history surfaces and, in this way, judge its significance.

However, what has gone on at some earlier time may be important for other reasons. On any occasion of joint working, a history of shared experiences may be helpful beyond resourcing straightforward continuity of task content. To see this, we need to recognise first the pervasive nature of the grounding effort that underpins everyday exchanges.

Krauss and Fussell (1991) develop the point that participants in routine communication are typically active and creative in their effort to establish common grounding. That is, when embarking on exchanges with unfamiliar others, we all readily make suppositions and draw inferences about common knowledge. For example, it might be established that someone was a 'New Yorker' and such understanding could be a useful resource for making inferences about what might be known in common with such a person. The importance of these loosely related histories is indeed to service a richly interpretative approach to communication. However, such shared experience may also be significant for its *affective* quality – for the potential to define a certain emotional content to the possibility of communicating. In particular, the awareness of common histories may *motivate* engagement with someone in the immediate present: it may drive the necessary effort required for collaborative construction. This more affective aspect of grounding and communicative co-ordination has not been pursued by psychologists. However, it is apparent in Anderson's (1983) discussion of the appeal of knowing that one shares with others a common contact with, for example, items of popular culture (such as independently watching some television soap opera).

For the case of pupils collaborating at a classroom task, the realm of such shared history is considerable. This is because classrooms throw pupils together in close and continuous contact. While such overlap clearly is important for the first reason given above (continuities of content with the task-at-hand), I suggest it may also be important for this second reason. That is, it can resource a greater motivation for attaining joint engagement. It can resource task partners to move towards a more active state of collaboration. Or, put at greater length: it affords a more disciplined and motivated commitment towards constructing an object of mutual knowledge – one that relates to some current classroom activity being shared.

This brings us to my main point: namely that there is some significance in participating in the life of a given classroom *community*. Research is needed which will consider how far any 'productivity' within some pupil collaboration arises from the partners enjoying a common history of classroom life.

The idea that educational practice should be theorised in terms of a community of learners happens to be very current. For example, one distinguished researcher (Brown, 1994) has described her own intellectual journey through various paradigms towards this conception. It is a journey that seems to have been taken by many others active now in educational research. Its attraction may arise in part from the influence of those who have written about the boundaries between formal and informal learning (e.g., Lave and Wenger, 1991; Rogoff, 1990). Perhaps many theorists are drawn to talk of classrooms as 'communities' because they are first drawn to the idea of learning as a socially managed apprenticeship, or to parallel claims that learning must be based in authentic activity (which must emerge from real community concerns). Certainly, theoretical reference to 'communities of learners' often accompanies accounts of interventions that stress resourcing pupils to carry out investigations that are authentic (e.g., Cognition and Technology Group at Vanderbilt, 1994).

Yet theorising in this manner has further to go. It may be true that engaging problems (say, in geography or mathematics) are more likely to be precipitated within social structures that resemble the actual worlds of practitioners (say, geographers or mathematicians). But claiming that pupils' experience should be 'communal' must mean more than that. This claim should draw our attention to the possibility and the significance of sustained interpersonal exchange in some (schooling) place. In particular, it should clarify whether and how an accumulation of loosely shared classroom experiences can become a learning resource for the participants. This requires research that investigates how shared experience is identified and deployed in actual classroom contexts. What, therefore, should be studied; and in what manner?

There are two broad themes to be pursued. The first is focused on talk. Here the issue is how do teachers and pupils use language to mark shared experience and subsequently recover it. The fact that so much of talk in primary classrooms seems dedicated to these purposes is well illustrated in the ethnographic study of Edwards and Mercer (1987). A second research theme might be more focused on artefacts and structure in the material environment. For a reminding of earlier experiences also depends on the paraphernalia and organisation of the classroom as physical space. Thus, it would be appropriate to consider wall displays, pupil work trays, exhibits, photograph albums and other material that keeps previous activities visible and that serves as a referential anchor for new forms of talk. Although the relevance of artefacts to collective remembering has been acknowledged (Radley, 1990), it is a topic that has been neglected in studies of classrooms. Indeed, beyond studies of teacher talk (Edwards and Mercer, 1987), the processes whereby the shared experiences of classroom life become recorded and mobilised has been addressed by very few researchers (but see Roth, in press).

In the following section, I shall briefly describe a computer application that is relevant to the issues that have been introduced above. Items of software are often characterised as valuable for supporting collaborative work. But what is usually meant by 'collaboration' relates to the particular circumstances identified at the start of this chapter: localised interaction within a small group working at a computer. The software I shall describe here is directed more towards sustaining the collaborative purpose at the more diffuse level we have been discussing here – i.e. acting to represent and make available an array of shared experiences. What is captured in this manner is thereby rendered available to resource 'collaborations'. In this sense the present software is directed at what I have been referring to as the broader social context, or the extended territory that situates collaborating.

A classroom resource to support collective remembering

My title for this section borrows from a book of essays in which 'memory' is discussed in terms of the sociocultural processes that create, transform and sustain a community's shared experiences (Middleton and Edwards, 1990). The notion of 'collective remembering' expresses fairly fully the social psychological phenomena supported by the software to be described here. However, what is distinctive about this software might also be captured by locating it in relation to a taxonomy of the various ways in which computers can enter into joint pupil activity. Elsewhere (Crook, 1994a), I have suggested four varieties of such mediational intrusion; the present case relates to the fourth (and perhaps least familiar) of these. The full taxonomy may be summarised as follows.

First, interactions *at* computers may acquire a collaborative quality where two or more learners gather at a particular place to solve a problem together. This is the most familiar and most studied sense of collaboration. Second, interactions may occur *around* computers. In this case, a loosely knit group of people are sharing a number of workstations housed in a common space. This ecology allows a degree of more casual and improvised exchange. Third, interactions *through* computers are possible when the social organisation is asynchronous. Here the partners are separated in time and space but a networking of the technology creates a novel opportunity for users to construct some degree of common knowledge. Fourth, and finally, interactions may occur *in relation to* some computer application. Here I have in mind circumstances where the crucial feature of the computer's mediation is not dependent on current interaction with the technology. Instead, the building of common knowledge is resourced by collaborators being able to reference some experience that was previously shared at the technology (Pea, 1992). The computer merely offers a vivid case of such occasion: one that might later impinge upon some current collaborative discussion. The computer may also mediate in this manner when the social referencing occurs in relation to learning events which the technology has been programmed to represent and preserve in some way. For example, a university teacher might assemble a record of a lecture course on some computer network (say as world-wide web pages); what results is a hypertext document summarising lecture notes, seminar discussions, reading lists and so on. In casual discussion, students may choose to make reference to such a resource.

Where this happens the technology is providing an anchor for collective remembering of a course that they have taken together. The students' collaboration would then be an interaction 'in relation to' the computer resource.

I find these distinctions useful because they remind us how the role of computers within collaborative learning is complex. Always, the psychological issue is how common knowledge gets constructed. However, my taxonomy above indicates how the nature of artefact mediation may vary within this core activity. Such an analysis therefore encourages looking beyond the circumscribed sessions of joint computer activity that define the interest of most research on this topic (interacting *at* the machine). What makes a computer a very interesting classroom object in this respect is the powerful representational capacity of the technology. If it were just another piece of specialised apparatus (and in some classrooms perhaps it is), then the range of interactions that would be organised 'in relation to' it might be limited. However, it is a more versatile, multi-purpose technology and this means experiences with it potentially can be appropriated into a wide variety of collaborative interactions. Moreover, the vivid and localised character of much classroom computer experience may serve to encourage this appropriation. For example, teachers may find it a potent reference point in their various discussions with pupils (at least they might in classrooms where pupil access was frequent enough to make this sensible).

My own interest has been in capturing this representational versatility and using it to fashion a generic item of software that more effectively serviced 'in-relation-to' kinds of collaborative possibilities. Such an application would capture, organise and make available more of the creative activity that defined the collective achievements of a classroom. Thus, the concerns of a classroom community would be represented in this medium. That representation could then offer a resource in relation to which a whole variety of learning interactions might be organised. In a modest way, it would allow some of the history of a community to be archived and referenced. Unlike other classroom records of activity, a computer-based archive has the added feature that the single computer system is also the place where *new* work is carried out. Thus, at times that pupils were working on new projects they could be incidentally confronted with some shared history: records of projects that have gone before.

The broad nature of this ambition is not original. What has been sketched above is what might be created on school computers that were configured into a local area network (LAN), with access to a common file-server. The 'archive' would be held on this server; it then could be referenced from any station on the network. My own experience of establishing and maintaining such a community resource in a primary school over a seven-year period suggests that, in practice, the LAN infrastructure does not readily provide what is needed (Crook, 1994b). The overheads of maintaining such a system are considerable. Others have done so more successfully (Scardamalia *et al.*, 1994). However, the technology comprising such interventions still requires careful routine management, and the expense of installation remains beyond the budget of most schools. If there is a distinctive aspect of the computer program described below, it is its accessibility. The program runs on typical UK classroom computers and is painless to manage and use. It achieves the basic functionality of networking but at the level of the solitary classroom computer (which represents the typical extent of current UK primary school provision). In short, it might be characterised as a 'virtual network' – a network on a single computer hard disc.

The program makes prominent use of a spatial metaphor to represent the location and organisation of work done in the classroom (and beyond). So when the computer is turned on, the pupil sees a picture of the solar system. Through a series of mouse-click selections, it is possible to converge on one's country, town, neighbourhood streets, school and classroom. This journey entails a sequence of pictures or maps, any one of which allows 'sideways' routes to be designed (say, into geographical project work). Although this journey is appealing to children, there is a shortcut from the opening graphic directly to the pupil's own classroom (the classroom home 'page'). Classroom pages comprise a message area managed by teachers, links to portfolios of class work, and links to pupils' own home pages. The links to class work are organised in respect of current activity and the activity of previous years. The opportunity to access work done by an earlier genera-tion of pupils is particularly intriguing. For it is rare for classroom communities to leave these kinds of tracks. Thus, the present design allows pupils an unusual opportunity to reflect on how their predecessors struggled with similar sets of problems to those they themselves are engaged with.

Pupils' own home pages give them access to suitable directory windows for saving and loading their own files. (All the proprietory interface metaphors of the host computer are deployed at this level of activity.) A personal password system gives some degree of protection over work that has been saved in this way. Pupils may place all or some of their work into topic-defined portfolios which then become accessible through various lists and menus accessed on classroom home pages. Pupils also have access to two kinds of communication tool. They can send short messages to other pupils – who are suitably notified of waiting mail the next time they use their home page. Or it is possible to send the contents of whole files as mail. In which case, the recipient is similarly notified and the relevant file then can be accessed by them. Because this system is being studied in eight schools in two separate towns, there is also the possibility of sending material between sites. Such 'mail' is passed to a floppy disc in the host computer; the disc can then be posted to other schools.

In short, the program avoids some of the cost and complexity of real networking while offering the advantages of an organised and friendly system for accessing a central archive. Both the conception and implementa-tion have good continuity with existing classroom resources and practices.

However, what is more important in relation to the present discussion is how such a resource supports collaboration. Evidently, at one level it simply furnishes another site for pupils to interact *at* a computer. But this is not the form of computer support for collaborating that I have been foregrounding in the present chapter. I have argued that what happens on any particular occasion of joint activity is resourced by and motivated by pupils' awareness of shared events experienced at the level of classroom community. The potential of a program such as that described above arises from the way in which it represents the 'location' of that community (in time and space) and how it captures and organises some of the products of the activity within the community (items of pupil work). Of course teachers already act in these kinds of ways: it is common for classroom walls to bear witness to the context of that classroom and the work done within it. However, whether and how such resources guide or motivate what pupils are doing on any particular occasion is as uncertain for traditional practices as it is for a new computer-mediated version of such practice. In the next section of this chapter I shall discuss briefly some research options that help us approach these questions.

Studying computer-mediated representations of a classroom community

Earlier in this chapter, I proposed that when we analyse routine sessions in which pupils work collaboratively, we should look to the broader social context in which these occasions are located. This is because the productivity of such sessions might partly depend on more extended histories of shared activity – experiences that pupils derive from common membership of their classrooms. Certainly educational communities will be characterised by the variety of shared experience that they create and, intuitively, it seems likely that something about such history should make a difference for pupils as they embark on each individual classroom task. While this may indeed seem intuitively sensible, these phenomena do remain hard to pin down for study. One approach to making such processes visible has been discussed here. That approach involves introducing a resource (a generic piece of software) that relates to the production and representation of shared classroom experience. Controlled observation could then make it possible to expose something of these community effects – as they might become visible in relation to a novel and distinctive resource.

So, what effects would one be looking for? In making more specific the argument for taking seriously a community structure to classrooms, I proposed two sorts of influence arising from shared experience. The first was a simple continuity between something in a current collaborative task and some earlier classroom-based events or actions that are relevant to reasoning about the present. The collaborating partners are mutually aware of this shared experience and this allows them to deploy it in their current cognitive co-ordinations. How would the computer program described above support this kind of continuity? If it has been effective in capturing and representing aspects of community activity, then what we would expect is to find reference to its representations in the interaction of our collaborators. We might also expect teachers to make such reference as part of their instructional interaction with pupils.

However, I suggested a second kind of influence arising from shared experience. Aspects of community membership might influence the *motivational* dimension of how routine collaborative sessions are managed by pupils. Collaborations involve a state of engagement in which people mobilise their natural capacity for building common knowledge and direct it towards some purpose defined by an educational setting. Enthusiasm for adopting this attitude may vary greatly. Moreover, such variation will have many sources. Some relevant influences will surely derive from partners recognising their involvement in the classroom community. This involvement affords them a degree of shared experience that helps promote some of the mutual commitment collaborative engagement demands.

The problem with this second variety of influence is that symptoms of its presence might not be so straighforwardly apparent. Ethnographers of classroom life are particularly prone to study talk; yet one of the awkward features of shared community experience is that it renders unnecessary certain routine forms of communication (such as certain things that might otherwise get *said*). Indeed this may explain some of the affective dimension that I have associated with collaborative exchanges: such affect arises from the intimacy of not *needing* to say certain things. For the participants in a collaboration, shared experience is a great asset – it removes the need to be so explicit. For research observers, shared experience creates problems – because, typically, researchers will not be party to the sharing process and thus they will be hard pressed to detect its influence. To some extent, psychologists have sidestepped this problem by studying collaborations at tasks that are self-contained, short and relatively decoupled from a flow of classroom life. Pupils' occasional experiences together at the classroom computer have many of these seductive qualities.

The intervention outlined in this chapter presents us with problems of this kind, although the character of the intrusion does make them less severe. The public way in which community activity is represented by this program allows a greater degree of access for relative outsiders. This illustrates one research strategy demanded by the current perspective: an effort to gain access *oneself* to community knowledge in order that interpretation of localised interactions can be informed by this. In the present context, the raw material of research remains familiar enough. It is the exchange of collaborators in action – although any interpreting of that exchange is more likely to be informed by participatory documentation of what pupils have access to as shared history. Otherwise, research strategy has to depend more than usual on probing conversations, in which an effort is made to judge the impact of the pertinent community feature (in our case, the program they all have access to). This is partly to ask about simple 'visibility' (although usage logs built into the software itself help address this also). These inquiries with pupils could also be about more evaluative issues. For example, such conversations have revealed in the present case that some children are uneasy about the way in which personal identity is marked through the notion of 'home page'. In particular, a decision to decorate these pages with pupil photographs (taken with a GIF camera) may have been mistaken: most pupils react shyly or resentfully towards their image – however good we judge the photograph to be. Such small things are very relevant to how a resource of this kind can extend or consolidate the sense of common purpose in a classroom.

There are other distinctive features of the research strategy that is demanded by this kind of project. One is to take fuller account of the institutional context in which such an intervention is situated. Cole (1995) has illustrated this very effectively for the case of an out-of-school intervention. In our own school-based case, the relevant context comprises reactions from others outside of the institution such as pupils in neighbouring classrooms, the head teacher's reaction to the resource, the IT co-ordinating teacher's attitude, and the interest of parents and others visiting the classroom. All such things make a difference to the status and reach of a feature that acts on the community defined as a place of 'shared knowing'.

Finally, projects of the present kind benefit from a *comparative* approach. In contrast to much research on collaborative learning, the approach here is not factorial. Psychological processes are not being teased apart and studied as isolated variables in controlled observations or experiments. What is under observation is more of a system. The characteristics and behaviour of this system are more likely to become apparent when it is possible to make global comparisons across different intervention sites. So, in the present case, an important part of research strategy has been to carry out traditional methods (the observing, recording and talking) in a number of different schools. This allows a co-ordinated picture to be constructed – at least, if the intervention is allowed to settle over a suitable period of time. But it is the taking of this time that has been neglected in psychological research; there is reluctance to accept that important aspects of learning experience are only visible over extended periods of observation in the community itself.

Concluding summary

Collaboration is a rich seam of activity within classroom life. I have argued here that we must understand this concept of collaboration in terms of the organised building of shared understandings. As such, teachers are persistently engaged in collaborative relationship with their pupils – they are for ever constructing common knowledge (Edwards and Mercer, 1987). Pupils are also deeply involved in this enterprise, but I suggested that the status of pupils as collaborators has been distorted by psychological investigation. In seizing upon the occasion of computer-based pupil interaction, we have focused too much on a certain kind of circumscribed, decontextualised exchange. I argued that the central place of collaborating in educational practice can only be properly recognised once we view classrooms as communities – with social action unfolding over time and sensibly located in a distinctive physical place.

Yet capturing the form and working of this community is difficult. In the present chapter I have described a modest computer-based resource that relates to this problem in two senses. First, it is a device designed to amplify the collaborative potential of classroom life – as our culture has defined this (small stable gatherings of learners). In this way it might be a help to the participants in such an enterprise. Second, the program is a kind of research probe. It creates an opportunity to bring the processes of community-driven knowledge-building into clearer view. As hinted at the start of the chapter, the research methods that are then demanded are not radically different when you get close to them: there remains observation, consultation and counting of events. However, the reach of the research enterprise must become greater – it must extend in time, and engage more fully with the cultural niche of the intervention.

References

Anderson, B. (1983) *Imagined Communities*, London: Verso.

Brown, A. L. (1994) 'The advancement of learning', *Educational Researcher* 23: 4–12.

Bruner, J. S. (1996) *The Culture of Education*, Cambridge, MA: Harvard University Press.

Clark, H. H. (1985) 'Language use and language users', in G. Lindzey and E. Aronson (eds) *Handbook of Social Psychology* (third edn), New York: Random House.

Clark, H. H. and Brennan S. E. (1991) 'Grounding in communication', in L. Resnick, J. Levine and S. Teasley (eds) *Perspectives on Socially Shared Cognition*, Washington DC: American Psychological Association.

Clark, H. H. and Schaefer, E. F. (1989) 'Contributing to discourse', *Cognitive Science* 13: 259–294.

Cognition and Technology Group at Vanderbilt (1994) 'From visual word problems to learning communities: changing conceptions of cognitive research', in K. McGilly (ed.) *Classroom Lessons: Integrating Cognitive Theory and Classroom Practice*, Cambridge, MA: MIT Press.

Cole, M. (1995) 'Socio-cultural-historical psychology: some general remarks and a proposal for a new kind of cultural-genetic methodology', in J. Wertsch, P. Del Rio and A. Alvarez (eds) *Sociocultural Studies of Mind*, Cambridge: Cambridge University Press.

Crook, C. K. (1994a) *Computers and the Collaborative Experience of Learning*, London: Routledge.

—— (1994b) 'Electronic communications in two educational settings: some theory and practice', in C. O'Malley (ed.) *Computer-Supported Collaborative Learning*, Berlin: Springer Verlag.

Doise, W. (1985) 'Social regulations in cognitive development', in R. Hinde, A-N. Perret-Clermont and J. Stevenson-Hinde (eds) *Social Relationships and Cognitive Development*, Oxford: Oxford University Press.

Dunn, J. (1993) 'Social interaction, relationships, and the development of causal discourse and conflict management', *European Journal of Psychology of Education* 8: 391–401.

Edwards, D. and Mercer, N. (1987) *Common Knowledge*, London: Methuen.

Hoyles, C. and Sutherland, R. (1989) *Logo Mathematics in the Classroom*, London: Routledge.

Krauss, R. M. and Fussell, S. R. (1991) 'Constructing shared communicative environments', in L. Resnick, J. Levine and S. Teasley (eds) *Perspectives on Socially-Shared Cognition*, Washington, DC: American Psychological Association.

Lave, J. and Wenger, E. (1991) *Situated Learning: Legitimate Peripheral Participation*, Cambridge: Cambridge University Press.

Middleton, D. and Edwards, D. (1990) *Collective Remembering*, London: Sage.

Pea, R. D. (1992) 'Augmenting the discourse of learning with computer-based learning environments', in E. de Corte, M. Linn, H. Mandl and L. Verschaffel (eds) *Computer-Based Learning Environments and Problem Solving*, Berlin: Springer Verlag.

Radley, A. (1990) 'Artefacts, memory and a sense of the past', in D. Middleton and D. Edwards (eds) *Collective Remembering*, London: Sage.

Rogoff, B. (1990) *Apprenticeship in Thinking: Cognitive Development in Social Context*, New York: Oxford University Press.

Roth, W-M. (in press) 'Inventors, copycats, and everyone else: the emergence of shared resources and practices as defining aspects of classroom communities', *Science Education*.

Scardamalia, M., Bereiter, C. and Lamon, M. (1994) 'The CSILE project: trying to bring the classroom into world 3', in K. McGilly (ed.) *Classroom Lessons: Integrating Cognitive Theory and Classroom Practice*, Cambridge, MA: MIT Press.

Tizard, B. and Hughes, M. (1984) *Young Children Learning, Talking and Thinking at Home and at School*, London: Fontana.

Webb, N. M (1986) 'Microcomputer learning in small groups: cognitive requirements and group processes', *Journal of Educational Psychology* 76(6): 1,076–1,088.

8 Sociocognitive interactions in a computerised industrial task

Are they productive for learning?

Danièle Golay Schilter, Jean-François Perret, Anne-Nelly Perret-Clermont and Franco de Guglielmo[1]

Introduction

Through the 'in vivo' study of professional training, we intend to contribute to the understanding of complex learning procedures. We have formulated the hypothesis that learning procedures of this sort incorporate factors not only of a cognitive and technical nature but also factors relating to identity and relationships. The chapter is concerned with the sociocognitive interactions observed in a real-life training situation in the workshops of a technical college. Students, working in small groups, are familiarising themselves with computer-aided production. Our aim is to analyse which interactive dynamics are deployed and to examine when these interactions can be considered to be effective.

In approaching these interactions and attempting to grasp the dynamics involved, it is possible to draw upon a number of studies which come from very different theoretical and methodological directions (e.g., Dillenbourg *et al.*, 1995). Nevertheless, these studies can be placed along two axes, distinguishing between, along the one, those works which describe the *interactions between learners*, and along the other, those which highlight the important task of *interpreting the meaning of the situation*, an interpretation which the participants must put into operation in order to manage their activity.

How do the learners interact?

Work on collaborative learning is most often concerned with primary school pupils who carry out different types of tasks in groups. With young adults undergoing professional training, will we find the same processes? For example, which of the different interaction patterns identified by Granott (1993) can be seen in the context of this activity? In the training situations studied, will we see any or all of the following:

Sociocognitive conflicts of the same nature as those observed from a psycho-sociogenetic perspective and about which a series of experimental research studies has shown that they could be at the origin of cognitive restructurations (Perret-Clermont, 1980; Emler and Valiant, 1982; Doise and Mugny, 1984; Perret-Clermont and Nicolet 1988; Light and Blaye 1989; Bearison, 1991). In what ways might young adults benefit from the confrontation of different points of view? Do they relate to cognitive re-elaborations of the task and its aim, or do the conflictual interactions produce changes in solution strategies (Gilly *et al.*, 1988; Blaye, 1989)?

Approaches to collaboration in which the partners each bring complementary elements. Do the learners observed enter into a dialogue when engaged in joint action? Discussion and explanation are considered to be favourable for the solving of tasks for two main reasons. On the one hand, they permit common goals to be established with regard to defining the problem and the interplay of meanings (which should facilitate an effective educational shift, according to Healy *et al.*, 1995). On the other, discussions help to bring about an analysis of the problem to be solved (Pontecorvo, 1990; Howe *et al.*, 1995; Mercer, 1996; Pléty, 1996), a sharing of ideas, and what is more an evaluation of those ideas in view of a communal decision. Will our observations present the characteristics of exploratory talk described by Mercer (1996, pp. 138–140)? In fact, some research has also shown that negotiations and dialogues of a 'resolution of conflict' type sometimes have little effect upon the immediate task performance of the groups studied (Perret-Clermont, 1980; Jackson *et al.*, 1992; Hoyles *et al.*, 1992, p. 255, etc.). What will the outcome be here?

An explicit or implicit distribution of different roles and tasks to each participant Experimental research on group work reviewed by Moscovici and Paicheler (1973) and research in an ergonomic perspective (Leplat, 1993) have both clearly shown that in order to be carried out efficiently, different tasks necessitate different social organisations of the group. What happens when groups are faced with a complex industrial computing task? Is there a distribution of roles and does it take place in a conscious or implicit manner? Does it evolve alongside familiarisation with the task? In a task of co-resolution of an arithmetical problem, Saint-Dizier *et al.* (1995) have shown that this distribution is reflected more particularly in turn-, decision- or power-taking, as well as in their evolution throughout the interaction. Is it also the case here? Are the respective places and status of the participants negotiated before or during the activity? Do we observe power-taking and is this effective or not in relation to the collaboration objectives? Are there any leaders, and of what type? A good deal of research has highlighted the sheer amount of attention subjects pay to 'place maintenance' and face saving, and more generally to identity, in situations apparently dedicated to the resolution of cognitive problems (Flahaut, 1978; Vion, 1992; Schubauer-Leoni 1986; Grossen *et al.*, 1997; Muller and Perret-Clermont, in press).

Asymmetric interactions   When are interactions explicitly experienced as asymmetric, with certain participants in the position of expert and others in the position of novice? When, on the contrary, are relationships symmetrical? Following from Vygotsky and, more widely, from a number of Russian researchers (notably Leontiev, Galperin and others), numerous studies have attempted to describe the relationships between novices and experts (McLane and Wertsch, 1986; Wynnikamen, 1990; Mercer and Fisher, 1992; Forman and McPhail, 1993; Rogoff, 1995). The 'a priori' theory adopted in this line of research is that knowledge is transmitted by the expert to the novice, the latter appropriating it in successive stages, deploying behaviours scaffolded by his/her expert partner. Are these phenomena found within the framework of learning to master a complex computing device? If interactions of this sort do establish themselves, is it only with the teacher or also between the students? Which events solicit modelling or scaffolding: breakdowns, the particular requirements of the teacher, the necessity to stand out on the part of young people seeking social acceptance, or is it simply a question of a common mode of interaction and thus normal and frequent?

Certain authors advocate 'cognitive apprenticeship' as a pedagogical method (Collins *et al.*, 1989), especially in the context of technologically complex environments (Järvelä, 1995). However, others (e.g. Trognon, 1993) have highlighted the fact that in certain problem-solving situations, partners can be observed supporting each other not in an asymmetric but in a reciprocal manner, each leaning on the reasoning of the other in order to progress towards an efficacious solution.

Interactions influenced by the characteristics of the task and software   The characteristics of the computer tool used are equally susceptible to influencing the modes of collaboration adopted. The way the use of the keyboard and mouse is (or is not) distributed is a major issue, as observed by Blaye *et al.* (1992). The nature of the software (and in particular visual feedback and error messages) is also worthy of attention. As revealed by Hoyles *et al.* (1992), the fact that a piece of software allows for open exploration (as is the case with Logo) favours reflection upon rules and dialogue as well as a means of resolving conflicts, whilst this is not the case if the software proposes a guided 'computer assisted learning' type of approach.

How do the learners interpret the situation?

In our research, the task presented to the student technicians seems clearly defined. Referring back to teaching encountered some months beforehand and working in groups of three, the students are required to use a piece of CAM (computer assisted manufacturing) software to specify the machining of a part which has already been designed. Subsequently they will set up the machining cell which will automatically manufacture the part. At all times they can refer to the teacher for assistance if they are stuck and for help if they should need it. After four hours of practical work, they have to provide a brief report on their work to be handed in to the teacher along with the machined part. The instructions are complete, the working conditions defined and the object of the exercise clearly designated. This apparent clarity does however merit closer examination.

Research alerts us to the fact that even apparently simple conversational situations (for example asking a question in a test situation) may reveal themselves to be complex polysemic social situations (Rommetveit, 1979; Hundeide, 1985; Grossen, 1988; Säljö, 1991). In effect, the students do not always endow the situation, the task and the instructions with the meaning anticipated by the teacher (Donaldson, 1978; Perret, 1985; Schubauer-Leoni, 1986; Light and Perret-Clermont, 1989; Bell *et al.*, 1985; Perret-Clermont *et al.*, 1991). The observation of subjects in interaction reveals that they deploy a breadth of cognitive activity to enable them to grasp not only what has to be done, but also the meaning of the situation in order to place themselves in a position to undertake the role most favourable to them. In scholastic situations, in particular, we know the extent to which the institutional framework plays a role in structuring the images that teachers and students have of their roles and expected performances (see Gilly, 1980; Brossard and Wargnier, 1993; Säljö and Wyndhamn, 1993; Schubauer-Leoni, 1993; Iannacone and Perret-Clermont, 1993). Is the industrial computing task with which we are concerned here also open, behind its apparent clarity, to diverse interpretations? This appears to us to be the case for two complementary reasons:

1   The procedure to be followed is open, at least to the extent that numerous options and decisions regarding the appropriate route are to be taken along the way. There is no standard procedure which can simply be faithfully applied. The software is complex, and presents some unexpected limitations. For example, error messages are not given in a systematic manner. All this gives rise to an element of uncertainty amongst the students at different stages of the activity with regard to the type of knowledge and strategies to be put into action.

2   In order to manage this element of uncertainty, the students will spontaneously rely upon their previous experience and the similarity that they perceive as existing (or not) between what is required in the present situation and what has been required in the past. From the point of view of the learners, the proposed task and their interpretation of it cannot therefore be isolated from the whole sequence of practical work being carried out throughout their training. The forms of scholastic work, and in particular the modes of collaboration which establish themselves do not reinvent themselves day by day. On the contrary, constants are observed in each activity, linked to the expectations and working rules which are generally established implicitly but which are components of the didactic contract (Schubauer-Leoni, 1986; Schubauer-Leoni and

Grossen, 1993). This framework of interpretation that the students have forged out of their previous experiences cannot be ignored if we wish to understand their reactions when faced with a new task in their practical work.

We therefore expect to see reflected here, at this level of micro-analysis and through the meanings that the learners attribute to the task, a number of psychological and social factors which bear upon the lives of the students and of the school. Other authors have already shown such articulations of different orders of phenomena within the same observed pedagogical 'micro-reality' (Woods, 1990; Benavente *et al.*, 1993; Garduno Rubio, 1996).

Learning a technical trade today: the case of computer-assisted manufacturing

The opportunity to study sociocognitive interactions in a technical college is linked to our participation in the Swiss National Research Programme on 'The efficiency of training systems'. The programme as a whole was set up to examine the possibility of improving training systems through a better understanding of the ways in which they evolve. In this context we are interested in the impact of new production technology on the redefinition of knowledge and know-how to be taught to future technicians. First this necessitated a knowledge of the institutional framework of the technical college studied, in order to grasp the principal elements of its history and evolution linked most notably to technological developments (Golay Schilter, 1995). It was also a matter of getting to grips with the professional and pedagogical motivations of those members of the college management and teaching staff who were affected by this evolution, as well as the financial conditions surrounding an undertaking of this sort (Perret, 1997). Interviews and a questionnaire given to the students (aged between 16 and 25) enabled us to grasp certain important elements of the scholastic, professional and existential problems encountered by them (Kaiser *et al.*, 1996).

This approach to the reality of a professional training establishment has revealed the existence of pedagogical choices which are difficult to make and manage when having to take into consideration multiple factors, each pulling in a different direction. Some of these are of a material order (financial constraints, but also architectural ones linked to the fitting-out of training facilities); others are professional, between on the one hand a *traditional view* of the trade, almost as a craft, albeit an industrial one (shown by, for example, the importance given to experience and 'hands-on skill'), and on the other, an *emerging view* based upon the development of automation, the future form of which we still know very little about. Other tensions also appear amongst the trainers (whose experiences of the professional world are diverse and often very different from those of their colleagues) and amongst the students who, in their working environment or during periods of work experience, glean information and opinions which feed their own perceptions of the industrial world and its evolution. Other dimensions which complicate managerial and pedagogical choices even more include sometimes anachronistic state regulations; competition between colleges; the pressures of the employment market and the fear of unemployment.

In this context, introducing students to automated manufacturing is a mirror which provides a particularly clear reflection of these tensions, even in view of the fact that this teaching only occupies a relatively restricted place in the training curriculum as a whole (an initial approach is of course already offered at the beginning of training at 16, but it is above all in the two years of preparation leading to the main qualification for technicians that systematic teaching in the subject is given). This is why we have chosen this learning area in particular, as a privileged observation point from which to identify the factors present in such training, the different modalities possible, as well as the respective roles of traditional know-how and more formal knowledge which requires the entirely mediated conception of a technical activity of this sort (Martin, 1995; Rabardel, 1995; Verillon and Rabardel, 1995).

The situation observed: a practical training session

The automation practicals take place one half day each week and cover different technical devices. The session at the centre of our observation required the students, working in small teams, to program the machining of a piece of synthetic resin, using computer assisted manufacturing (CAM) software. As we have already indicated above, the aim of the practical work is to carry out the complete manufacturing of a part (shown in Figure 8.1). This task must be performed in a short period of time and in order to carry it out, the students must refer back to data and processes covered several months beforehand. It is thus an opportunity for them to revise and use a large body of knowledge in a practical context. In this, it differs from their typical practicals which are generally more directly linked to a particular textbook chapter. This activity is also closer to an actual work situation than usual.

At the beginning of the practical, the teacher gives oral and written instructions to the students. He describes the three main stages of the procedure as well as some of the technical constraints. He also states the assessment criteria: the time taken to complete the machining should be as short as possible and during the practical session the students should work independently of the teacher as much as possible. All the members of a given group will receive the same mark. The teacher addresses them collectively.

At the first stage, activity is focused on the screen; a large number of variables have to be specified. The software interface shows a long series of running menus including sub-menus. Data are input by opening the running menus and clicking on the desired options. The program then provides a series of windows and dialogue boxes. Each time a window has been

124   *Golay Schilter et al.*

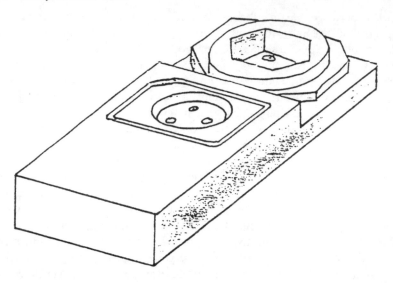

Figure 8.1 The part machined

completed correctly (by clicking on the options chosen or by filling in values), the next one opens. Windows and dialogue boxes are complex and require a lot of data input. The program indicates the next general process at the bottom of the screen (e.g. 'select outlines'). It also transmits error warnings and includes a thematic help menu. Finally, it enables users to visualise and monitor work already done on the part (see Figure 8.2).

The students

Ten male student technicians, aged between 20 and 25 years, were observed. These students were organised into four working groups, all of whom had worked together during previous practical sessions. In the present chapter we will focus our attention on one of the groups in particular but without losing sight of the others. The students' knowledge of machining processes varies depending upon their former training. Some have had practical experience in the use of traditional and/or computer numerical control (CNC) machine tools, while others have only followed a thirty-hour course in computerised machining.

Selection and transcription of the sequence to be presented

The activity as a whole, from its conception to the effective machining of the part, takes place over four hours. The session was recorded and filmed using two cameras in order to obtain an image of each team and the computer screen they were using. These recordings allowed us to capture a series of difficulties encountered by the students during this activity. One such diffi-

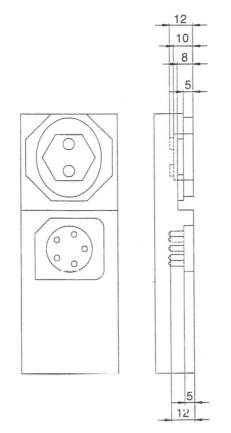

Figure 8.2 View of the part as it appears on the screen of the computer and side view
with the dimensions of the shapes to machine

culty regards the relative definition of the values corresponding to different
machining plans which have to be specified to the machine: the surface of
the part called the 'reference surface'; the depth of a hole; the depth of a
hole in the interior of an already machined cavity; without forgetting the
'security plan' and the 'rapid approach plan' which regulates the approach of
the reamer even before it starts machining. It is the reaction to this particular difficulty and the examination of the management of it that we have
singled out for the present study. We focus in particular on one group made
up of Ted, Guy and Didier.

Working from the video recordings, as well as notes taken by one of the
researchers, the relevant passages were transcribed in their entirety following
the normal conversation format. 'Turn taking' is indicated by a new para-
graph. Data input activity as well as the reactions of the software (changes,
messages) have been indicated in order to report on the interaction between
the students as well as between the students and the computer.

The sequence presented below is particularly interesting because it shows different aspects of the dynamics involved in collaboration at the following levels:

- Task-solving procedures; i.e. the way in which the students plan each stage, define aims, take and assess decisions, deal with the information provided by the program and proceed when faced with a problem.
- Division of labour and roles; the way in which the students share the computer commands, take part in the conversation and make suggestions, the nature of their exchanges, and the roles they assume during the working and decision-making processes, in terms of who initiates and concludes important decisions, who contributes decisive arguments, who takes the final decision and what feelings and emotions are expressed.
- The meaning given to the task; this sequence in effect allows something of the meaning that the students attribute to the learning situation to show through.

The sequence in progress

The sequence presented here lasts roughly ten minutes, during which time a team of three is programming the drilling of five holes in the part to be machined. This sequence can be divided into a number of stages.

Stage 1: initial choices

The three students, Guy, Ted and Didier, have already been at work for roughly fifteen minutes. Since the exercise commenced, Guy has been monopolising the commands of the PC. Ted is sitting on his left, in front of the screen, while Didier has placed himself on the outer edge of the group, furthest from the computer. The instructions and a sample of an already machined part are in front of Ted. Didier has offered to write the report to be handed in at the end of the training session. This division of roles was not preceded by any explicit negotiation.

The first stage of production lasts roughly ninety seconds, during which the students (Guy and Ted) input various data. Then, in the following excerpt, the students decide the values in millimetres for each working level of the drill. These values correspond to the distance between the surface of the part, taken as level zero, and each level reached by the drill from its initial position (see Figures 8.3 and 8.4).

Key machining terminology

Security level (at tightening): level on which the machine positions the drill above the part.

Reference surface: surface of the part, on which the tool makes contact with the raw material.

Fast approach: level reached by the drill in its quick descent from the security level towards the part, still without touching it.

Depth of the hole:

at the diameter: depth reached by the part of the drill determining its diameter (above the tip)
at the tip: depth of drilling at the tip of the drill

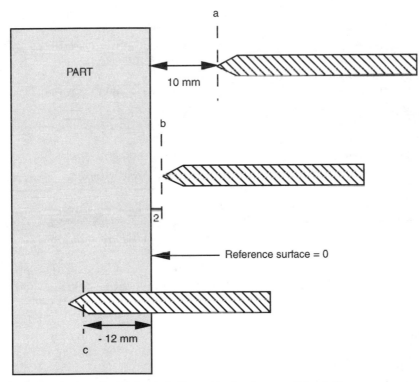

Figure 8.3 The successive levels indicated in the descent of the drill
Key:
a= Security level
b= Fast approach level
c= Depth of the hole

The correct solution would require that the values for each level deeper follow a decreasing order. For instance: Security level: $Z = 10$mm. Fast approach $Z = 2$ mm. Reference surface $Z = 0$. Depth $Z = -12$, given at the diameter. In this case, the students use a drill, for which the program automatically integrates the length of the tip into its calculations. Therefore a depth indicated as -12 'at the diameter' becomes an actual depth of -17.5.

G1:[2]   *(He reads the screen, then speaks without turning towards the others)* Security level. Pfff. *[Goes on to the next box without filling the first.]*

G2:   *(He reads)* Fast approach . . . *(turning to T)* Down to Z 0, OK?

T3:   No, less, I mean more! +2.

G4:   Down to Z 2. Yeap, that's right. *[He types +2.]*

T5:   Now, depth (looking at the screen).

G6:   *(Reading, without paying attention to T)* Surface level, 0. *[He leaves the 0.]*

T7:   And now depth . . .

G8:   *(Reading)* depth of the hole . . . *(both look at the instructions in front of T)*

T9:   *(Reading the instructions)* 12. *(Turning to G)* It is −12. −12 or +12?

G10:   *(Looking at the screen)* Z −12. *[He types −12.]*

G11:   *(Reading)* Fast: at tightening.

T12:   *(Skipping to the next stage, looking at the screen)* Careful, 'depth of hole' is meant for the diameter, not for the tip.

G13:   *[Accept the default option 'Fast: at tightening' and clicks on the 'diameter' option for the depth.]*

G14:   *(Checks the values indicated for each level, going up with the pointer)* Surface, OK. 'Security level, at tightening', what's that?

T15:   That, I don't think we have . . .

G16   *(Turning briefly towards T)* I don't think we have used that.

T17:   No, never.

G18:   *[Leaves 0 for 'security level' and clicks on OK to indicate that the window has been completed.]*

P19:   Recalculates the depth from −12 to −17.5 and changes the option 'depth at the diameter' for 'depth at the tip'. Beeps. Remains on the same window.

All the verbal exchanges take place between Guy and Ted. By his attitude and his glances, Didier shows that he is paying attention, but he does not intervene during this first stage.

As for the working procedure, we notice that Guy, almost always looking at the screen, reads the headings of the dialogue boxes aloud, following the order suggested by the program. Decision making is partly based on what the students remember of the processes used in the exercises done during the year preceding the practical work. Decisions are not justified through discussion (G4, G10, G13), this makes it difficult for an external observer to discern their motives. In the exchange from G14 to G18, it is clear that the point of reference is the curriculum, and not the computer program, nor the future drilling situation. The dialogue determining the choice of the value for the security level (from G14 to G18) is important, because the decision

Depth calculated at the tip of the drill

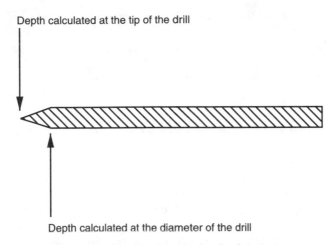

Depth calculated at the diameter of the drill

Figure 8.1 Two ways of indicating the depth of the hole

taken gives rise to a serious mistake in the drilling of the part. What is happening here? Guy's question might have led to a conceptualisation (G14 'security level, what's that?'), but the tone used rather indicates irritated surprise ('What is that thing I don't know about?'). The decision is based on the idea, shared by both, that having never used it (i.e. in their former training experience) they should not pay attention to it. G18 translates into action the conclusion that if something has never been used, the zero value should be left as it is.

Regarding status, Guy seems to occupy a high position. Sitting at the commands, he plays the role of an intermediary between the program and his team mates. He alone determines the reading rhythm of the program and the filling in of answers. Twice (in T5 and T7), Ted tries to introduce the concept of 'depth', against the order indicated both by the program and by Guy, but the latter ignores Ted's interventions until his own reading of the screen brings him to the same point. Guy passes judgement on Ted's proposal (G4: 'Down to Z. Yeap, that's right'), and chooses what answer he will feed to the computer. In the transcribed passage as well as in the preceding exchanges, he seems to be able to recall the proceedings with greater confidence, a capacity he expresses in normative assertions: 'That's how it's done'; he has a greater influence on the decision taken. As for Didier, he follows what is going on, but he does not express himself verbally, nor do either of his team mates address him directly in this excerpt.

Stage 2: reactions to an error warning

The students have given 0; 2; 0; −12; and the 'depth at the diameter' option. The program automatically recalculates the depth of the hole at the tip of the tool, beeps and does not move on to the next stage.

G20:   (*Looking at the screen*) What crap is it telling me!? Depth of the hole, what's that codswallop?

T21:   (*Slightly irritated and looking at G*) That's because you haven't defined the depth of the part, you can't make a hole in a sheet!

G22:   (*In a low voice, and looking at the screen*) Well, perhaps it wasn't like that.

In G20, Guy poses as the main interlocutor of the program, which addresses *him* ('telling *me*'). He also seems to indicate the program to be the cause of the problem (the computer is talking crap). Is it an attempt at face saving? At the same time, he wants an explanation.

Ted answers, confirming that Guy is indeed the main interlocutor of the program and indicates *him* to be the cause of the problem ('*you* haven't defined . . . '). At this point in their collaboration, the mistake is not considered as having been made by the team, but by one of the protagonists. From a cognitive point of view, it is interesting to note that in his question Guy already mentions an interpretation of the problem: the trouble is the depth of the hole; and Ted implicitly accepts this suggestion when he starts explaining (in T21) what is wrong with the depth.

How did they arrive at this idea? In P19, the program simultaneously gives several indications: it moves from the 'depth at the diameter' to the 'depth at the tip' option, then it recalculates the depth and it beeps. This signal reacts to the fact that the students have given a security level that is lower than the fast approach level. But the students do not interpret the beep in that way, because they think the problem is linked to the recalculation made by the computer, i.e. to the depth of the holes. Apparently, they have not noticed that the 'tip' option has replaced the 'diameter' option and, like other teams observed, they do not seem to remember that the program makes this conversion automatically. They are also backed up in their opinion because the software, in this case, does not give them a written message specifying what mistake they have made, whereas it has done so on other occasions.

We shall see that Ted and Guy's (incorrect) understanding of the problem influences many of their attempts to solve it in the next six minutes.

Stage 3: various attempts

For six minutes Guy, Ted (and to a lesser degree Didier) embark upon an intense search for solutions. Besides the systematic exploration of the menus, twice repeated by Guy, they perform nine separate interventions on the program in vain. Their procedures in this search[3] prove to be very varied: checks and changes in the computer image of the part, changes in the piercing options, consultation of the menus and 'help' option. The main line of their research aims at making sure that the part, as defined for the program, is indeed 20 mm high. This height already worried them when they started, and has been the topic of a fruitless interaction with the teacher. Now, still unsatisfied, they focus on this point. Ted also suggests some modifications relating to previous choices. Does this reveal the fragility of both the decisions taken and of the knowledge and agreement underlying them? Or is it a simple trial-and-error approach, often described in people accustomed to seizing the opportunity allowed to them to modify former choices, which is facilitated by computerised instruments?

In this part, Ted plays a more important role: most proposals come from him, and are followed by Guy. Moreover, Ted does not like Guy's silent dialogues with the program and he interrupts him twice, asking him what he is doing. Didier briefly goes away.

The students show signs of stress and irritation: sighs, violent blows on the keyboard, and disparaging comments: 'A real treat, this practical work, isn't it!' Didier says to Ted, who later comments: 'We haven't touched this subject for a year, why do we have to do this all of a sudden?' Some of their remarks to each other are made harshly, while at other times they scold the program for not 'agreeing'.

Stage 4: towards a (wrong) solution

After the various attempts described above, Ted makes a suggestion from which they will elaborate a means of solving the problem.

T101.	Try to fill the field with the zeros,[4] write some mock values, to see if it accepts them. If it does, it means that we have forgotten to indicate a depth.[5]
G102 G111:	[Following Ted's indications, Guy puts 3 for security level, for fast approach and for reference surface.]
P112:	'Refuses' their parameters by keeping the same window on the screen. Beeps.
T113:	(Sounding exasperated) Ooooh! That's not it!
G114:	[He feeds 0's everywhere, even for the depth of the drilling.]
P115:	Moves on to the next window, which means that the values offered have been accepted.
T116:	(Surprised, laughs ironically and speaks to D) We've put 0's everywhere and it works! That thing's stoned!
G117:	(Scratches his head and moves from one box to the next with the pointer. When he is on 'bottom of the hole', Ted suggests . . .)
T118:	Try it with -20 (stressing the word 'minus'), well, -12, then check the diameter as well.
G119:	[Follows T's proposals.]
P120:	Accepts and moves on to the next window.
T121:	Well, we only have to check the fast approach, now; normally it's $+2$.
G122:	Let's drop the fast approach!

T123	Come on! If we are above . . . *(gesture of one hand pointing down towards the other, level hand)*
G124:	*(Grunts dismissively, with a gesture inviting T to drop the issue)*
T125:	No, it won't work, we must try to approach fast.
G126:	We won't approach fast, that's all.
T127:	OK, go ahead.

As far as collaboration is concerned, we notice that up to G119, Ted takes the initiative. Indeed, the alternation of the speakers in T101–G102, T113–G114, T116–G117 and in T18–G119, shows that his suggestions are followed by Guy. This passage confirms Ted's role as 'proposer'. Since he cannot, like Guy, search the menus for ideas, he seems freer to elaborate suggestions that are not directly linked to what appears on the screen. In G114 Guy, again, modifies the values without previous discussion but Ted, who watches him, comments on the program's feedback and directs the next action.

What solution do they come to? In T101, Ted finally takes into account the values given to the parameters and suggests a test that ought to show if they must replace one of the 0's with another value ('it means that we have forgotten to indicate a depth'). That he should suggest putting random values, and then be surprised by the program's refusal, reveals an important aspect in his visualisation of the problem: he considers each level as a discrete unit, as it appears on the screen, and not as a stage in the descending movement of the drill, where values must follow a decreasing order, as in the actual drilling situation. In this instance, the program, which does not offer error warnings concerning the security level, backs him up in his mistake.

After P112, which indicates the failure of the T101 proposal, Guy, in turn, seems to carry out a test by putting 0's everywhere, but his test concerns the program's feedback; thus they notice that it accepts solutions that are wrong for the actual machining (a drilling depth of zero). But the team does not grasp the full implications of this phenomenon (i.e. that an incorrect solution can be accepted) and afterwards they opt for the following procedure: starting from the solution accepted by the program (0 for all parameters), they add the value needed for drilling (the depth of -12), which is so evident that it does not give rise to any discussion. Here, apparently, their aim (and consequently their interpretation of the task) has momentarily changed: now they no longer refer to the machining process but want to give the program a solution it will accept. Nevertheless, Ted thinks they still have to give a value for the fast approach: 'Normally, it is $+2$'. When Guy, unimpressed by this appeal to respect a norm, refuses, Ted goes back to the previous interpretation and defends his idea by describing – verbally and with gestures – the machining situation, and then by defining more precisely the action concerned, i.e. to approach fast. In G126 Guy insists: 'We won't approach fast, that's all', as if for him not approaching fast was not a mistake and, besides, it was not important to approach fast. Ted gives in, abandoning for the moment the goal set by the teacher, i.e. that the machining time should be as short as possible. In the end, the program accepts their solution and the students think they have got away with it. They go on to use the same procedure for all the operations programmed. When their part is machined, it is scratched by one of the tools as a result of the lack of positive values for the security and for fast approach levels.

Analysis of the observations: the interactions between learners in this sequence

Throughout the activity, verbal exchanges, which are at times very lively, accompany the students' work. What is the nature of these verbal exchanges and how should they be characterised?

As we anticipated, sociocognitive conflicts were observed at certain times between individuals holding different points of view. However, the confrontation between learners does not seem to be valued or methodically thought through at any time. Rather than really confronting each other with their points of view (as they do in, for example, excerpt T121 to T127), they tend to ask the computer to settle the argument by means of the immediate feedback that it provides (feedback which still needs to be interpreted correctly). The computer is expected to confirm or contradict the soundness or otherwise of each operation or course of action. Requiring this of the software risks, as can be seen at times, short circuiting the cognitive restructuring processes necessary for the integration of different points of view, processes which, in psychosociogenetic research, are precisely identified as being fruitful.

Nevertheless we observe, notably because of negative feedback from the software, certain cognitive re-elaborations on the part of the participants. Their understanding of the task can, in effect, evolve along the way; the aim of the activity is itself at times prone to modification. This is for example the case when, following persistent blocks, the initial task aimed at *machining a part* is manifestly transformed into a task aimed at *satisfying the program*, that is circumventing it as the need arises by introducing incoherent data with the aim of progressing with the task despite everything.

In the sequence analysed, the distribution of roles is equally worthy of attention. The work is carried out by two students, leaving the third outside the sphere of activity. However this marginalisation of Didier's role should be examined within the context of the work carried out as a whole during that afternoon. In group work, it can happen that the person who appears to be 'left out' is in fact at a distance which facilitates a more reflective overview, a 'meta-view' of the action taking place. From this position, it is possible to give points of view and make proposals which are pertinent to the activity and useful in its development. This contribution, neglected by the duo in command, did in fact, at a later stage, play an essential role in the solution of the task.

Everything takes place as if, for this third partner, the fact of not having to act (through lack of power), allows him to develop a meta-cognitive space for reflecting upon what is happening. He may not have sufficient social weight to impose his point of view, but it is through the persistence of his observation that in the end he plays an essential role.

The tool which is at the centre of the activity has an important place in this distribution of roles. In effect, the computer only has one mouse and holding it is, de facto, a form of seizing power. During the exercise however, we see a changing distribution of roles, most notably as difficulties are confronted.

The characteristics of the software also influence the nature of the interactions which develop between learners. In this practical work session, one can question whether or not the program used incites them to resort to methods of trial and error. In effect, the rapid presentation of countless windows and the large number of choices cause the students to take risks, and this all the more because the time available to them is relatively limited. To orientate themselves they sometimes seem to click on options or data almost at random, counting on the feedback to readjust their choice. It should also be noted that other aspects of this software, in particular the possibility of simulating and visualising the state of machining at any given time is little exploited by the students. It can be hypothesised that the use of the visualisation options could have given rise to other interpersonal relations orientated less towards forging ahead with the activity and more towards close examination of work that had already been carried out.

Without doubt, these observations as a whole reveal that the students do in fact collaborate, but the form that this collaboration takes is quite particular: it is essentially a pooling of resources, in which the partners do not appear to require justifications or explanations from each other. Given the perceived sense of urgency, proceeding in this manner is probably the most rapid strategy. The work is thus carried out in constant dialogue (at least in the excerpts presented here), without argumentation or exploratory talk being observed. We see the students neither planning each stage nor establishing partial objectives. The activity is considered globally. Everything occurs as if responsibility for this is left to the machine, given the job of 'testing' the worth of decisions taken. What is more, one of the participants is perceived as the computer's main interlocutor; having this responsibility does not encourage him to integrate the third partner into the collective dynamics. We never see them offering opinions 'in turn' for example. Studies have already reported that working by trial and error does not encourage social grounding (Blaye *et al.*, 1992; Hoyles *et al.*, 1990).

To sum up, there is collaboration, there is practically continuous interaction, and there is a pattern of role distribution strongly dependent upon the nature of the software and tools being shared (a screen, a keyboard, a single mouse) and probably upon the students' perception of the limited time available. Confronting and deepening their comprehension of programming machining does not appear to be central to the learners, as we shall see now in the part which deals with their interpretation of the meaning of the proposed activity.

The students' interpretation of the meaning of the situation

The naive observer who arrives in a workshop could be under the impression that s/he is placed in a situation from which to observe interactions aimed mainly at broadening knowledge of a technical operation. This is not the case. The impression released from an attentive examination of the reality of the exchanges transcribed is of a scene which includes other factors, even though learning does nevertheless take place. What representation of the task do the students make for themselves? They seem to understand their role as being essentially one of correctly carrying out the machining of a part during the afternoon and respecting certain limitations, most notably that of finding an optimal machining time. In a way, this is what the teacher asked of them during the initial instructions. Nobody speaks of what else might be learned here, nor takes any action in that direction.

In keeping with an implicit didactic contract, and no doubt present in all their past school experience, these students expect that the task presented to them by the teacher will require the application of knowledge learned and practised previously in class. They refer to this several times: either positively, to base themselves upon it, or negatively to complain about this task for which they do not feel adequately prepared.

The students do not bring this up in the excerpts reported here, but the mastery of this Flexible Manufacturing System cell does not in fact form part of the final examinations which certify their level of professional competence. Thus it only had the status of a college exercise. This 'college' interpretation of the task probably caused them sometimes to operate in the abstract, without basing themselves upon their knowledge of machining. However, this practical knowledge is essential for the correct use of the software and to give full meaning to the numerous parameters to be introduced.

But the task that they set themselves that afternoon is not only a cognitive one: one senses at all times the need for one or the other of them to save face when confronted with a difficulty. They play power games. Thus, for example, when Ted attempts to win control of the situation by giving Guy orders one after the other, the tension mounts, aggression towards the machine and towards one another manifests itself, each blaming the other for the impasse.

A further interesting element concerns the students' perception of the software. The software has imperfections, but the students do not appear to think about this seriously. They implicitly expect the software to work perfectly, requiring it to test everything. When its reaction appears absurd, they think it has broken down (cf. T116: 'We've put 0's everywhere and it works! That thing's stoned!'). This perhaps reflects only a partial under-standing of the nature of the tool that they are using and of the logic behind its working. The software can allow solutions which lead to errors and does not reject fruitless avenues of research; it is an open-ended instrument, conceived in the first place for use in a professional context and not for training beginners who still need to be led step by step, much in the style of a tutorial.

The slight apprehension of the strange 'partner' the machine represents for them probably also causes them to miss using certain symbolic resources, such as the possibility of simulating on the screen the machining that they have already programmed in and to visualise the successive stages of the part. What is striking is that throughout the length of these sequences they use the visualisation possibilities very little as a means of alleviating uncer-tainties or checking the adequacy of the work they have already carried out.

The meaning which these technician students give to different events experienced during the task thus appears to be influenced on the one hand by the college framework and on the other by their utilitarian rapport with the technical device which they are spending time getting to work, even if without understanding it. Where do the representations that the students manifest here come from?

Reflections upon wider psychological and social factors

The arrival of automated systems of production has not been without the creation of uncertainty and even worry for those directly concerned. To what extent will the machine replace human labour? Is there a risk of human activities becoming subservient to the machine or, on the contrary, will these machines enrich them? Who will really benefit from the changes taking place? What level of skill will the worker, the technician or the engi-neer have to achieve in order to take part in this change and not pay the price? These questions may seem philosophical, they are however very everyday and concrete, in that everyone is familiar with firms that have restructured with the introduction of computerised tools, putting people out of work. But there is also some awareness of other firms which are growing because of their know-how in computing and automation.

The introduction of new computer-assisted manufacturing techniques, and the perception of it that those concerned have, has repeatedly called into question the status of traditional industrial know-how that can be described as a craft. Is it still necessary? To what extent is the mastery of machine tools an indispensable prerequisite to a technical training? Can automated manufacturing be learned without passing through this stage? These ques-tions are not specific to the Sainte-Croix Technical College but have been posed since the introduction of the first generation of computer numerical controlled machines (Martin, 1991). In the excerpt reported here, we see the students waver between treating the problem in a concrete way (thus at certain times, they have recourse to a language of gesture in order to make themselves understood, cf. T123), but at other times (for example, just after the use of gesture mentioned above), we see them formally trying to manage data which do not appear grounded in reality. In fact, this second type of data management predominated in the group. This admittedly allowed them to 'fill in' all the windows provided by the software, and in doing so, to advance in their work. However, the end product was scratched due to a lack of realism in the specification of values on the screen. From a psychological point of view, the question is thus to discern under what conditions the concrete experience of the working with tools and the reaction of materials can be a resource facilitating the programming of the machining of a part.

This finding brings us back to the question of efficacy. Is efficacy a matter of carrying out the work demanded of them quickly, or does efficacy reside in the quality achieved? Efficacy could also be found in knowledge which can be acquired through difficulties encountered and thus through the solutions worked out in order to overcome them. It is not certain that the students consciously asked themselves this question, perhaps because their lengthy schooling never required an ability to evaluate their own performance, its efficiency and its costs.

Other important aspects of the technical college are also reflected in the observations which we have reported here. The study of the curriculum structure has permitted us to perceive the highly symbolic and nevertheless marginal aspect of this practical work. Shown off to advantage by the college each time that its public image is at stake, the training activities on the Flexible Manufacturing System form only a small part of the course and are not part of the final assessment for the technicians' diploma (mainly because state regulations and professional training have not yet integrated all the technological changes in their assessment systems).

The marginalisation of this practical work is also evident in the way the students think about it. Through numerous remarks, they indicated that they were not sure that this was a real machine and a real industrial exercise. They machine resin and not metals (for reasons of security and visibility of operations). Also, use of this software is not widespread in the factories in the area. Moreover, as there is no standard in this regard and each automation system has specific characteristics, the students do not see the relevance of this learning situation. Some of them are interested in the possibility of getting a complicated device to work (this is shown in the attraction, sometimes even excitement, which the final automatic machining engenders), but others, not having been invited to reflect upon the specific or general characteristics of the machine and software, remain sceptical regarding the point of working on a device which they are unlikely to encounter in quite this form in their future professional life.

This takes us back to a problem of identity; we have seen the students struggling to save face and place themselves in a high position in the group. Without doubt this has a connection with their insecurity regarding their professional image which leaves them doubting whether the most important thing for a technician is understanding or know-how. The ethos of the profession of precision mechanics requires the acquisition, over years of apprenticeship, of the almost perfect mastery of classic machine tools. However, this requirement cannot be transposed onto new devices which are still in development and in relation to which the college only has introductory objectives. What is it then to show yourself to be a good student or worker in this situation? Thus we can see that diverse psychological and social factors traverse these learning situations.

Conclusion

In this chapter, we have presented a piece of research based upon the observation of a live training situation within a technical college. Its goal was to study the training problems which arise from the introduction of new manufacturing technologies and the way in which student technicians construct the new skills currently expected of them in this domain. This led to a particular interest in the sociocognitive interactions deployed during the practical sessions on automation.

A precise work sequence was placed under the 'microscope', without losing sight of the institutional and social context within which this sequence took place, with the aim of making apparent the interdependence of two phenomena: the micro-processes of the interactions and the more macro-pedagogical, technical and social elements present in the lives of the students and of the school.

The learning situations observed revealed themselves, in an even more pronounced way than expected, to include not only cognitive and technical elements but also questions of relationship and identity. When facing difficulties in finding a solution, the students do apply their knowledge, but we also see them pushing themselves to finish quickly, trying to save face, showing ambivalent attitudes towards the automation, or even questioning themselves about the meaning or relevance of the task proposed. The detailed analysis of what happens or is said within a working group reveals traces of these diverse elements which, in one way or another, mark the modes of collaboration adopted.

In this context of activities containing multiple elements, it is important to grasp the manner in which the student technicians interpret the task required of them. The meaning which they gave to this practical work situation appeared to be strongly influenced by the scholastic framework of their training; the students seemed to focus essentially upon carrying out the work asked of them as quickly as possible and obtaining a good mark. They show a utilitarian rapport with the technical device, using a method of trial and error to get it to work without necessarily seeking to understand how it works. The objective, which could be to deepen their understanding of the device, escapes them, moreover this objective is not made explicit in the teacher's instructions.

Regarding the question of the efficiency of sociocognitive interactions, our study shows that it is interesting to consider two levels of reality: on the one hand, the different pedagogical changes that our observations suggest: notably learning objectives to be redefined, evaluation criteria to be made explicit, time management and organisation of group work to be restructured. On the other hand and more subjectively, the impression that the students have of the efficiency of their own activity as a function of their understanding of the objectives to be achieved. The goal of training technicians to master sophisticated tools with rapidly evolving technology necessitates the rethinking of both the pedagogical activity involved and the understanding of the profession and its demands.

Notes

1 This chapter was written in collaboration with Jean-Philippe Chavey, engineer and teacher at the Technical College of Sainte-Croix (Switzerland), responsible for the teaching of automation.

Thanks to Claude Béguin and Anne-Marie Rifai for their help with the translation. A grant from the Fonds National Suisse de la Recherche Scientifique has made this research possible (Programme National de Recherche No 33 'Efficacy of our teaching systems', grant No 4033–035846 to A-N. Perret-Clermont, R. Bachmann and L. O. Pochon). We are grateful to Ronald Bachmann, director of the Technical College of Sainte-Croix (Switzerland), for inviting us to work at his school, and to the students, who kindly agreed to be filmed and interviewed.

2 Guy = G; Ted = T; program = P. Data input activity is in square brackets and is italicised and the other actions are in round brackets and are italicised.

3 The transcription of this section is not reported here due to word length constraints.

4 In the window concerning the drilling levels.

5 For one of the levels, the correct value is not 0.

References

Bearison, D. J. (1991) *Interactional Contexts of Cognitive Development: Piagetian Approaches to Sociogenesis*, Norwood, NY: Ablex.

Bell, N., Grossen, M., and Perret-Clermont, A-N. (1985) 'Sociocognitive conflict and intellectual growth', in M. W. Berkowitz (ed.) *Peer Conflict and Psychological Growth*, San Francisco: Jossey Bass.

Benavente, A., da Costa, A. F., Machado, F. L., and Neves, M. C. (1993) *De l'autre côté de l'école*, Berne: Peter Lang.

Blaye, A. (1989) 'Nature et effets des opposition dans des situations de corésolution de problèmes entre pairs', in B. E. Garnier (ed.) *Construction des Savoirs-Obstacles et Conflits*, Québec: Cirade, d. Agence d'Arc.

Blaye, A., Light, P., and Rubtsov, V. (1992) 'Collaborative learning at the computer: how social processes "interface" with human–computer interaction', *European Journal of Psychology of Education* 7(4): 257–268.

Brossard, M., and Wargnier, P. (1993) 'Rôle de certaines variables contextuelles sur le fonctionnement cognitif des élèves en situation scolaire', *Bulletin de Psychologie*, XLVI(412): 703–709.

Collins, A., Brown, J. S., and Newman, S. (1989) 'Cognitive apprenticeship: teaching the crafts of reading, writing and mathematics', in L. B. Resnick (ed.) *Knowing, Learning, and Instruction*, Hillsdale, NJ: LEA.

Crook, C. (1995) 'On resourcing a concern for collaboration within peer interactions', *Cognition and Instruction* 13(4): 541–547.

Dillenbourg, P., Baker, M., Blaye, A., and O'Malley, C. (1995) 'The evolution of research on collaborative learning', in P. Reimann and H. Spada (eds) *Learning in Humans and Machines*, London: Pergamon.

Doise, W., and Mugny, G. (1984) *The Social Development of the Intellect*, Oxford: Pergamon Press.

Donaldson, M. (1978) *Children's Minds*, Glasgow: Fontana.

Emler, N., and Valiant, G. (1982) 'Social interaction and cognitive conflict in the development of spatial coordination', *British Journal of Psychology* 73: 295–303.

Flahaut, F. (1978) *La Parole Intermédiaire*, Paris: Le Seuil.

Forman, E. A., and McPhail, J. (1993) 'Vygotskian perspective on children's collaborative problem-solving activities', in E. A. Forman, N. Minick, and C. A. Stone (eds) *Contexts for Learning: Sociocultural Dynamics in Chidren's Development*, New York, Oxford: Oxford University Press.

Garduno Rubio, T. (1996) *Action, interaction et réflexion dans la conception et la réalisation d'une expérience pédagogique: l'Ecole Paidos à Mexico*, Université de Neuchâtel.

Gilly, M. (1980) *Maître-élève: Rôles Institutionnels et Représentations*, Paris: Presses Universitaires de France.

Gilly, M., Fraisse, J., and Roux, J. P. (1988). 'Résolutions de problémes en dyades et progrès cognitifs chez des enfants de 11 à 13 ans: dynamiques interactives et socio-cognitives', in A-N. Perret-Clermont and M. Nicolet (eds) *Interagir et Connaître*, Cousset (FR): Editions Delval.

Golay Schilter, D. (1995) 'Regards sur l'organisation et les enjeux de l'enseignement à l'Ecole Technique de Sainte-Croix', *Document de recherche No. 4*, Séminaire de Psychologie: Université de Neuchâtel.

Granott, N. (1993) 'Patterns of interaction in the co-construction of knowledge', in H. Wozniak and K. W. Fischer (eds) *Development in Context: Acting and Thinking in Specific Environments*, Hillsdale, NJ: LEA.

Grossen, M. (1988) *L'intersubjectivité en Situation de Test*, Cousset (Fribourg): Editions Delval.

Grossen, M., Liengme Bessire, M-J., and Perret-Clermont, A-N. (1997) 'Construction de l'interaction et dynamiques socio-cognitives', in M. Grossen and B. Py (eds) *Pratiques Sociales et Médiations Symboliques*, Berne: Peter Lang.

Healy, L., Pozzi, S., and Hoyles, C. (1995) 'Making sense of groups, computers, and mathematics', *Cognition and Instruction* 13(4): 505–523.

Hennessy, S., and McCormick, R. (1994) 'The general problem-solving process in technology education', in F. Banks (ed.) *Teaching Technology*, New York and London: Routledge, The Open University.

Howe, C., Tolmie, A., Green, K., and Mackenzie, M. (1995) 'Peer collaboration and conceptual growth in physics: task influences on children's understanding of heating and cooling', *Cognition and Instruction* 13(4): 483–503.

Hoyles, C., and Forman, E. A. (1995) 'Introduction', *Cognition and Instruction* 13(4): 479–482.

Hoyles, C., Healy, L., and Pozzi, S. (1992) 'Interdependence and autonomy: aspects of groupwork with computers', *Learning and Instruction* 2: 239–257.

Hoyles, C., Healy, L., and Sutherland, R. (1990) *The Role of Peer Group Discussion in Mathematical Environments*, Department of Mathematics, Statistics and Computing: Institute of Education.

Hundeide, K. (1985) 'The tacit background of children's judgements', in J. V. Wertsch (ed.) *Cuture, Communication and Cognition: Vygotskian Perspectives*, Cambridge: Cambridge University Press.

Iannacone, A., and Perret-Clermont, A-N. (1993) 'Qu'est-ce qui s'apprend? Qu'est-ce qui se développe?', in J. Wassmann and P. Dasen (eds) *Les Savoirs Quotidiens*, Freibourg (Schweiz): Universitätsverlag Freibourg.

Jackson, A. C., Fletcher, B., and Messer, D. J. (1992) 'When talking doesn't help: an investigation of microcomputer-based group problem solving', *Learning and Instruction* 2: 185–197.

Järvelä, S. (1995) 'The cognitive apprenticeship model in a technologically rich learning environment: interpreting the learning interaction', *Learning and Instruction* 5(3): 237–259.

Kaiser, C., Perret-Clermont, A-N., Perret, J. F., and Golay, D. (1997) 'Apprendre un métier technique aujourd'hui: représentations des apprenants', *Document de recherche No. 8*, Séminaire de Psychologie: Université de Neuchâtel.

Leplat, J. (1993) 'Ergonomie et activités collectives', *Revue Roumaine de Psychologie* 37(2): 103–118.

Light, P., and Blaye, A. (1989) 'Computer-based learning: the social dimension', in H. Foot, M. Morgan, and R. Shute (eds) *Children Helping Children*, Chichester: John Wiley.

Light, P., and Perret Clermont, A-N. (1989) 'Social context effects in learning and testing', in D. Gellatly, D. Rogers, and J. A. Sloboda (eds) *Cognition and Social Worlds*, Oxford: Oxford University Press.

Linhart, F. (1994) *La Modernisation des Entreprises*, Paris: Editions La Découverte.

Martin, L. M. W. (1995) 'Linking thought and setting in the study of workplace learning', in L. Martin, K. Nelson, and E. Tobach (eds) *Sociocultural Psychology: Theory and Practice of Doing and Knowing*, Cambridge: Cambridge University Press.

Martin, L. M. W., and Scribner, S. (1991) 'Laboratory for cognitive studies of work: a case study of the intellectual implications of a new technology', *Teachers College Record* 92(4).

McLane, J. B., and Wertsch, J. V. (1986) 'Child–child and adult–child interaction: a Vygotskian study of dyadic problem systems', *The Quarterly Newsletter of the Laboratory of Comparative Human Cognition* 8(3): 98.

Mercer, N. (1996) 'The quality of talk in children's collaborative activity in the classroom', *Learning and Instruction* 6(4): 359–377.

Mercer, N., and Fisher, E. (1992) 'How do teachers help children to learn? An analysis of teachers' interventions in computer-based activities', *Learning and Instruction* 2: 339–355.

Moscovici, S. and Paicheler, G. (1973) 'Travail, individu et groupe', in S. Moscovici (ed.) *Introduction à la Psychologie Sociale*, Paris: Librairie Larousse.

Muller, N., and Perret-Clermont, A-N. (in press) 'Negotiating identities and meanings in the construction of knowledge', in J. Bliss, P. Light, and R. Säljö (eds) *Learning Sites: Social and Technological Contexts for Learning*, Oxford: Pergamon.

Perrenoud, P. (1994) *Métier d'élève et Sens du Travail Scolaire*, Paris: ESF éditeur.

Perret, J. F. (1985) *Comprendre l'écriture des Nombres*, Berne: Peter Lang.

—— (1997) 'Introduction de nouvelles technologies dans un établissement d'enseignement professionnel: logique d'équipement et logique de formation', *Document de recherche No. 5*, Séminaire de Psychologie: Université de Neuchâtel.

Perret-Clermont, A-N. (1980). *Social Interaction and Cognitive Development in Children*. London, New York: Academic Press.

Perret-Clermont, A-N. and Nicolet, M. (1988) *Interagir et Connaître*, Cousset (FR): Editions Delval.

Perret-Clermont, A-N., Perret, J-F., and Bell, N. (1991) 'The social construction of meaning and cognitive activity in elementary school children', in L. B. Resnick, J. M. Levine, and S. D. Teasley (eds) *Social Shared Cognition*, Washington, DC: American Psychological Association.

Pléty, R. (1996) *L'apprentissage coopératif*, Lyon: Presses Universitaires de Lyon.

Pontecorvo, C. (1990). 'Social context, semiotic mediation and forms of discourse in constructing knowledge at school', *Learning and Instruction* 2: 1–27.

Rabardel, P. (1995) *Les Hommes et les Technologies*, Paris: A. Colin.

Rogoff, B. (1995) 'Observing sociocultural activity on three planes: participatory appropriation, guided participation, and apprenticeship', in J. Wertsch and A. Alvarez (eds.) *Sociocultural Studies of Mind*, Cambridge: Cambridge University Press.

Rommetveit, R. (1979) 'On common codes and dynamic residuals in human communication', in R. Blakar (eds) *Studies of Language, Thought and Verbal Communication*, London: Academic Press.

Saint-Dizier, V., Trognon, A., and Grossen, M. (1995) 'Analyse interlocutoire d'une situation de corésolution d'un problème arithmétique' in *Congrès des Sciences Sociales Suisses. Atelier de la Société Suisse de Psychologie*, Berne.

Säljö, R. (1991) 'Piagetian controversies, cognitive competence, and assumption about human communication', *Educational Psychology Review* 3(2): 117–126.

Säljö, R., and Wyndhamn, J. (1993) 'Solving everyday problems in the formal setting: an empirical study of the school as context for thought', in S. Chaiklin and J. Lave (eds), *Understanding Practice: Perspectives on Activity and Context*, Cambridge: Cambridge University Press.

Schubauer-Leoni, M. L. (1986) 'Le contrat didactique: un cadre interprétatif pour comprendre les savoirs manifestés par les élèves en mathématique', *European Journal of Psychology of Education* 1(2): 139–153.

—— (1993) 'L'algèbre vue par des professeurs du secondaire inférieur: démarche comparative en fonction des contextes institutionnels', in J. F. Perret and E. Runtz-Christan (eds), *Les Manuels font-ils école?*, Cousset (Fribourg): Delval/IRDP.

Schubauer-Leoni, M. L., and Grossen, M. (1993) 'Negotiating the meaning of questions in didactic and experimental contracts', *European Journal of Psychology of Education* 8(4): 451–471.

Stroobants, M. (1993) *Savoir-faire et Compétences au Travail. Une Sociologie de la Fabrication des Aptitudes*, Bruxelles: Editions de l'Université de Bruxelles.

Trognon, A. (1991) 'L'interaction en général: sujets, groupes, cognitions, représentations sociales', *Connexions* 57(1): 9–26.

—— (1993) *Résoudre Conversationnellement un Problème Technologique*, Nancy: Laboratoire de Psychologie, GRC Université de Nancy.

Verillon, P. and Rabardel, P. (1995) 'Cognition and artifacts: a contribution to the study of thought in relation to instrumented activity', *European Journal of Psychology of Education* 10(1): 77–101.

Vion, R. (1992) *La Communication Verbale. Analyse des Interactions*, Paris: Hachette.

Woods, P. (1990) *The Happiest Days? How Pupils Cope With School*, London: The Falmer Press. Wynnikamen, F. (1990) *Apprendre en Imitant?*, Paris: Presses Universitaires de France.

Wynnikamen, F. (1990) *Apprendre en Imitant?*, Paris: Presses Universitaires de France.

9   Learning as the use of tools

A sociocultural perspective on the human–technology link

Roger Säljö[1]

Introduction: studying learning

Issues concerning how people learn and appropriate knowledge are very much the focus of attention today. Technological, economic and social development have resulted in more sophisticated work processes that require a broad range of skills of a technical as well as interpersonal nature. Moreover, knowledge and information have become prominent features of life in general; we expect citizens to acquire at least a certain degree of computer literacy and to be able to orientate themselves in a complex world by using the resources offered through modern information technology. Such technology is also rapidly changing the ways in which information is distributed in society. Schools, for instance, have to accommodate to the new resources available. The traditional textbook, the core of modern schooling, comes of age rather quickly, but new information on almost anything can be collected from databases available on the internet, on CD-ROMs or through other channels.

It has also been assumed that computers and modern information technology will revolutionise human learning and create what is sometimes referred to as a learning society. This impact on learning is assumed to be visible on different levels. We will have information sources from literally across the world available on line when working with problems in our homes or at school, and this will make our thinking and problem solving more efficient. Another feature of such technologies is that they make it easier to co-operate across physical distances. We can keep in touch with colleagues and with experts even though we are geographically separated. It is assumed that life in classrooms will be very different when the potentials of information technology are made full use of. Students will be able to reach outside the walls of the classroom with their questions and gain access to the most recent information on whatever issue they are working on. They can contact fellow students in other countries to get first-hand information on what is happening across the globe, and they may also engage in dialogue with experts in various fields. In such a process, where arguments can be gathered from many sources, the authority of the teacher as the most knowledgeable conversation partner will be challenged. The technology will also facilitate collaboration within the classroom itself and provide new ways of working together (see Crook, 1994, this volume).

At present, it should be stressed that some of these features of information technologies must be seen as potentials that have yet to be implemented in productive manners in contexts of learning. Computer-mediated learning and the use of resources such as e-mail have not always been success stories. Light and Light (this volume), for instance, point to some of the problems in promoting and sustaining communication via e-mail amongst students in higher education. Schofield (1995, pp. 3ff.) presents the various arguments regarding the impact of computers on schooling that have been expressed during recent years. Some, like the inventor of LOGO programming, Seymour Papert, argue that the 'computer will blow up the school' (quoted in Schofield, 1995, p. 3), while others take a much more restrained attitude to the introduction of computers in education and claim that the effects on teaching and learning will not be all that profound (see, for instance, Cuban, 1986). Light (1997) summarises this sway between unlimited faith in technology as a vehicle for revolutionising learning and downright scepticism about the promises of such developments in a somewhat ironic manner by pointing out that '[p]redictions were made to the effect that by the turn of the century computers would provide the major means of learning at all age levels and all subject areas'. But against 'such utopian enthusiasms', Light continues, lay a heavy weight of accumulated experience; many new technologies had been offered to education as panaceas in the past, and the judgement of many was reflected in the quip that 'the only successful piece of educational technology is the school bus'.

Rather than arguing for or against the merits of using information technology in contexts of learning at a general level, it would seem appropriate to inquire more precisely into what features of such resources are likely to have an impact on learning in the diverse range of settings in which people appropriate knowledge and skills. The issue might not just be one of facilitating teaching and learning as we conceive of these processes today. It might also be that what we conceive of as learning will be somewhat different when our communicative practices change.

The human–technology link in social practices: conditions of learning

The introduction of technologies into human activities, and the use of such resources for learning and for the mastery of complex activities, is nothing new, and this is the major point of this chapter. In fact, throughout history people have sought to develop technologies to help them solve intellectual as well as practical problems (Cole, 1996). To some extent this is almost a defining feature of the human species: the ability to create a broad range of powerful technologies transforming life conditions in almost any setting. For instance, when faced with the practical problem of moving heavy stones and other objects, people developed the technique of using levers to increase their power. The first users of such a device, way back in the history of humankind, discovered that by using a thick stick or a pole, the physical strength necessary to move a heavy object decreased dramatically. What had been too heavy to move could now be managed with much less physical strength.

It is also apparent that the development of tools has by no means been restricted to areas where physical strength is the main limitation. Throughout history there has been a continuous creation of devices and technologies that have changed the mode in which we communicate and use our intellectual resources. One very clear example of such a technology, with far-reaching consequences culturally, socially and psychologically, was the introduction of technologies of writing (Ong, 1982; Olson, 1994). Before writing was used to communicate and (re)produce messages, oral communication (and eventually, although quite late in the history of humans, pictures) was the only mode in which it was possible for people to share their ideas about the world. Information that was to be retained over time had to be stored in someone's head. Our preliterate predecessors could only learn from the people they met in person. Face-to-face interaction was the only alternative available for exchanging knowledge and information, since sound waves (unlike documents) do not travel very far.

When writing, in some form, entered the scene, the mode in which humans used their limited cognitive capacities changed. Writing can preserve and make permanent messages in a manner that talk does not (Ong, 1982). Unlike relying on highly limited human memory, there is no end to how much information can be stored when documents can be produced. The writing of different types of messages and documents, such as business agreements and various kinds of contracts, tax and census registers of the inhabitants of a town or a village, legal documents, information about nature, religion, society and so on in textbooks to be used, for instance, in schools, was a revolutionary information technology in its time. So later was the printing press in the sense that it allowed for the reproduction of messages at a reasonable cost to large groups of citizens (Eisenstein, 1985). Today, writing is so commonplace that we might not conceive of it as technology-based at all. But it certainly is; the technique for reproduction that we use for writing, in our case the alphabet, and the physical devices such as paper and pencil, typewriters and word-processing programmes, are artefacts. The desire to be able to communicate more efficiently through writing *per se* became a technological force that resulted in the production of new writing materials and artefacts. This development has by no means come to an end as the continuous flow of new and increasingly more powerful word-processing programmes illustrates (for an analysis of the development of word-processing programmes, see Grossen and Pochon, 1997).

The most interesting aspect of writing as a technology for communicating is that in a very obvious sense it reorganises the manner in which we deal with intellectual (and practical) problems (Hutchins, 1995). Just think of what it would take to divide 133.21 by 6.81 or to convert 253 German Marks into pounds or dollars, if you were not allowed to do it on paper. It would take a long time, and it might not even be possible to manage such tasks at all without the use of paper and pencil as aids to thinking. Similarly, how would we manage to remember the phone numbers and addresses of our friends and colleagues if we did not record them in writing? And how would we learn about nature and other societies, if we did not have access to texts? What would our lives be like without our diaries? Thus, the ways in which humans learn – i.e. retain, reproduce and produce information, knowledge and skills – changed dramatically when writing became used as a resource for communicating in social life. Some learning activities became more or less obsolete (like memorising verbatim long poems or stories), while other skills, for instance, the ability to produce coherent and intelligible texts or the skill of organising information, became important.

So, technological development runs through human history and it has contributed to changing our daily activities many times before. Human learning has always been a matter of mastering tools of different kinds, intellectual (such as, for instance, becoming competent in how to do a division or a multiplication by using algorithms) as well as physical (learning how to build a house or how to cultivate land). A fundamental assumption in a sociocultural understanding of human learning is precisely this: learning is always learning to do something with cultural tools (be they intellectual and/or theoretical). This has the important implication that when understanding learning we have to consider that the unit that we are studying is people in action using tools of some kind (see Wertsch, 1991, 1998; Säljö, 1996). The learning is not only inside the person, but in his or her ability to use a particular set of tools in productive ways and for particular purposes.

However, learning is not generally construed in this manner. Rather, the history of research into learning has been dominated by two different scientific traditions that at first sight appear contradictory, however both share a disregard of this ability of human beings to create artefacts and technologies. These two traditions have their origin in philosophical positions that were already formulated in ancient Greece, and they represent ideas regarding human knowledge and behaviour that stretch well beyond the specific issue of theories of learning and development. Because these ideas have been, and still are, so influential inside as well as outside education, it is worthwhile briefly presenting them in order to point out specifically how they disregard this significant aspect of human learning.

One of these traditions represents what philosophers call an *empiricist* stance to learning and knowledge. This position implies that learning is construed as a matter of registering and remembering sense impressions that come from the outside. People are like empty buckets or *tabulae rasae*, and they gain knowledge through observation and by being exposed to information. This empiricist tradition is generally linked to a powerful idea of the nature of knowledge which holds that knowledge is independent of human beings. This position on the nature of knowledge is referred to as *realism*, and its founding father is the Greek philosopher Aristotle (384–322 BC). The dominant empiricist-realist tradition in the history of modern psychology is *behaviourism*. To a behaviourist, learning is linked to changes in physical behaviours, and the assumption is that it is performance of new behaviours which is the true sign of learning.

The alternative position is called *nativism*. It implies that knowledge is viewed as the unfolding of capacities that exist in latent form, inside human beings. Our capacities for learning are given to us as members of the human species and it is the role of the environment, schooling and other resources to provide us with the experiences and psychological stimulation that allow for our talents to surface. The nativist position is generally linked to a view of knowledge which is called *idealism* or *rationalism*. The classical scholar who formulated this conception of knowledge is perhaps the most famous of all Western philosophers, Plato (428–348 BC). The idealist tradition makes a sharp distinction between the 'real', physical reality, and our knowledge of this reality. Knowledge – concepts, skills and so on – is held to be non-material, some kind of reflections or images of the world that exist as abstract entities in our minds. The physical doing of something, such as solving a problem or mending an artefact, is seen as an 'application' of knowledge in a practical setting. Modern cognitive psychology of recent decades with its emphasis on how people 'process' and 'store' information falls within this tradition.

What this brief introduction illustrates is that what is considered as knowledge and learning varies dramatically between different theoretical positions. A behaviourist and a cognitive psychologist do not agree on what is a relevant indicator of learning or how it should be measured; what is real and central to one theoretical position (for instance, mental phenomena such as concepts and psychological processes in idealist traditions) is of little, if any, interest to the other tradition (behaviourism) and vice versa (see Bruner, 1990). This observation is an illustration of a general precondition for the understanding of human learning and development; our observations are relative to the theoretical assumptions we hold regarding the nature of knowledge. Or, in philosophical parlance, our observations are theory-laden (Hanson, 1958). This observation on how our understanding of learning and knowledge is relative to our interpretations of what these phenomena are all about applies to teaching as well. We cannot simply teach without building on some assumptions regarding the nature of knowledge and how instruction should be organised so as to be productive. Here is one of the interesting challenges of the new information technologies to the way in which learning is organised and understood; do they support new forms of teaching and learning that radically transform the manner in which people appropriate knowledge? Or is the change less dramatic than it might appear? These are questions that do not as yet have any clear answer.

From a sociocultural perspective the problem of the traditional approaches to understanding learning is that they imply a disregard of the cultural side of knowledge. They treat knowledge and skill as if people were not operating with tools when solving problems and when managing social activities. People learn and develop by making use of artefacts, and as we move across societies and historical periods, the nature of the tools that people have available will differ. It is one thing learning to do multiplications and divisions when there are calculators around, it is another thing doing it with paper and pencil. It is yet another type of task when doing it without any physical artefacts whatsoever. To take another example, modern agriculture with its use of tractors and a range of mechanical devices to cultivate land, a wide variety of chemicals to increase production, freezing as a technique for preserving products, and information technologies for complex activities such as book-keeping, the filling in of forms etc. require very different learning processes from those associated with agricultural work a few decades ago when the technologies were less differentiated.

Knowledge as the use of tools: exploring learning beyond the dualism between mental and material

It follows from what has been said so far that in order to study how people learn, we must have a clear and theoretically grounded definition of what counts as learning we have to know what we are looking for. An important element of what I refer to as a sociocultural view of human learning is the conscious attempt to avoid seeing knowledge either as purely mental (as would be the idealist/rationalist tradition) or as physical and independent of human activities (which would be the realist perspective). Instead of making this division the basic premise for our understanding of how people learn, a sociocultural view builds on the assumption that learning has to do with how people appropriate and master *tools for thinking* and *acting* that exist in a given culture or society (Wertsch, 1991). Learning is located in the interplay between culture and individuals, and it implies the *transformation* of individuals and collectives in terms of the nature of the tasks they master.

Two different kinds of tools can be identified: *physical* (or technical) *tools* on the one hand, and *psychological* (or mental) *tools* on the other (Vygotsky, 1986). In almost any situation in modern society, people rely on physical tools to help them accomplish their goals; when writing we use paper and pencil, a typewriter or a word processor, when communicating we use telephones, faxes and computers, when mending a car we use wrenches, screw drivers and many other tools. In a complex society (Hannerz, 1992), we can no longer expect people to master all the sophisticated physical tools that are available. Unlike the case some hundred years ago in an agrarian type of society, when the range of complicated tools was not that extensive, many modern physical tools require considerable expertise before they can be handled efficiently. The computer in the office, the echo-sounder on board the ship, and the gas chromatograph in the chemistry laboratory, exemplify the kind of powerful physical tools imbued with sophisticated knowledge that require considerable training before they can be handled competently.

A prominent feature of the human species is our ability to develop psychological tools – i. e. resources for thinking and acting that are stored in language, or, rather, in discourse. This is why talk is, and always will be, such a prominent feature of human knowledge and learning. Knowledge is not merely stored in our minds, it circulates between us when we communicate with each other in concrete activities. Even more importantly, to a significant extent it is created in such interactions when we convert our experiences and reflections into language and make them public. The most prominent medium for communicating what we hear, see and experience in life is ordinary talk (see Mercer, 1995). An important ingredient in the development of knowledge in society, however, is the creation of specialised forms of discursive practices that allow for precise communication about the world in specific settings. Already at an early age in school, children encounter elements of the conceptual constructions characteristic of the study of nature, history, language and social life in general in a range of school subjects. In mathematics, students have to learn about how to compute the area of a parallelogram or a triangle by using the appropriate formulae and other tools. In a similar vein, they are introduced to the analysis of language by learning certain grammatical concepts that communicate an understanding of the more general features of how language works. In a historical perspective, many of the concepts (i.e. psychological tools) and procedures (for instance on how to do divisions with decimal numbers) that children are taught fairly early on in their educational career must be seen as quite complex and they have taken humankind a very long time to develop. It is primarily in relation to the learning of such knowledge that formal teaching is geared, and it is also in this context that new technologies may provide experiences that are productive.

Psychological tools stored in language are used as resources in all kinds of activities. When we analyse a problem of how to estimate the surface of a floor or how much interest we have to pay annually when we borrow money to buy a new car, we rely on a number of such tools: measurements expressed in centimetres or metres, algorithms for multiplying and for calculating percentages, and so on. Thus, psychological tools in the form of concepts, definitions and procedures are not to be opposed to practical knowledge, as is commonly done when discussing the alleged conflicts between 'theory' and 'practice'. Even in practical activities, such as the mending of a car engine or in producing handicraft, psychological tools are essential. The mechanic has to analyse the nature of the malfunction of the engine (which is done largely by means of concepts) and form hypotheses about what the problem might be (which is also largely a conceptual activity) (see, for instance, Trognon and Grusenmeyer, 1997). Keller and Keller (1993) provide an interesting analysis of the prevalence and significance of conceptual and discursive knowledge in what might be seen as the most physical of all activities, that of the black-smith. The forging of iron by the smith while 'thinking hot' relies on sophisticated perceptual and intellectual skill.

But even more importantly in this context, the mastery of concepts implies being able to do something (Harré and Gillett, 1994). Human actions to a significant extent are communicative and discursive in nature; activities such as being able to calculate percentages when making purchases or measuring the surface of a wall when ordering wallpaper, or a teacher explaining to a student the sexual system of plants, or the salesperson convincing a potential buyer about the advantages of a particular kind of computer or photocopier, are all discursive in nature and simultaneously they constitute concrete actions of people in everyday life. Human beings to a large extent act by means of communicating.

Technology as mediational means in human activities

A sociocultural perspective, the alternative to the dominant dualist position on knowledge and learning, takes as its point of departure the *mediated* nature of human knowledge and action as already noted. The mediational means – psychological and physical tools – that people use in concrete activities must be understood as simultaneously physical and intellectual in nature. Let us illustrate this by means of some examples. When young children at the age of 5 or 6 learn to read the clock, they at some level learn how to interpret the digits and the positions of the arms on the face (or, in recent times, the digits on the digital clock). Prototypically, this learning process starts out by the children being able to identify the time on the hour ('at 12 o'clock both the arms point upwards', 'at six o'clock the long arm points upwards and the short arm downwards', and so on), and eventually their skills develop so that they can read the clock in a more general sense. This, of course, is the mastery of something very concrete and practical, and this skill is one of the most fundamental that people have to acquire in modern society in which time is such an important dimension of social order. At the same time, however, the learning of how to read the clock is much more than the learning of a limited skill; it is the introduction of the child to a way of conceiving many activities in life in general. Thus, as the children appropriate the concepts of seconds, minutes and hours, they acquire mediational means that are artificial in origin but which they come to see as 'natural' and 'real' in a very obvious manner ('I don't want to work for so little per hour' or 'time is money, so we should not waste more time on this'; see Lakoff and Johnson, 1982, for an analysis of the commodity metaphors of time in the English language). Very likely, many will never consider that there are any alternatives to this way of measuring and experiencing time; that time is something you measure in seconds, minutes and hours will be their reality. A substantial proportion will even risk developing ulcers and other bodily health problems since they are trying to achieve too much within too limited a time! The particular system for mediating time that is inherent to the clock is thus social in origin, and learning in this example implies mastering simultaneously the skill of reading an instrument and the conceptual distinctions upon which it relies. The conceptual distinctions that we use for measuring time in a literal sense have been built into the artefact, which is material and conceptual at the same time.

In modern times, the most apparent example of the interrelationships between mental tools and physical objects would be the computer and information and communication technology in general. Information technology is a very clear illustration of how human conceptual constructions have been built into physical artefacts and their support devices (such as software). If we just think of what we now consider as a relatively simple device such as a calculator, we find that sophisticated knowledge about mathematical operations (how to divide and multiply, for instance), about the notational system (the use of the zero and decimals) and about how to perform certain frequent operations (such as calculating percentages, finding inverse numbers or square roots) has been incorporated into the machine. Thus, when pupils, even in the lower grades in school, press the buttons of the calculator, they are literally operating with conceptual tools that have developed over thousands of years (and that are unknown in many cultures), and that have been incorporated into the calculator. In this sense, the material reality and the intellectual distinctions are integrated into the technology.

Discourse, technology and the mastery of conceptual tools

The mastery of mediational means is thus an essential aspect of the process of learning. By means of variations in the psychological and practical tools, different features of a problem become visible for the learner. But what, then, are the potentials of information technologies to provide learning experiences that may transform people and provide them with skills and insights that expand their capabilities? As I have already pointed out, this is an issue about which opinions diverge widely; some argue that schools will be closed down in the near future, others see no profound impact on schooling of information technologies. But if we disregard these major social issues about the future of education, and limit the discussion to learning in the sense of the mastery of tools by individuals, there are signs that some kinds of learning processes will be facilitated.

What is new about information technology as a resource for learning?

There are several potential features of information technologies that allow for them to serve as tools for the appropriation and understanding of conceptual knowledge. One type of work that has attracted a lot of attention over the past decade or so is the *simulation* of events and processes by means of computer models. A particularly popular mode of simulating events and processes has been the construction of so-called *micro-worlds* (Nickerson, 1995). A micro-world is a representation of a phenomenon or process that can be explored by students. Thus, the basic laws of motion, energy and force in mechanics can be illustrated in terms of a simulated micro-world in which objects behave in accordance with the rules of Newtonian physics. Such a micro-world can also be built so as to challenge students' understanding of motion by contrasting 'naive' conceptions with those formulated within Newtonian physics (White, 1984). Thus, the program can explicitly inform students about the differences between our everyday understandings of how objects move and those acceptable to physics.

A very obvious feature of computers is that they allow for powerful *visualisation* of models and all kinds of complex phenomena. This is a feature that is prominent in the use of information technologies outside education as well, and it has changed the nature of work in, for instance, engineering and design. While objects and processes can be visualised on drawings by means of paper and pencil as well, which would be what engineers used to do until recently, modern computer-assisted design software produces sophisticated visualisations of a much more powerful kind. The body of a car or the structure of a house can be presented from any angle and in any detail when working with a powerful design software. There is no need to engage in the time-consuming process of making a new drawing if one wants to see what the car or the house looks like from a different angle, as would be the case with the old technology of using paper, pencil and a drawing board. When the relevant data have been entered, any perspective on or enlargement of the object can be produced within seconds.

In educational settings, computer technology has been used to visualise many different kinds of phenomena. This is obviously a significant aspect of the creation of micro-worlds that 'make "observable" what is in nature "unobservable"' (Snir *et al.*, 1995). At first this might not seem that different, but the mode in which, for instance, abstract concepts that can never be observed in any direct sense (such as force and momentum), can be 'made visible' and manipulated in simulations offers new pathways for learning. Also in mathematics teaching, where there are no tangible objects out there in the world that correspond to the concepts to be learned, concepts such as function, vectors and so on can be quite easily visualised by means of images on computer screens. A function can also be described both in mathematical notation and be presented as a graph, and the parallels between these formats for presenting mathematical relationships can be explored by students (see Schwartz *et al.*, 1993). As many authors have argued, this exemplifies how information technologies simplify the production of *multiple representations* that potentially support student understanding.

Underlying all of these features of information technology is the psychologically very interesting feature that it allows for new forms of *interactivity* between the learner and what is to be learned. In some sense, the educational software is half-way between a text (which does not by itself respond to the reader) and a human being (who reacts in an active manner to initiatives) when it comes to attempts to interact. The computer can respond, although always within the limits given by the alternatives that the program designer managed to put into the software, and it can provoke active reflection on the part of learner who has to consider alternatives, manage concepts and representations and so on in order to work through a task. Thus, this quality of interactive software is not something mystical that will dramatically enhance learning, but it is a promising feature that has potentials in relation to some learning tasks.

To add some substance to the general arguments presented so far, I will limit myself to discussing one particular aspect of this general issue, namely how the interactive nature of information technologies provides room for experiences that are, at least potentially, productive for the specific case of appropriating abstract and difficult concepts. I will exemplify this with a short illustration from two empirical, and related, studies, one relying on hands-on experimentation of children with physical objects, and the second one simulating a similar problem by means of a computer-mediated micro-world.

Making the abstract tangible: hands-on experimentation with and without information technology

A very elegant series of studies illustrating the general assumption of a sociocultural perspective of the dependence between cognition, learning and mediational means in the context of elementary geometry has been carried out by Sayeki *et al.* (1991) and by Wyndhamn (1993). In their original study, Sayeki *et al.* (1991) set out to test the possibilities of presenting the principles of how to calculate the area of a parallelogram in a conceptually more accessible manner to students. Traditionally Japanese schools (and probably schools in many other parts of the world as well) use the so-called paper-cut model. This model implies that a section (a triangle) of the parallelogram is cut and then fitted on to the opposite side of the parallelogram to produce a rectangle. However, this model is conceptually not very elegant, and it is often not clear to children what is significant about this transformation in a more general sense. In addition, this model does not generalise to all parallelograms as the authors show. It is also problematic, since it does not make explicit what is the critical variable when calculating the area (i.e. the height of the parallelogram, which in the special case of the rectangle coincides with the side). Thus, there is a tendency for children to say that as one deforms the rectangle into a parallelogram as shown in transformation A to C in Figure 9.1, the area does not change. The argument is that nothing is added or subtracted from the figure, and, thus, on grounds of conservation, the area (and the perimeter and all other elements) must remain the same.

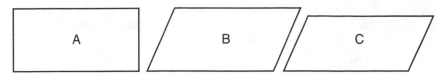

Figure 9.1 Comparison between two types of deformation of a rectangle.
Transformation A to B maintains the area but not the perimeter,
while A to C maintains the perimeter but not the area (which now
becomes approximately 90 per cent of that of rectangle A).
(Following Wyndhamn, 1993, p. 205.)

In order to make it easier for the children to understand the relationships
between the areas of rectangles and parallelograms (and the relationships
between perimeters and areas), the authors made explicit use of two
contrasting mediating devices that they referred to as the frame (or hinge)
model (Figure 9.2) and the deck-of-cards model (Figure 9.3), respectively.

When the deck-of-cards model is deformed to produce a parallelogram
(which the children did hands-on in this study), the area of course remains the
same, since the height does not change in this case, as the participating children realised. As a consequence it became clear that this was not the case with
the frame model (which was the side of matchbox being deformed as shown
in Figure 9.2), since it was different from the deck-of-cards model. The study
illustrates that this particular mediating device (the deck of cards), and the
realisation of the difference between this model and the frame model, made it
clear to students – at least in relation to this particular type of task – that the
height of the parallelogram is the essential variable when it comes to finding
the area, since no matter which type of deformation you make, it will always
result in the same area. The differences in performance between children
taught by this approach and those taught in a conventional manner could be
observed also on tests several weeks after the teaching.

Wyndhamn (1993) developed these ideas concerning how the relationships between perimeter and area could be mediated in a computer setting

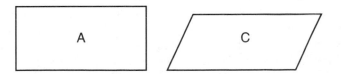

Figure 9.2 Deformation following the hinge or frame model

Figure 9.3 Deformation following the deck-of-cards model

allowing for active manipulation on the part of participants (students of the age of 12). He tested the effects on learning of specially designed computer software by means of which children could work on these kinds of problems of the relationships between areas and perimeters of parallelograms and rectangles. Even though the children in this case did not physically manipulate the objects as they did in the Japanese studies, these two mediational figures or metaphors – the deck-of-cards and the frame model respectively – were effective for the same reasons as will be evident from below; the figures were visible and they could be manipulated to illustrate what happened to the area as the shapes were changed.

Also in this study, in which children worked in pairs in front of the computer, there were signs that some participants approached this problem from a 'logical' rather than 'empirical' point of view. Consider the following statement from one of the students, Diana (who was classified as an average performer in mathematics by her teacher):

> Diana: There is no difference between the 'deck of cards' and 'the hinges'. Area and perimeter are the same all the time. It ought to be so.
>
> (Wyndhamn, 1993, p. 213)

This 'logical' approach to the problem – since nothing is taken away and nothing is added, everything must stay the same – was one of the preconceptions which provided resistance for students to accept the fact that the surface changed between the figures (and this was the same problem that some of the Japanese children had). However, the computer simulation, where rapid changes between figures could be made with the mouse, made practically all participants in this study accept that transformations of the parallelogram may affect the area. On the screen it became visually evident that in some transformations, such as when the angle between the vertical and horizontal side became very small, the surface also became significantly smaller than had been the case with the 90 degree angle.

Two further observations from this study merit consideration in the present context. Even though learning should be described in contextual terms as the mastery of tools in situated practices, the students in this case were able to generalise from the computer modelling to the situation in which they worked with identical tasks using paper and pencil (which was used as part of a post-test). What is also very interesting to note in this study are the conceptual aspects of the students' work, and the interplay between what is shown on the screen (or written and drawn on paper) and how students communicate. The critical aspect here, in terms of understanding, is being able to conceptualise and explain the relationships between the sides (or the perimeter) of the figures when being deformed, and what happens to the area as a consequence of the transformations. The following list exemplifies how students accounted for what they saw and did (right column), and the particular aspects of the figures (how they looked, how they changed, and what happened to the height).

Reference to	*Examples of utterances from students*
Appearance	It looks like a deck of cards.
	The deck of cards is thick and standing more 'upright'.
	This resembles a deck of cards.
Difference (between transformations of figures)	The hinges press down more than the deck of cards.
	The hinges put down more.
	The hinges slope more quickly.
	(The statements often reinforced by accompanying movements of hands.)
Constancy of heights	This is the same . . . (pointing to the height in the case of the deck of cards picture).
	[The height of] The deck of cards remains the same . . . (showing constant distance between the thumb and the forefinger and simultaneously moving the hand over the drawing).

As can be seen, the students use the concepts of deck of cards and hinges as resources for explaining what they see and what happens in the transformations. These terms are incorporated into everyday discursive accounts ('hinges press down more than the deck of cards') that participants produce. It is equally interesting, however, to see that throughout the work at the computer, and with the tasks performed as post-tests, there were no completely convincing signs that students actually appropriated the more general concept of height as it would be defined in geometrical discourse. Thus, even though they could point to and account quite effectively for what happened to the area and perimeter when figures were transformed, there were no clear signs that students realised that the concept (or psychological tool) of height in geometry is the element that is critical when understanding how the areas change between figures. From a sociocultural perspective, one would be inclined to say that the knowledge students expressed was situated in, and may be dependent on, the particular context they were operating in. They showed that they could explain what happened to the area in the transformation, they could carry out the relevant calculations (at least when operating with the standardised figures and numerical values in the computer program), but we cannot assume that these performances necessarily are indicative of mastery of the concept of height in any more general sense, nor of the principled role it plays for estimating the area.

But the analysis offered by Wyndhamn also illustrates how learning will never be automatised even when using technologies. The most significant repository of human knowledge is language, or, rather, discouse. As Mercer

(1995) so aptly phrases it, talk is a 'social mode of thinking' (p. 4), and if one looks at the concrete verbal interaction between the students as they work at the computer, one can easily detect the qualitative differences in their grasp of what appears on the screen. Simultaneously, one can also see that what technologies provide are experiences, but they do not guarantee a specific interpretation of these experiences that would amount to learning what was intended. To facilitate understanding, the expertise of a teacher or a knowledgeable conversation partner would still be required.

The following table illustrates the different levels at which students communicated about what appeared on the screen (adapted and modified from Wyndhamn, 1993, p. 216). The colours mentioned by students refer to the symbols that had to be manipulated to change the shapes of figures.

Category of talk	*Characteristic utterances by students*
Demonstrative level	(Pointing to the screen and simultaneously saying:)
	Take this one.
	Put the pointer here.
	Increase that.
	More there.
	Try that first.
Visual level	Take the blue spot, I think.
	Decrease with the yellow.
	Run with red.
Metaphoric level	Change with the deck of cards.
	Try the hinges.
Formal level	We try to hit the area first.
	Change both area and perimeter in one go.
	Reduce the area.
	The perimeter is far from correct. Add.

As can be seen, the students operate by means of concepts and utterances that are sometimes completely tied to what is shown on the screen (demonstrative level). Here talk just supplements pointing and carries very little meaning. The students do not make explicit what aspects of the figures they are referring to. At the metaphoric and formal level, however, there are signs that students are using some elements of the conceptual tools that are decisive for understanding the geometrical aspects of the task. At the metaphoric level, they use the concepts of hinges and deck of cards introduced by the program to alert the users to the differences between the two models. This, of course, does not qualify as geometric discourse proper, but it indicates that students in their interaction make use of a distinction that carries a particular meaning discriminating between two models. At the formal level, the world of geometry appears in the terminology used. We cannot be sure that students are able to define area and perimeter in a formal sense, but they are using these concepts to make sense of what appears on the screen, and this is an important indicator of the fact that these concepts have a functional meaning for them in relation to the task.

But, and as I already pointed out, it is still apparent that the students do not arrive at an explanation of the differences between the transformations in which they explicitly single out the height as the critical variable. Even though they can reason as if this were the case, they do not generalise at this level spontaneously. However, it would not appear particularly far-fetched to assume that a teacher engaging in a conversation with the children, and knowledgeable about the general nature of these conceptual difficulties, could have turned this kind of exercise into an even more powerful learning exercise. By somehow focusing the students' attention on the critical variable of height, a teacher could probably have provoked an explicit discussion in which students would have been able to formulate the principled nature of what differed between the two models in their geometrical properties. When students were communicating at the metaphoric or formal level, such a continuation of the interaction would probably have been quite natural.

As this little example illustrates, working at the computer with this kind of task does not automatically produce learning and understanding. There is no mysterious flow of conceptual knowledge from the screen to the learner. But the technology provides opportunities for manipulating models and concepts in a manner that might be conducive to learning, provided that students are involved in conversations with competent partners who can assist in articu lating the general conceptual issues involved in what is presented. Again, a sociocultural interpretation of this would be that learning is in the co-ordination between language and experience. What the technology does is that it increases the range and nature of experiences that can be provided for the learning of subject matters that are complex and abstract. The interactive character of modern technology can support reasoning by amplifying the nature and boundaries of scientific models of objects and events. But the full realisation of the potentials of such experiences will still rely on students' access to conversation partners who carry on discussions in which these models and concepts are validated. The creation of knowledge is essentially a matter of learning to argue, and no technology will ever replace the need for learners to participate in ongoing conversations with partners sharing inter-ests and commitments. Technology should not be seen as replacing such communication but rather as providing a resource for supporting it.

Note

1 *Acknowledgements:* The research reported here has been financed by the Swedish Council for Research in the Humanities and Social Sciences. The final version of this chapter was written while the author was a Belle van Zuylen professor at the Department of General Social Science at the University of Utrecht.

References

Bruner, J. (1990) *Acts of Meaning*, Cambridge, MA: Harvard University Press.
Cole, M. (1996) *Cultural Psychology*, Cambridge, MA: Harvard University Press.
Crook, C. (1994) *Computers and the Collaborative Experience of Learning*, London: Routledge.
—— (1998) 'Computers in the community of classrooms', in this volume.
Cuban, L. (1986) *Teachers and Machines: The Classroom Use of Technology Since 1920*, New York: Teachers College Press.
Eisenstein, E. (1985) 'On the printing press as an agent of change', in D. R. Olson, N. Torrance and A. Hildyard (eds) *Literacy, Language and Learning: The Nature and Consequences of Reading and Writing*, Cambridge: Cambridge University Press.
Grossen, M., and Pochon, L-O. (1997) 'Interactional perspectives on the use of the computer and on the technological development of new tool: the case of word processing', in L. Resnick, R. Säljö, C. Pontecorvo and B. Burge (eds) *Discourse, Tools and Reasoning: Essays on Situated Cognition*, Berlin and New York: Springer Verlag.
Hannerz, U. (1992) *Cultural Complexity: Studies in the Social Organization of Meaning*, New York: Columbia University Press.
Hanson, N. (1958) *Patterns of Discovery*, Cambridge: Cambridge University Press.
Harré, R., and Gillett, G. (1994) *The Discursive Mind*, London: Sage.
Hutchins, E. (1995) *Cognition in the Wild*, Cambridge: MIT Press.
Keller, C., and Keller, J. D. (1993) 'Thinking and acting with iron', in S. Chaiklin and J. Lave (eds) *Understanding Practice: Perspectives on Activity and Context*, Cambridge: Cambridge University Press.
Lakoff, G., and Johnson, M. (1982) *Metaphors We Live By*, Chicago: The University of Chicago Press.
Lave, J. (1988) *Cognition in Practice: Mind, Mathematics, and Culture in Everyday Life*, Cambridge: Cambridge University Press.
Lave, J., Murtaugh, M., and de la Rocha, O. (1984) 'The dialectic of arithmetic in grocery shopping', in B. Rogoff and J. Lave (eds), *Everyday Cognition: Its Development in Social Context*, Cambridge, MA: Harvard University Press.
Light, P. (1997) 'Computers for learning', *Journal of Child Psychology and Psychiatry* 38: 1–8.
Light, P., and Light, V. (1998) 'Analysing asynchronous learning interactions: computer-mediated communication in a conventional undergraduate setting', in this volume.
Mercer, N. (1995) *The Guided Construction of Knowledge: Talk Amongst Teachers and Learners*, Clevedon, England: Multilingual Matters.
Nickerson, R. S. (1995) 'Can technology help teach for understanding?' in D. N. Perkins, J. L. Schwartz, M. M. West and M. S. Wiske (eds) *Software Goes to School: Teaching for Understanding with New Technologies*, New York: Oxford University Press.
Olson, D. (1994) *The World on Paper*, Cambridge: Cambridge University Press.
Ong, W. J. (1982) *Orality and Literacy: The Technologising of the Word*, London: Methuen.
Säljö, R. (1996) 'Mental and physical artefacts in cognitive practices', in P. Reimann and H. Spada (eds) *Learning in Humans and Machines*, Oxford: Pergamon.

Sayeki, Y., Ueno, N., and Nagasaka, T. (1991) 'Mediation as a generative model for obtaining area', *Learning and Instruction* 1(3): 229–242.

Schofield, J. W. (1995) *Computers and Classroom Culture*, Cambridge: Cambridge University Press.

Schwartz, J. L., Yerushalmy, M., and Wilson, B. (1993) *The Geometric Supposer: What is it a Case of?*, Hillsdale, NJ: Lawrence Erlbaum Associates.

Snir, J., Smith, C., and Grosslight, L. (1995) 'Conceptually enhanced simulations: a computer tool for science teaching', in D. N. Perkins, J. L. Schwartz, M. M. West and M. S. Wiske (eds), *Software Goes to School. Teaching for Understanding with New Technologies*, New York: Oxford University Press.

Trognon, A., and Grusenmeyer, C. (1997) 'To resolve a technical problem through conversation', in L. Resnick, R. Säljö, C. Pontecorvo and B. Burge (eds) *Discourse, Tools, and Reasoning: Essays on Situated Cognition*, Berlin and New York: Springer Verlag.

Vygotsky, L. S. (1986) *Thought and Language* (A. Kozulin, trans.), Cambridge: MIT Press.

Wertsch, J. (1991) *Voices of the Mind*, Cambridge: Cambridge University Press.

—— (1948) *Mind as Action*, Oxford: Oxford University Press.

White, B. Y. (1984) 'Designing computer games to help physics students understand Newton's laws of motion', *Cognition and Instruction* 1: 1 4.

Wyndhamn, J. (1993) 'Mediating artefacts and interaction in a computer environment. An exploratory study of the acquisition of geometry concepts', in J. Wyndhamn, *Problem-Solving Revisited. On School Mathematics as a Situated Practice*, Linköping: Linköping Studies in Arts and Science.

10 Analysing asynchronous learning interactions

Computer-mediated communication in a conventional undergraduate setting

Paul Light and Vivienne Light[1]

Introduction

Information technology is often seen as promising (or threatening) a radical transformation of higher education. For example, one UK university vice chancellor recently wrote in the higher education press that information technology investment: 'will free education from the constraints of time and space. It affords the chance to create a distributed community of teaching and learning' (M. Fitzgerald, *Times Higher*, July 1996). Picking up on this reference to community, a critic responded in the following issue that such developments threaten the sense of community inherent in conventional institutions that is so valuable to students. But what exactly is it that conventional institutions of higher education have to offer as 'communities of teaching and learning'? How does information technology fit into such communities? Can it serve to foster such communities, or only to threaten them?

While the bulk of information technology investment for higher education has gone into the packaging of learning resources for student use, our focus here is on the content-free resources afforded by computers as vehicles for interaction and communication. Most of the research to date on the educational uses of computer-mediated communication has been concerned with distance education. Here we are concerned with its use within a conventional full-time university setting, asking both how productive interaction in this medium can be, and also how such productivity can be analysed and understood. First we shall review some of the relevant literature. Then we shall draw upon case-study material from an evaluation of 'skywriting', a form of electronic supplement to tutorial interaction, to explore methodological and substantive issues arising in this field of research.

Student learning and computer-mediated communication

Given that the overwhelming majority of social scientists work and teach in universities, university education itself seems to have attracted surprisingly little social science research. Moreover, sociological research (on, for example, student culture and experience) has not typically had much to say about how students learn, while psychological research has been almost exclusively concerned with the individual cognitive and metacognitive attributes of learners. Recent interest in more ecologically grounded or 'situated' approaches to learning (e.g. Lave and Wenger, 1991; Crook and Light, in press) suggests the possibility of integrating sociological and psychological approaches around a notion of learning as *activity*. The research task becomes one of establishing how particular environments or resources constrain or afford particular learning activities.

Information technology is sometimes seen as threatening to cut learning off from the interpersonal contexts which give it meaning and utility. A counter-argument that might be offered is that the community practices of student life are actually more threatened from other directions. In the UK, in common with a number of other European countries, the 1990s have seen a rapid expansion in access to university-level education, with rapidly diminishing funding per student. This has jeopardised traditional modes of teaching and learning to the extent that information technology might actually offer the best hope of preserving and developing what was valuable in them.

Though they have not attracted a high proportion of the available investment, some of the more interesting applications of information technology in higher education are those involving computer-mediated communication. This technology affords a possible means of providing for interaction between tutors and students and between students themselves. Interest in the use of electronic mail and computer conferencing in the context of distance education has been considerable, perhaps the largest scale evaluation of student use of a conferencing system being that undertaken in relation to an Open University course concerned with information technology (Mason, 1989, 1991; Yates, 1992).

The results of this evaluation have been generally rather discouraging. Most students regarded the conferencing system as less helpful than available alternatives for contacting their tutor and for getting help with the course. While exchanges about practical computing matters 'took off' relatively quickly, exchanges about more theoretical subjects proved to be a different matter, and there was very little extended discussion of course issues. Local tutor conferences (the membership of which corresponded to tutorial groups) were marked by variable but mostly low levels of activity, and Mason (1991) notes 'the inability of even the most diligent and enthusiastic tutors to stimulate sustained interactive discussion'.

Part of the reason for this may be that computer-mediated communication fails to offer some of the supports for interaction offered by face-to-face communication. In face-to-face conversation speaker and listener share organisational responsibility. In computer-mediated exchanges students may feel less obligation or pressure to respond than when interacting face to face. Mason (1991) concluded that weaker and 'less verbal' students were disadvantaged by computer-mediated communication as it was used in the Open University context.

In other respects, though, computer-mediated communication might seem to offer a more accessible medium than face-to-face interaction, especially face-to-face interaction in a group setting. Graddol (1989), for example, notes that in face-to-face settings, successful participation is often a competitive business, relying on speed, confidence and a variety of conversational skills. Contributing to a computer mediated exchange does not depend in the same way upon interruption and attention-getting skills.

Another difference between face-to-face and electronic communication is that contributions in the former are usually fairly fleeting, and accessible only to those present at the time. Grint (1992) observed that for many of the Open University students a major factor was feeling exposed to ridicule if they 'said something silly' in the computer conference. Messages can be carefully preprepared, but this tends to produce 'sanitised' contributions, lacking in spontaneity and immediacy. Students may play safe by just asking questions of the tutor rather than offering opinions or entering into arguments. Henri analysed nearly 300 messages from six distance-learning 'teleconferences' and found that only a small minority of students' messages were parts of genuinely interactive exchanges. Henri suggested that computer mediation only serves to echo traditional role relations in education: 'It is exactly as in traditional learning situations: the student speaks; the teacher answers, confirms, approves, reinforces' (1995, p. 158).

A number of researchers have raised the possibility that students might participate more *equally* in electronic than in face-to-face communication. Harasim (1989), for example, noted that the written mode of communication may reduce the salience of physical and social cues such as gender and race, which may constrain communication in various undesirable ways in face-to-face settings. Bannon (1995) has suggested that computer-mediated communication can provide opportunities for those students who are too inhibited to 'speak out' in face-to-face situations.

Girls are widely reported to show more negative attitudes to computers than boys, and to have less experience with them (e.g. Martin, 1991; Culley, 1988). However, Yates' research (in press) with adult Open University students indicates that, although female students tended to start with lower levels of computing experience, they were equally positive in their response to computer-mediated communication. Once students began using the system, there are very few differences in utilisation, and in fact levels of use were not related to levels of previous experience.

There are thus mixed messages in the available research on computer-mediated communication in distance education. Some of the issues raised in this research might be expected to apply with equal force in relation to the use of such technology in a conventional university setting, while others might not. As yet, there has been little research on this, and it is this consideration which motivated the research reported here. In the context of the present volume, it is also important to note that little of the research to date has given much explicit attention to the question of the 'productivity' of computer-mediated communication. How is productivity to be understood and measured in relation to such forms of learning? We shall offer some reflections on this question, even if we are not able to offer any very definite answer.

Skywriting: a case study

At the University of Southampton an electronic-mail-based innovation called skywriting has been introduced into a variety of courses in all three years of the undergraduate psychology curriculum. The term 'skywriting' was introduced by Harnad (1990) to refer to the use of multiple-reciprocal-e-mail in the service of academic discussion. Harnad argues that electronic mail retains many advantages of the written form of language, such as overcoming memory and attention span limitations by providing an enduring record which can be consulted whenever it is needed. At the same time, though, it offers speed and the possibility of addressing any number of recipients simultaneously. It also allows a form of response (namely text capturing, quoting and commenting) which has the potential to support highly focused conversational interaction. Harnad (1995) has suggested that 'the inspirational power of skywriting depends upon a population of skyreaders'. Insofar as there is an audience of others to whom the discussion is accessible, the interaction can come to resemble a symposium or discussion.

Attempts to build skywriting into a number of undergraduate courses in psychology at the University of Southampton have taken somewhat different forms with different courses. Here we will focus upon a lecture course entitled 'Explaining the Mind' taken over a twelve-week period by eighty psychology honours students (plus fifty other students) in their first year. There was a single lecturer throughout, but the fortnightly tutorials were taken by a number of different tutors. Skywriting was offered as an optional extra, supplementing the usual lectures and tutorial meetings.

Having been given a fairly thorough induction into how to use the computers for communications purposes, students were encouraged to use skywriting to ask questions, offer opinions and enter into debate with the tutor and with one another about issues relating to the course. In all cases the messages were sent on e-mail to a list which included the lecturer/tutors concerned and all the students on that course, and all replies also went to the list. To supplement this, the tutor extracted the messages from the list as they came in and placed them in a hypermail archive on the World Wide Web. Here readers could sort them by author, by date, by subject or by 'thread' (temporally ordered sequence of related messages on the same subject).

Skywriting, in this form, offers one example of how computer-mediated communication might be implemented in a full-time conventional undergraduate setting. Our interest in studying it arose from a wider interest in how the use of new technology outside of the formal curriculum impinges on the informal patterns of everyday student life (Crook and Light, in press). If universities can be considered as 'communities of learning', it is important to appraise the possibilities offered by new technology for sustaining and fostering the students' effective participation in such communities.

In considering how to evaluate and learn from skywriting, we had a number of concerns:

1   We wanted to know who made use of the skywriting facility and who did not. In regard to sending messages, this is simple, since all messages are automatically logged. In regard to reading the messages such logging was unavailable, and we had to rely on asking students about their 'reading habits'.
2   We wanted to know how far the students' general attitudes towards, or previous experience with, computers would shape their response to skywriting. To this end we used a questionnaire, given to all students before the course began.
3   We wanted to know how the pattern of contributions to skywriting related to the pattern of verbal contributions in face-to-face tutorials. For this we undertook some limited direct observation of face-to-face sessions.
4   We were interested whether gender and/or age made a difference in relation to students' participation in different media of interaction, and also in whether the reasons that they gave for studying would be related to their participation. We used a standard questionnaire-based 'approaches to study' inventory for this purpose.
5   Finally, we wanted to know how skywriting was perceived and received, and we approached this through extended semi-structured interviews with individual students (selected on the basis of their contribution/ non-contribution to skywriting) at the end of the course.

In general, the quantitative methods were designed to generate a 'rough-and-ready' but comprehensive picture of how this innovation worked out on this occasion, while the qualitative analyses of interview material were intended to offer some insight into underlying processes which might explain why things worked out as they did.

Quantitative analyses

At least three-quarters of the students were 18-year-olds, entering university straight from UK full-time schooling. The remainder mostly comprised mature students (typically in their thirties). Overall, some three-quarters of the students were female, a proportion not untypical of UK social sciences courses.

Attitudes and experience

Despite the UK having one of the highest levels of computer provision at secondary school level in the world, students still frequently arrive at university with low levels of hands-on experience with computers, and considerable anxieties about their competence in this area (Anderson *et al.*, 1993; Crook, 1994). Within a week or so of arrival, we gave all the students a questionnaire relating to their attitudes to, and previous experience with, computers, based on an instrument developed by Davis and Coles (1993). Responses were obtained from sixty-two of the eighty honours students.

The first section of the questionnaire concerned previous experience with computers. Students were asked about the frequency with which they had used computers for various purposes, including games, programming, art and music, word processing, data handling, and sending and receiving messages. All students had at least a little previous experience of computer use, either at school, at home or at work. Almost all had experience of using computers for both word processing and games, but experience in other areas of computer use was patchy. Whereas in a similar survey the previous year none of the students reported experience of using computers to send or receive messages, about 20 per cent of the 1995 entry group reported at least some experience in this area. An aggregate measure of experience (indexing the extent of experience both across situations and across applications) showed a statistically significant gender difference favouring males. The area of use showing the most marked gender difference was, not surprisingly, computer games. About a third of the students said that they owned and had access to a computer during term time, and this was not significantly associated with gender.

The second section of the questionnaire addressed students' attitudes towards computers. Most students expressed broadly positive attitudes towards computers. There was no significant difference in this respect between the male and the female students, though overall, greater degrees of experience were significantly associated with more positive attitudes. The mature students did not differ significantly from the other students in terms of their experience or attitudes.

Face-to-face interactions and skywriting

In order to make a comparison between the frequencies of different students' contributions to face-to-face discussion and to electronically mediated discussion, we had an observer sit in on one complete 'round' of tutorial sessions, observing the sixty-two students for whom we had questionnaire data. The tutorial sessions were conducted with groups averaging ten students, by three different tutors. Levels of student participation were coded very crudely in terms of frequency of verbal contribution, excluding directly solicited contributions. 'Scores' ranged from zero (two students) to 21 (two students), with a mean of 5 contributions in a forty-minute session.

The mature students contributed more often than the younger students, and the male students (with a mean of over 8) contributed on average more than twice as often as the female students (with a mean of less than 4).

At the half-way point in the twelve-week course, when the data were sampled, the skywriting logs indicated that some 30 per cent of the students had contributed no messages at all, a further 30 per cent only one, and the remaining 40 per cent had contributed between two and twelve messages. These were typically short (about 100 words) and addressed to the course lecturer. All contained questions, while only about half contained any expression of opinion. Most related to issues raised in the lectures. Since most messages took the form of questions to the lecturer, and almost all were replied to, about half of all messages on the list were from the course lecturer. These tended to be longer because they used a quote/comment format to respond to particular aspects of the student's question. Few student messages generated any response from fellow students.

Analysis focused upon establishing whether the two discussion media produced differential patterns of participation. A repeated-measures analysis of variance was conducted with gender and age (younger vs. mature) as factors, and participation in skywriting and face-to-face tutorials as dependent variables. In the case of gender, there was a significant main effect reflecting a higher overall level of activity by male students, and more interestingly a significant interaction between gender and discussion medium. While male students contributed substantially more than females in face-to-face interactions, the female students contributed just as much as males in electronic interaction.

Mean levels of participation were higher for mature students than for others in both media, but given the numbers involved the differences were not statistically reliable. The small number of non-UK students contributed relatively more in skywriting than in face-to-face sessions, perhaps because of fluency constraints in spoken English.

Some of the more striking findings of this quantitative work concerned the *absence* of relationships. There was no correlation at all between the frequencies of contributions in skywriting and in face-to-face tutorials. Moreover, neither attitude to computers nor experience with computers as assessed at the start of the year significantly predicted the extent of subsequent involvement in skywriting.

Approaches to study

The Revised Approaches to Study Inventory (RASI; Tait and Entwhistle, 1996) was given to a randomly selected group of twenty-four students, twelve of whom had participated in the skywriting (eight female, four male) and twelve of whom had not (eight female, four male). Twelve were from the 'Explaining the Mind' course and twelve from another lecture course using skywriting. Those who had participated actively in skywriting scored significantly higher on the 'Deep Approach to Study' subscale, and in particular on the groups of items labelled 'intention to understand' and 'use of evidence'. The non-participants scored significantly higher on the 'Surface Approach to Study' subscale, and in particular on the items grouped as 'fear of failure' and 'passive learning'. The RASI is designed to tap fairly stable aspects of approach to study. Thus even though it was administered *after* the students' exposure to skywriting, it seems likely that approach to study influenced participation rather than vice versa.

'Deep' scores on the RASI were weakly but positively correlated with higher course assessment outcomes ($r = +0.17$), while 'surface' scores showed a weak negative relation to assessment outcomes ($r = -0.25$). Frequency of skywriting contributions showed a modest positive correlation with assessment outcomes ($r = +0.32$), whereas the frequency of face to face tutorial contributions was hardly correlated at all with such outcomes ($r = +0.13$). Curiously, in both cases active contribution was more strongly associated with assessment outcomes for the male students ($r = +0.60$ for tutorial contributions and $+0.50$ for skywriting) than for female students ($r = +0.01$ for tutorial contributions and $r = +0.29$ for skywriting).

Qualitative analyses

To help explain the observed patterns of participation we conducted individual semi-structured interviews of about thirty–forty minutes each with a sample of the students. We deliberately targeted non-participants as well as participants, and sought a spread of age and gender. Targeted students were offered a small sum of money for their participation. We obtained eight interviews with students who had not sent messages, and eleven interviews with students who had done so.

The interviews were fully transcribed. Although there was a schedule of questions to be addressed in the interview concerning what the students saw as the strengths, weaknesses, opportunities and threats associated with skywriting, the form of discussion was fairly free, and students raised issues in different ways and at different points. In analysing the material, therefore, we sought to identify the principal recurrent themes across the interviews as a whole. Quotations from the transcripts were grouped under provisional headings, which shifted somewhat as the process continued. This approach to analysis and exposition aims to give the reader as full a sense of the material as is possible in the space available.

Temperament and tempo

Skywriting was seen as having particular benefits for those students who 'couldn't get a word in edgeways' in tutorials. Thus, for example: 'I seem to be more reserved in my student tutorials, probably because they talk quite a lot, they sometimes seem to know more, and it makes me nervous';

'Self-conscious people like me prefer not to talk'; 'I'm a shy person. I think I prefer typing up and then waiting for the answer.'

The pace and timing of interaction emerged as a central issue for many: 'It's good for people who tend to be quiet who tend to wait for the argument and tend to spend a long time thinking about it, or would like to go and research something before saying anything'; 'On skywriting you can take as long as you want'; 'You can think of something three hours later and say "I wish I had said that in the tutorial" and you can't do anything about it because it's gone, whereas in skywriting you can think "I have just thought of something else" and send it, and still be incorporated at the end of the day'; 'Often when somebody says something to you and you reply, you say something before you've really thought out what you're going to say to them, but when you're arguing with someone over the computer, you can really think about what you want to say, and you can make sure your message is clear'; 'Using the skywriting you have more time to think about your question; the answers you get are better thought through. The lecturer has more time to think it through and give a good answer too.'

For others, though, considerations of timing militated against skywriting. 'Time consuming waiting for the computers' was a frequent comment. Some of the skywriting messages were long: 'Such long essays in answer to a simple question', and working at the screen for a long time was a problem for some: 'I can't do it for more than two hours, it hurts my eyes too much.' But the main timing issue was to do with the slow 'turn-round time', or pace of discussion: 'You don't get any sense of discussion because you have got sometimes a day difference between the answer and the question and then other people have to read and contribute.' In tutorials, by contrast: 'You don't have to wait for the answers, you can get everyone's ideas, then and there.'

Exposure and self-protection

While shyness was seen as a problem for some in tutorials, or in asking questions in lectures, it was also a big issue for many in relation to skywriting, since many of the students felt very 'exposed' when they put their ideas or questions in writing: 'You have to be brave to do it'; 'You feel as if you have to ask an intelligent question, you can't just say that you don't understand what is being talked about.' The permanence of contributions was alarming: 'It's going to be up on that Web page for the rest of time in the archives.' An option for anonymous contributions was not available; it will be available, though not encouraged, in future.

At the beginning, some students took a flippant attitude to skywriting: 'Some people were asking ridiculous questions. They were using it as an opportunity to just play about.' The tutors' response was to adopt a very 'no nonsense' style, but this in turn set up another dynamic: 'I think the responses of the tutors are so harsh – I think that absolutely terrifies people.' Some took a philosophical attitude: 'Sometimes I was demolished into bits but at least I got some answers so . . . ', while others decided that discretion was the better part of valour: 'After that first one I tended to do a bit more research and ask questions instead of giving opinions.'

Many students were concerned about presentation, as indeed their lecturer had encouraged them to be: 'You have to be competent with spelling'; 'It would be very embarrassing if you made a really silly grammatical mistake'; 'There are loads of messages on the Web with spelling mistakes, syntax and grammar etc. Everyone can communicate in English, but a lot of people have difficulty putting it on computer; it puts you off.' Compared to contributions to tutorial discussion, messages tended to be almost obsessively well prepared, spell checked and were sometimes read over by friends before being sent: 'Before people write on the skywriting they really research their stuff and they have a query and they polish their query so that it looks sensible and it sounds right, whereas in a tutorial you just kind of come out with stuff.'

For most, it is the other students in their year who are the important audience: 'It frightens me, the fact that what I'm saying is going to go back to everybody in my year'; ' A hundred people being able to read and criticise what you have written is quite daunting.' Others seemed to feel exposed to the whole world, as in a sense they were, because access to the Web site was not restricted: 'Trying to express an opinion on something that you don't know much about anyway can be a bit daunting when the whole world can see you making a real wally of yourself.' Occasionally the whole world made its presence felt, as when one student had a query about one of his contributions from someone in the USA.

The predominant mode of exchange became one of question and answer, and students rather rarely commented on one another's offerings 'in print'. Typical comments were: 'I wouldn't like to criticise anyone else's work really, especially as you end up with your name next to it'; 'I don't know, it seems almost impolite to have a go at someone else'; 'People don't want to tread on anyone's toes'. So much for the culture of critical debate! It seems as if the students at this level are still having difficulty in separating personal criticism from criticism of ideas. There was a definite sense that the tutors' answers were definitive: 'I tend to concentrate more on his answers'; 'I'd wait until [lecturer] gave the proper answer.'

Reading skywritings

Even amongst the students who did not send any messages themselves, most did none the less read at least some of the skywriting exchanges. As first years, they had had relatively little feedback via assessed work since starting their course, and concern as to their ability or level of work relative to their peers was fairly widespread: 'It is good to get everyone else's messages, to find out what level everyone is on'; '[It] lets you know that other people don't understand as well'; 'It clarifies who is having what sort of difficulties in the course; you're not alone with the problems you're facing.'

Many found that other students tended to ask much the same questions and in much the same way that they would have done: 'People ask all the same questions, and it is always asked in a similar way to the way you would ask it yourself. The reply comes back at the level the question is asked'; 'I wasn't very motivated to send [messages]; I would just read the answers and hope that someone had written a question that I would have wanted to ask'; 'A lot of other people would ask the questions you have thought of and then forgotten, or thought of and then didn't have time to ask it in the lecture so you almost get the stuff twice.'

Of course there were times when this feedback was not so encouraging: 'There seemed to be a couple of people that were talking about things way over my head and I didn't know where I was; I felt I was really fumbling.' Some of those who participated heavily in skywriting were clearly seen to be 'a class apart': 'There are a few people who are real shining lights'; '[Some] people who wrote on the e-mail were enthusiasts. They'd read deeply into it and come out with some very obscure questions that I hadn't thought of. Those were the ones I just flip through, because I just want to pass the course, I'm not that interested in it. I just wanted things that came up in the lectures clarified.'

Though students did not tend to comment on each other's 'skywritings' in print, skywriting itself did become a topic of conversation amongst the students: 'A lot of people talk about it, they give their opinions on it'; 'At some point most people didn't like it so then we had something to talk about!' It needs to be remembered that these students didn't know one another very well at this stage, and skywriting seemed to offer a good icebreaker: 'It's a really good conversational topic: "Did you read that skywriting thing? Did you understand it? Wasn't it long?", or "I understood that, it was really good". People will say if they've seen anything of yours on there.' At least one student reported making a friend this way! Sometimes, productive interactions happened around the computer itself: 'The person I was reading it with had already scanned through them so he had a vague idea of what they were about and he was pointing out the ones that were good answers or bad answers. We talked about it together so that we understood it.'

Downsides of reading skywriting exchanges included the need to work in crowded and noisy surroundings: 'It's annoying because I have to sit in front of the computer and take down notes. If it was in my room it wouldn't be so bad, but here it's noisy.' Printing everything off was prohibitively expensive for most: 'You might want to highlight things, which you can't do on the computer. You have to copy it or print it off, but that's expensive.' Many found reading a lot of material on screen disagreeable: 'I find being presented with lots and lots of things on screen really difficult.'

Skywriting and tutorials

Although skywriting was offered to the students as a supplement rather than an alternative to tutorials, in the interview we asked students about how they saw the balance of advantage as between these two forms of interacting and learning. The overwhelming answer was: 'No contest, tutorials are much better'; 'It's nicer to speak to people'; 'Nothing beats contact'; 'Because it is spontaneous'. The immediacy of interaction in the tutorials was probably the most often mentioned factor: 'In a tutorial you've got more prompting. If the person's there, you can ask a question. They'll get you to ask questions, get feedback from you'; 'You can't see people's reactions on the computer'; 'With tutorials you have more room to manoeuvre around the subject, and push it in different directions. With skywriting you can't have that constant discussion, so it doesn't progress further.'

Students get to know the other members of your tutorial group: 'If you are talking in tutorials you can get to know their face and the name and how they feel about things in general and interact from there.' By contrast, in skywriting: 'You don't know who the people are and you never get to know who they are.' Finally, a more instrumental consideration is that the students expect the tutor to use the tutorial to guide them to what they need to know: 'We're being told stuff that will be important and you can ask questions, whereas skywriting seems to be about [questions] that just spark off a discussion which may not be relevant to what we're going to have to do.'

On the plus side, skywriting was seen to have the advantage over tutorials in that it generated a permanent record: 'With tutorials you don't have it written down, so you can't learn it'; 'You might forget the steps of thought you went through while in the tutorial.' A similar observation was made by another student in relation to lectures: 'I think skywriting has made a big impact. You take it in without realising. It's not that strenuous to sit there and read for a little while.'

The continuity of access to skywriting across the course was seen to have some advantages in terms of keeping up the work: 'In a sense it does make you work more throughout the whole course'; 'It's like revising before you even finish the course – you can go over that material as many times as you want to.' Indeed, a majority of students interviewed (including many of those who did not send any messages on skywriting) said that skywriting should be available for more courses, and that, if it was, they would use it in the future. Indeed, one observed: 'I think I would be lost not to do it now.'

Conclusions

We opened this chapter by quoting a futuristic vision of computer-mediated communication as 'freeing university study from the constraints of time and place'. What we have been looking at as a case study is rather more limited and prosaic, and does actually highlight some ways in which 'time and place' (and in particular being together at the *same* time and place, in face-to-face interaction) can support rather than constrain university study.

Did skywriting succeed in offering opportunities for 'productive interaction' to these students? The answer to such a question depends on a judgement as to what 'productivity' consists in, of course, but it also depends a bit on what is meant by interaction. The students who contributed messages which elicited responses were obviously involved in skywriting interactions. Less obviously, but perhaps equally importantly, those students who read the exchanges without ever contributing to them were also party to the interactions. So too were those who talked to one another about skywriting contributions that others had made, or that they themselves had made, or were considering making.

The extent of contribution to skywriting showed a small positive correlation to course assessment outcomes in the present case. Cause-and-effect relationships cannot, of course, be assessed from such correlations. More importantly, even if we were to discover no such correlation at all, we would not be justified in concluding that the skywriting facility made no difference to assessment outcomes. After all, as other data reported here underline, many students (especially female students, it seems) who say little or nothing in tutorials go on to do very well on their courses. We would be rash to conclude from this that their tutorials are serving no purpose.

Moreover, it is by no means clear that doing well in the end of course assessments is all that people have in mind when they discuss the 'productivity' of learning interactions in this medium. Enthusiasts for computer-mediated communication have often portrayed it as having the potential to *transform* the experience of learning, not merely to enhance it. For example, Riel (1995) sees the technology as shifting the role of the teacher from controlling the transmission of information to providing intellectual leadership in challenging conversations among a community of learners. Other benefits looked for from such technology might include a strengthening of the sense of being part of a discipline, or a fostering of skills in critical argument. If these are the envisaged benefits, then ways will have to be found of achieving agreed measures of them before we can test any claims about productivity.

As Bannon (1995) has noted, however, there is often a tension between the radical potentials of the technology and the conservative instincts of some of those involved in education. In the case we have been studying, this conservatism is certainly reflected in some of the views expressed by the students, and neither the patterns of usage nor the interview responses showed much indication of radical transformative potentials. Rather, they supported Henri's (1995) observation, quoted earlier, that such exchanges tended to reflect and perhaps even reinforce traditional patterns of teacher–student relationship.

Skywriting did come to be perceived by most of the students as a useful vehicle for question-and-answer exchanges. Moreover, the accumulated body of questions and answers was used as a resource by a considerable number of students. There are indications here that a kind of 'vicarious learning' through accessing the tutorial dialogues of other students with the tutors might be pedagogically effective. As Mayes and Neilson (1995) have pointed out, there is an obvious development possibility here. If student–tutor question-and-answer dialogues are really useful and usable for other students, then across the years a considerable resource could be built up with modest effort, which could evolve with the course. Instead of replying at length, the tutor could then simply guide the questioner to an appropriate answer. Indeed, an artificial 'intelligent system' might be designed to do this. When compared to the huge investment of time and money required to develop effective content-based courseware, this could still prove cost effective.

The form of 'tutor-centred' skywriting which emerged on the course described here may involve very low start-up costs, given the technological infrastructure now widely available, but it is, of course, expensive in tutor time. Given the pressure on teaching resources, it may be unrealistic to envisage any widespread adoption of skywriting without cost to other forms of teacher–student contact. Yet as we have seen, none of the students would willingly have sacrificed face-to-face sessions in favour of skywriting.

The role and style of the tutors involved in the course we have observed was clearly a major factor in shaping the outcome. In general it seems that the role of the tutor in computer-mediated tutorial interactions has been neglected in the available research (O'Malley, 1995). Our own initial assumption was that it was as a medium for student–student interaction and discussion that skywriting would hold its greatest potential. Our observations of skywriting used in relation to other courses (Crook and Light, in press; Light *et al.*, 1997) suggest that the size of the group, the shared knowledge and mutual familiarity of the students and the tutor's stance are the principal factors determining whether such activities 'take off'.

Returning to the present case, an unanticipated feature of skywriting to which the students drew attention was that it rendered the other students' levels of attainment or ability more visible. A nice example came from a young student who said she had been in awe of the mature students until she saw from their skywriting that 'Some of them couldn't even do punctuation properly!' Similarly, as we saw, the students' anxieties about their contributions were very much linked to how they would be seen by their fellow students.

These issues of self-presentation and social comparison loomed much larger in the students' minds than any more general attitudes towards computers. It is therefore understandable that attitudes towards, and experience with, computers turned out to be unrelated to levels of participation in skywriting in this group. In particular, gender differences in previous experience with computers had no effect, and skywriting in fact produced a more equitable basis of contribution than face-to-face classes in this respect. Participation was associated with a tendency towards a 'deep' as against a 'surface' approach to study, but it was not just a matter of the more able or advanced students participating; participants did not outperform non-participants in terms of assessment outcomes.

The fact that these students were in their first year, that they were a large group, and that they were new to skywriting may all have conditioned the phenomena we have observed. Likewise, all manner of variations, such as anonymity of contributions, might have made a difference to the outcome. Thus, the 'natural history' of cases will vary a good deal. The greater the number of particular cases we know about, however, the better able we will be to identify the sources of variability. Moreover, the 'high-level' issues identified in any such case study (such as the significance of social comparison, mentioned above) are likely to be relevant to all such cases, though they may manifest themselves in different ways.

Skywriting, as with any innovation, may be particularly 'plastic' at the outset, capable of taking on a wide variety of forms and significations. Habits and mores set in fast, though, as was reflected in one of our student's musing as to what she would do if her next course didn't use skywriting: 'There will be nothing to log on for! It sort of becomes what you do everyday.' Some variant on skywriting might 'sort of become what we do everyday' for many in higher education over the next decade, we suspect. But the form which it eventually takes may depend less on curricular or technological considerations than on what one might refer to as the 'ecology' of student learning, an ecology which remains all too little understood.

References to 'natural history' and to ecology highlight the sense in which learning is a matter of adaptation to context, and thus underline the need to take context fully into account in any characterisation of learning. Observable interactions have many and often unobservable determinants in the histories of individuals, groups and institutions, and a variety of research methods will be needed to address these factors. The present case study has used an eclectic mixture of quantitative and qualitative analyses to reveal something of 'what went on and why' in a novel but naturally occurring situation. The rate of technical and educational innovation in this field will ensure that further opportunities for research will not be in short supply.

Note

1 *Acknowledgements:* The work reported here was assisted by a grant from The Leverhulme Trust and a Senior Research Fellowship from ESRC. Thanks are due to Jayne Artis for assistance with the interviews and to Stevan Harnad and Chris Colbourn for their co-operation with the research and their helpful comments on drafts of the chapter.

References

Anderson, C., McLeod, H. and Haywood, J. (1993) 'Entrant undergraduates' experience of using computers', in N. Hammond and A. Trapp (eds) *CAL into the Mainstream: CAL93 Conference Handbook*, CTI Centre for Psychology, University of York.

Bannon, L. (1995) 'Issues in computer-supported collaborative learning', in C. O'Malley (ed.) *Computer Supported Collaborative Learning*, Berlin: Springer Verlag.

Coombs, N. (1989) 'Using CMC to overcome physical disabilities', in R. Mason and R. Kaye (eds) *Mindweave: Communication, Computers and Distance Education*, Oxford: Pergamon.

Crook, C. (1994) *Computers and the Collaborative Experience of Learning*, London, Routledge.

—— (1995a) 'Educational practice within two local computer networks', in C. O'Malley (ed.) *Computer Supported Collaborative Learning*, Berlin: Springer Verlag.

—— (1995b) 'Computer networking and collaborative learning within a departmentally focused undergraduate course', *British Psychological Society, Developmental Section Annual Conference*, Strathclyde, September.

Crook C. and Light, P. (in press) 'Information technology and the culture of student learning', in J. Bliss, P. Light and R. Säljö (eds) *Learning Sites: Social and Technological Contexts for Learning*, Oxford: Pergamon.

Culley, L. (1988) 'Girls, boys and computers', *Educational Studies* 14: 3–8.

Davis, N. and Coles, D. (1993) 'Students' IT experience on entry to initial teacher education', first report to the *Association for Information Technology in Teacher Education*, Croydon.

Goodyear, P., Steeples, C. and Johnson, R. (1993) 'Flexible learning in higher education: the use of computer-mediated communication', in N. Hammond and A. Trapp (eds) *CAL into the Mainstream: CAL93 Conference Handbook*, CTI Centre for Psychology, University of York.

Graddol, D. (1989) 'Some CMC discourse properties and their educational significance', in R. Mason and R. Kaye (eds) *Mindweave: Communication, Computers and Distance Education*, Oxford: Pergamon.

Grint, K. (1992) 'Sniffers, lurkers, actor networkers: computer-mediated communications as a technical fix', in J. Benyon and H. McKay (eds) *Technological Literacy and the Curriculum*, London: Falmer Press.

Harasim, L. (1989) 'On-line education: a new domain', in R. Mason and R. Kaye (eds) *Mindweave: Communication, Computers and Distance Education*, Oxford: Pergamon.

Harnad, S. (1990) 'Scholarly skywriting and the prepublication continuum of scientific enquiry', *Psychological Science* 1: 342–344.

—— (1991) 'Post-Gutenberg galaxy: the fourth revolution in the means of production of knowledge', *Public Access Computer Systems Review* 2: 39–53.

—— (1995) 'Interactive cognition: exploring the potential of electronic quote/commenting', in B. Gorayska and J. Mey (eds) *Cognitive Technology: In Search of a Humane Interface*, Oxford: Elsevier.

Henri, F. (1995) 'Distance learning and computer-mediated interaction: interactive, quasi-interactive or monologue?', in C. O'Malley (ed.) *Computer Supported Collaborative Learning*, Berlin: Springer Verlag.

Hoyles, C. (1988) *Girls and Computers*, University of London: Institute of Education, Bedford Way Papers, 34.

Kaye, A. (1995) 'Computer-supported collaborative learning in a multi-media distance education environment', in C. O'Malley (ed.) *Computer Supported Collaborative Learning*, Berlin: Springer Verlag.

Kirkup, G. (1992) 'The social construction of computers', in G. Kirkup and S. Keller (eds) *Inventing Women: Science, Gender and Technology*, Oxford: Polity Press.

Lave, J. and Wenger, E. (1991) *Situated Learning: Legitimate Peripheral Participation*, New York: Cambridge University Press.

Lea, M., O'Shea, T., Fung, P. and Spears, R. (1992) 'Flaming in computer-mediated communications', in M. Lea (ed.) *Contexts of Computer Mediated Communication*, Hemel Hempstead: Harvester Wheatsheaf.

Light, P., Colbourn, C. and Light, V. (1997) 'Computer-mediated tutorial support for conventional university courses', *Journal of Computer Assisted Learning* 13: 228–235.

Lovegrove, G. and Segal, B. (1991) *Women into Computing*, Heidelberg: Springer Verlag.

Martin, R. (1991) 'School children's attitudes towards computers as a function of gender, course subjects and availability of home computers', *Journal of Computer Assisted Learning* 7: 187–194.

Mason, R. (1989) 'An evaluation of CoSy on an Open University course', in R. Mason and R. Kaye (eds) *Mindweave: Communication, Computers and Distance Education*, Oxford: Pergamon.

—— (1991) 'Refining the use of computer conferencing in distance education', in O. Boyd-Barrett and E. Scanlon (eds) *Computers and Learning*, Wokingham: Addison Wesley.

Mason, R. and Kaye, A. (1989) *Mindweave: Communication, Computers and Distance Education*, Oxford: Pergamon.

Mayes, T. and Neilson, I. (1995) 'Learning from other people's dialogues: questions about computer-based answers', in B. Collis and G. Davies (eds) *Innovative Adult Learning with Innovative Technologies*, North Holland: Elsevier Science.

Muter, P. and Manrutto, P. (1991) 'Reading and skimming from computer screens and books', *Behaviour and Information Technology* 10: 257–266.

O'Malley, C. (1995) 'Designing computer support for collaborative learning', in C. O'Malley (ed.) *Computer Supported Collaborative Learning*, Berlin: Springer Verlag.

Riel, M. (1995) 'Cross-classroom collaboration in global learning circles', in S. Star (ed.) *The Cultures of Computing*, Oxford: Blackwell.

Tait, H. and Entwhistle, N. (1996) 'Identifying students at risk through ineffective study strategies', *Higher Education* 31: 97–116.

Yates, S. (1992) 'Gender and computer-mediated communication: an analysis of DT200 in 1990', *CITE Report, 158*, The Open University, UK.

—— (in press) 'Gender, language and computer mediated communication for education', *Learning and Instruction*.

11 Productivity through interaction

An overview

Karen Littleton

Introduction

In any area of research, ideas develop through collective as well as individual efforts. The preceding chapters themselves illustrate the ways in which ideas are argued over, contested, borrowed and shared as our collective understanding is advanced. Such understanding is a discursive phenomenon, and its achievement a fundamentally social process. To this extent, this volume is an illustration of its own thesis. This final chapter will seek to pull together some of these threads, drawing mainly on the contributions which have preceded it. Unless otherwise specified, references to contributors refer to their contributions to the present volume.

Collaborative learning in context

The advent of educational computer technology did not suddenly result in the generation of new collaborative learning practices. The benefits of groupwork were being advocated long before the computer 'revolution', for example in the UK government's 'Plowden Report' (Central Advisory Council for Education, 1967). Classrooms were in many cases already lively places where students could learn together, in collaboration with their peers. As Crook observes, though, the introduction of computers into classrooms did render peer interaction visible to researchers. At younger age levels in particular, computers were a scarce resource. So, for pragmatic reasons, children were often to be found working together on the computer either in pairs or small groups. Often they were working without the direct involvement of a teacher, who was attending to the rest of the class. It was not only practical considerations which dictated this pattern of computer use. Many teachers believed that the introduction of computers into schools provided children with an excellent environment in which they could both learn to work together in groups, and work together in groups in order to learn. This situation of learners working together on the computer in relatively autonomous groupings in turn suggested to researchers a nicely bounded context in which to study collaboration and peer interaction.

Throughout the 1980s and 1990s a wealth of experimental studies of collaborative computer-based interactions appeared. Initially these studies were concerned with whether and when working together with a partner was more effective than working alone. Independent variables such as group size, composition of the group and nature of the task were controlled for, and attempts were made to assess their effects. However, as Dillenbourg *et al.* (1995) point out, the fact that such variables interact with each other in complex ways has meant that it has been virtually impossible to establish causal links between the conditions for and the effects of collaboration. Thus empirical studies started to focus less on establishing parameters for effective collaboration and more on the role(s) such variables play in mediating interaction (Dillenbourg *et al.*, 1995, p. 189). This shift to a more process-oriented account brought with it an interest in the talk and joint activity of learners working together on a task, an interest which is clearly reflected in the contributions to this volume. As the contributions make clear much energy has been expended in attempting to identify interactional features which are important for learning and cognitive change.

Researchers with different theoretical backgrounds and different method-ological approaches have emphasised different facets of interaction with some highlighting the important role of conflict, others planning, negotiation and so on (see Light and Littleton, this volume). Moreover, there is great diversity in what is conceived of as learning and as a learning 'outcome'. Howe and Tolmie, in common with Underwood and Underwood and others, see learning in terms of conceptual accomplishments at an individual level, demonstrable through appropriate individual post-tests. Talk and social interaction of various kinds may be a means to this end. Mercer and Wegerif, however, argue that talk and social interaction are a 'social mode of thinking'. That is, 'talk and social interaction are not just the means by which people learn to think, but also how they engage in thinking . . . discourse *is* cognition *is* discourse. . . . One is unimaginable without the other' (Resnick *et al.*, 1997, p. 2). As Resnick *et al.* make clear, the notion that concepts and ideas are constituted in interactive discourse is a challenge to traditional accounts of the nature of knowledge. It implies that talk is not just the mediating means for supporting individual development, rather: 'ways of thinking are embedded in ways of using language' (Wegerif and Mercer, 1997, p. 51). Seen in these term, the accomplishment of particular forms of educated discourse is an end in itself (Wegerif and Scrimshaw, 1997).

There is thus a latent tension here between a developmental psychological tradition, which tends to focus on the developing individual, and a situated approach to learning which emphasises learning as a collective activity in a cultural context. It is arguable that understanding individual psychological development in the context of such a situated approach remains problematic.

Approaches to studying collaborative activity

Many of the experimental studies of collaborative interactions, our own included (e.g. Barbieri and Light, 1992; Light *et al.*, 1994) have handled 'talk data' by effectively reducing them to pre-defined coded categories which in turn lend themselves to treatment by statistical analyses. Correlational techniques can be used, as for example by Howe and Tolmie, to determine whether there is any evidence of an association between particular features of the learners' talk and success on task or learning gain. Similarly, regression analyses enable Underwood and Underwood to determine which, if any, facets of the paired or group interaction are successful predictors of on-task performance. As well as allowing an examination of any associations between aspects of collaborative activity and measures of 'outcome', the use of coding schemes also affords other distinct advantages. For example, their use permits the handling of large corpora of data, affords explicit criteria for comprehensively categorising an entire data set and offers a basis for making explicit comparisons between the communicative behaviour of groups of learners (Mercer and Wegerif, this volume). Whilst this 'codifying' approach to the study of collaborative interactions has yielded many valuable insights, it is also important to recognise that there are serious weaknesses inherent in this approach.

Mercer and Wegerif highlight the specific problems encountered when using coding methods to study 'language-in-use'. These include problems in dealing with ambiguity, and the multi-functionality of utterances. There are also difficulties in determining the appropriate size of the unit of analysis – especially as the phenomenon under study involves a continual, evolutionary process of negotiation and renegotiation of meaning. Crook highlights a further difficulty, pointing out that a *failing* collaboration could be rich in instances of supposedly 'productive' talk, in the sense that there is evidence of conflict, predicting, questioning and so on. But what a simple count of such measures would miss is that, as the collaboration evolved, the corpus of talk may not get mobilised towards the particular goal of creating common knowledge (p. 106). It is in this important sense that coding schemes for talk clearly fail to capture the crucial evolutionary and temporal dimensions of collaborative activity, effectively reducing collaborations to atemporal 'inventories of utterances' (Crook, 1994, p. 150).

Studying and understanding the temporal dimensions of collaborative work represents a considerable theoretical and practical challenge. Categorical coding schemes are inappropriate tools to use for studying the processes by which learners build shared understandings, and the use of experimental studies involving brief circumscribed sessions of computer-based collaborative work is far from ideal. In order to gain a fuller understanding of the processes of collaborative work we need to recognise that collaborative experiences are typically more than just brief, time-limited, localised sessions of joint activity. When we observe a pair or group of learners working together, the interaction we observe is located within a particular historical, institutional and cultural context. Learners have relationship histories. As Crook notes, any productivity of interaction observed within a particular session may arise from circumstances that have previously been established (p. 107). This point is echoed by Light and Light who also assert that observable interactions are likely to have unobservable determinants in the histories of individuals, groups and institutions (p. 175).

The necessity and the difficulty of studying the temporal dimensions of collaborative activity are particularly highlighted in the contributions from Issroff, Crook, Golay Schilter *et al.* and Scanlon *et al.* Whilst Issroff analyses relatively short sessions of collaborative work, the time-based representations of interactions derived from the 'Timelines' software clearly illustrate the way in which paired activity evolves and changes over a period of time. At first sight the use of software such as 'Timelines' may appear to offer an attractive technological solution to the problems of studying the evolution of talk and joint activity over time. But, as Issroff makes clear, there are difficulties in deciding what constitutes an appropriate level of analytic granularity. The problem of studying the evolution of joint activity will not be solved simply by the development of increasingly sophisticated computer-based tools for analysis. Progress will instead depend on further conceptual work 'unpacking what is meant by the 'productivity' of classroom experiences, or characterising more carefully the interpersonal framework within which pupils organise joint activity' (Crook, this volume, p. 103).

Understanding the creation of shared knowledge over extended periods of time will bring with it many other challenges for researchers. For example, as learners establish a shared history and develop common knowledge, the need to be verbally explicit about their work declines. For the participants in a collaboration, this is undoubtedly an asset. For researchers of productive interaction, however, this 'backgrounding' is problematic. Intuitively we know that what is *not* said is sometimes as significant, if not more significant, than what is said. But how do we study and conceptualise the role of productive ambiguity, or even silence? The accounts of productive talk developed thus far rest fundamentally on learners practising various forms of verbally explicit reasoning. This focus on the explicit has arisen at least in part from the way we have chosen to study collaborative endeavour – in short, self-contained sessions. Researchers studying collaborative work in the context of authentic extended activity will increasingly need to develop an understanding of shared action as well as verbal interaction. They will also need to interpret and understand the role of periods of apparent *in*activity as well as observable activity.

As researchers, we are often quick to interpret periods of apparent inactivity negatively. This is especially the case if one member of a group appears to be somewhat remote or distant from the main sphere of group activity. We write of a learner's disengagement from the task and their isolation from the other group members. However, the work of Golay Schilter *et al.* invites us to question our assumptions about learners who appear to be 'being left out'. In their work the negative connotations associated with 'being left out' are replaced with the notion of a learner who is 'at a distance'. Golay Schilter and colleagues argue that in some cases distance can facilitate a 'meta-view' of the action taking place. In their study, a student who does not have to act (albeit through lack of power) appears to 'develop a meta-cognitive space for reflecting upon what is happening' (this volume, p. 133). Whilst this student did not have sufficient social weight to impose his point of view, through the persistence of his comments his contributions came to play an essential role in the solution of the task. As Golay Schilter and colleagues make clear, this notion of distance as opposed to marginalisation only emerged through a detailed analysis of the session of work as a whole. That is to say, it was only by studying the evolution of the collaborative activity over time that this characterisation of the learner emerged. In highlighting this example of productive apparent inactivity I do not wish to deny that isolation and disengagement *are* experienced by some, perhaps many, students who are being expected to work collaboratively. Rather, the purpose is to illustrate how the careful study of the evolution of joint activity can sometimes reveal the fruits of quiet critical reflection.

The importance of reflection for the development of understanding is highlighted by Azmitia (1997), who questions whether our fascination with peer interactive minds may have led us to underestimate the contribution of solitary work and reflection to cognitive development and learning, or at least fail to acknowledge that development and learning may require both. This question reminds us that as we move to studying more extended collaborative endeavours, particularly when these occur in authentic educational settings, we will need to develop an understanding of the ebb and flow of group activity. It is highly likely that not all members of the group will be engaged on all aspects of a lengthy task at the same time. Sometimes periods of intensive discussion and collaborative activity will be followed by periods of individual study and personal reflection, the results of which may or may not inform collaborative work undertaken at a later date. Understanding the interrelationships between, and the meshing of, these experiences will undoubtedly prove to be a challenge.

Throughout the volume it is clear that developing an understanding of authentic classroom activity requires access to a wide range of 'data', such as those collected by Scanlon *et al.* The need for different approaches to understanding the many facets of collaborative learning is also highlighted, and there are calls for multi-methodological approaches to its study. Less clear is how to balance the very different perspectives on the nature of meaning embodied in, for example, qualitative and quantitative approaches to talk data. The interpretative framework offered by Mercer and Wegerif neatly illustrates the tension between a desire to present talk accurately and in its full context and the need to generalise from particular incidents, in order to draw conclusions which other researchers find convincing (Wegerif and Scrimshaw, 1997, p. 5). For Mercer and Wegerif, the successful combination of different methodologies depends on the research being underpinned by a practical theory of discourse. By adopting such a theory, they argue, researchers are able to transcend particular methodological perspectives and make systematic complementary use of particular methods.

A practical theory of discourse may well take us further in our understanding of collaborative interactions. However, as these authors recognise, it is clear that such a theory needs to be broader than a theory of paired or group discourse. In and of itself such a theory is not sufficient. Learners do not work in isolation. Whether in the compulsory, further or higher education sector, teachers and tutors guide the construction of knowledge.

Scaffolding collaborative interactions

Whilst many of the contributions to this volume have chosen to focus on understanding collaborations between groups of learners working relatively autonomously at the computer, the contributors acknowledge that if we are to develop our understanding of the processes of productive interaction we need to go beyond the immediate interaction between learners and the computer-screen (Wegerif and Mercer, 1997). There is a need for accounts of groupwork that recognise the powerful influence of the teacher or tutor on learners' computer-based collaborative work. As Mercer and Fisher (1992, 1997) note, in discussing their work in schools, it is the teacher's responsibility to ensure that children's computer-based experiences contribute to their education and this is a responsibility that cannot be delegated to even the most sophisticated software or to the children themselves.

There is, therefore, a need for rich descriptions, conceptualisations and evaluations of the ways in which teachers and tutors attempt to support or 'scaffold' learners' collaborative learning with computers and how this in turn impacts on the processes and outcomes of their joint work. Such work will need to consider how group work is set up, how teachers and tutors intervene in such work and how they contextualise the work after the event (Wegerif and Scrimshaw, 1997). Moreover, such teacher–pupil interaction cannot be treated as just another self-contained aspect of the analysis. Learning is culturally based not just culturally influenced (Wegerif and Scrimshaw, 1997). Making a study of learning must amount to more than giving consideration to the particular facets of teacher–learner interactions. As Crook and Light (in press) so aptly put it, our traditions of organised education have evolved various forms of community structure and it is important that the impact of such structures is understood.

Situating collaborative learning: contexts for collaboration

As the contributors to this volume make clear, Vygotsky's work has provided a valuable starting point for an approach to understanding how peer interaction can facilitate learning and problem solving. This approach has highlighted the joint construction of solutions to problems, with solutions being achieved predominantly through discussion (Mercer, 1995). Vygotsky's work has, however, provided an important starting point for a wider theoretical development known as 'cultural psychology' (Crook, 1994). Cultural psychology focuses on thinking and reasoning as activities which take place in particular situations. This approach has come together with influences from anthropology (Lave and Wenger, 1991) and cognitive science (Suchman, 1987) to form the basis of what is now commonly termed 'situated learning'.

Situated approaches to understanding human cognition and learning encompass many diverse theoretical perspectives. Yet, underpinning all these perspectives is a recognition that human cognition and learning are embedded in specific contexts (e.g. Brown *et al.*, 1989) and are constituted through processes of interdependence, interaction and transaction between people and their environment (e.g. Sternberg and Wagner, 1994). Put quite simply, 'learning and thinking are always situated in a cultural setting and always dependent upon the utilisation of cultural resources' (Bruner, 1996, p. 4). Bruner's words remind us that the groups of children we study are not undertaking their joint work 'in a vacuum'. When focusing our research efforts on micro-genetic analyses of sessions of talk and joint activity we must be careful not to neglect the broader picture. We need to recognise that understanding contexts for collaborative learning involves more than understanding how the immediate joint activity is resourced. Learners' interactions are framed by, and therefore can only ever be fully understood within, the context of particular institutional structures and settings.

Different institutional contexts afford, and indeed constrain, different opportunities for interaction. The educational practices we see today are the result of a long period of historical development, and the activities of today's students are largely circumscribed by existing practices and established materials (Crook and Light, in press). The implication, then, is that collaborative interactions need to be understood within their cultural niche, that is, with specific reference to the broader social and historical context within which they are positioned. By studying interactions around computers conducted in educational settings, we are studying interactions in a particular 'niche' and are gaining a highly context-specific understanding of the process of collaborative work and interaction. For example, in classroom settings teachers and pupils engage in heavily contextualised discourse. Their interactions are influenced by a complex contextual system which is inseparable from how education is defined in our culture (Mercer and Fisher, 1992). Understanding collaborative interactions within the context of wider educational communities is undeniably difficult. It is not easy to capture the work of a community for study. Yet it is vital that we do so, not least in order to understand the motivational dimensions of the way in which routine collaborative sessions are managed by learners (Crook, this volume, p. 114).

At first sight the argument that we need to understand the wider social context of collaborative working around computers may only seem to apply to those who research collaborative work within authentic educational settings. But the need to contextualise the study of collaborative learning applies equally to the experimental tradition of research. For example, whilst they are not an integral part of on-going classroom activity, many experimental studies of collaborative activity are undertaken in school contexts (e.g. Issroff, this volume) and as such we need to address 'the relations between experiments and indigenously organised activities' (Cole, 1996, p. 250).

The phrase 'locating the experiment' was first coined by Scribner (1975) and it is a phrase which highlights that experimental tasks are not decontextualised occurrences. It also draws attention to the fact that joint activity undertaken in experimental sessions of work is shaped by broader levels of context. Responses to the experimental tasks undertaken in educational settings are determined by contextual systems, which extend far beyond the immediate interaction between experimenter and participants.

The computer as mediator of collaborative activity

At this point, the reader might be forgiven for thinking 'but where is the computer in all this?' The answer is, in essence, that many of the activities observed and described are mediated by the computer. The concept of mediation is central to 'situated' approaches to understanding cognitive activity and it is a term which refers to the fact that our relationship with the outside world is always mediated by signs and artefacts (Säljö, 1995; this volume). Put very simply, we think with and through artefacts. The choice of which artefact to use alters the structure of our work activity (Scribner and Cole, 1981) thereby fundamentally transforming the cognitive and communicative requirements of our actions (Säljö, 1995, p. 90).

Säljö (1995, p. 91) stresses that if we are to understand cognition and practical action, we must recognise that people and artefacts operate in a system that cannot be divided. The notion that there is co-functionality, whereby the mediational means form part of actions in situated practice, has considerable implications for the ways in which we study computer-supported collaborative learning. The computer is an artefact which is not only capable of supporting collaborative endeavour, but has the potential uniquely to transform the way in which collaborative activity is organised. It can reorganise the social processes of learners' joint problem solving (see Crook, and Light and Light, this volume). So, the central role of the computer in framing and mediating joint activity needs to be conceptualised.

The contributions to this volume begin this process of conceptualising the vital role of the computer in shaping collaborative activity. For example, Golay Schilter and colleagues discuss the impact of computer hardware in the distribution of roles – the computer has only one mouse and holding it is *de facto* a form of taking power. These researchers also consider how the development of interactions between learners is influenced by the particular piece of software in use. We are invited to consider whether the program used by the students in their study resulted in a trial-and-error method of working. Golay Schilter *et al.* argue that it was the rapid presentation of countless windows and the large number of choices available which, given the time constraints, resulted in the students' risk-taking behaviour. The learners did not seem to put their engagement with the software on hold whilst they reflected on their current situation and what their next move should be. It is the opportunity for such reflection which Mercer and Wegerif see as being of vital importance.

It is important to remember, however, that we never experience artefacts in isolation, but only in connection with a contextual whole: 'An object . . . is always a special part, phase or aspect of an environing experienced world' (Cole, 1996, p. 132). The *expectations* of learners as they interact with a computer tool are thus powerful mediators of activity too. Golay Schilter and colleagues are mindful of this as they discuss the contextualisation of their learners' joint activity. The students' work with the 'Flexible Manufacturing System' was framed in the curriculum as a scholastic rather than a professional activity. It is thus argued that the 'college' interpretation of the task sometimes caused them to operate in the abstract without basing themselves on their knowledge of machining. This abstract mode of operation was evident despite the fact that such practical knowledge was essential for the correct use of the software and that such knowledge was needed if the parameters which were introduced to the students were to be meaningful. As Golay Schilter and colleagues note:

> The meaning which they gave to this practical work situation appeared to be strongly influenced by the scholastic framework of their training; the students seemed to focus essentially upon carrying out the work asked of them as quickly as possible and obtaining a good mark. They show a utilitarian rapport with the technical device. . . The objective, which could be to deepen their understanding of the device, escapes them, moreover this objective is not made explicit in the teacher's instructions.
>
> (p. 138)

The importance of understanding the meaning which teachers and learners give to tasks, computer-based or otherwise, is also highlighted by Scanlon *et al.* who discuss how different interpretations of the task in hand led to conflict which hindered learning. As Scanlon and colleagues make clear, learners' 'readings' of task meaning impacts on their joint activity. Meaning is not a fixed or tangible commodity. Learners construct the meaning of a task, and that meaning may change dramatically over time.

Moreover, it may differ between peers, and may be at odds with that intended by the teacher. Meanings are constructed through a process of interpretation and reinterpretation, as a result of action and interaction. Mutual understanding of the purpose of the task may be of paramount importance for collaborative learning and such understanding will need to be achieved through the negotiation of meaning.

The need to analyse the role of the computer in supporting collaborative interactions and the understanding of task meaning is also stressed by Howe and Tolmie, who note that in many learning contexts it is the structure of work practices which provides opportunities for learners to develop views of what activities are about and become engaged with them. In highlighting the value of observation and peripheral participation in joint activity (Lave and Wenger, 1991), Howe and Tolmie (p. 42) stress that 'the important point about this perspective is that it suggests not only what the students were doing when they were involved in joint action, but what the *computer* was doing too, namely, creating the "structure of work practices" which was both helping to shape student action and providing information about what was involved'.

In talking about 'children' or 'learners' generally we must not forget that the significance of the computer and particular pieces of computer software is not the same for all learners. For example, in our own work (Light and Littleton, 1997) we have demonstrated that the imagery or metaphors used in the presentation of the task can have a marked influence on the performance of pairs of girls encountering the software. We also have findings that illustrate that, with a given piece of software, girls' performance can be substantially affected by the context in which that software is presented. Once more we are reminded that context effects exert a critical influence on cognitive performance and that it can affect not just the absolute difficulty of a task, but also its relative difficulty for different groups of children.

Identity and groupwork

Several authors in this volume comment on the need to conceptualise peer interaction in terms of affect and motivation as well as learning and cognition. Collaborations may be 'productive' in the sense that a task is accomplished, a problem is solved, or something is learned, whilst at the same time the process by which such outcome is achieved may be characterised by domination, disunity, hostility or even aggression. Under certain circumstances, then, learners may come to feel that peer interaction represents a threat rather than a potential opportunity. The possibility that working with others may pose a 'threat' is highlighted in the work of Golay Schilter and colleagues. They note that when the technical students they were observing working with a complex industrial computing task encountered difficulties, the students were most concerned with 'saving face' and securing a 'high position' in the group. Hostility towards one another and the computer became apparent as the students engaged in 'power games' borne of insecurity regarding their professional image and identity. Even if students are not hostile towards one another, they may often feel a sense of social unease. The results from the mixed-gender pairs in the first of Howe and Tolmie's studies, undertaken with school-aged students, testify to social unease which can be occasioned by gender. Such social unease may also account for the lack of discussion in the girl–boy pairs in Underwood and Underwood's studies.

Issues of personal identity, self-presentation and social comparison were also of paramount importance to the undergraduate students studied by Light and Light. Students felt exposed when putting their ideas or questions in writing, and the permanent visibility of their contributions within the computer conference was a source of anxiety for many. Students were concerned that they might be criticised, or make 'a wally' of themselves. The notion of personal criticism was not clearly distinguished from criticism of ideas. The students were also intensely interested in and sensitive to their own ability and the quality of their work relative to their peers. Messages posted to the conference were often used as a source of informal 'feedback' or a means of gauging 'what level everyone is on'. Such social comparison is unsurprising. From a very early age learners are highly skilled at making sense of educational contexts and activities. They construct and participate in discourses about ability and effort (Bird, 1994) and are motivated to understand what it means to be a learner and what it means to do and succeed at educational tasks. The social climate of comparison, competition, success, failure and issues of relative status in the classroom rapidly becomes established within the early years of schooling (Crocker and Cheeseman, 1988) and remains with students throughout their educational careers.

Whilst many of the approaches outlined in this volume have been concerned with the role of overt, observable processes of interpersonal interaction, findings such as those detailed above point to a need for studies of collaborative interactions which address issues such as self-presentation, social comparison and the relative status of pupils. The work of Monteil and colleagues is of relevance here (e.g. Monteil, 1993; Huguet *et al.*, 1994). This work, which stems from social rather than from developmental psychology, illustrates the extent to which children's expectations of their own success relative to their classmates can impact upon their learning. For example, Huguet and colleagues have demonstrated that an artificially raised expectation of success on a computer-based problem-solving task can lead to enhancement of children's performance. A not dissimilar line of work has been undertaken by Liengme Bessire *et al.* (1994) who have shown that attributions and perceptions of expertise can influence both group dynamics and learning outcome.

There are limitations, then, on how far we can expect to get with purely cognitive accounts of the benefits of groupwork. Undoubtedly, studies based on cognitive-developmental theories derived from the work of Piaget and Vygotsky can take us some considerable distance in understanding how and when peer interaction facilitates children's understanding. As we have seen, however, a unified model of productive groupwork will need to embrace an understanding of collaboration as a situated activity, mediated by artefacts. The role of shared action and the interrelationship of action and interaction need to be conceptualised. It is also imperative that a fuller understanding of children's social perceptions and emotional responses is incorporated with our cognitive accounts of 'how groupwork works'. The challenge, then, is how best to develop an understanding of collaborative learning environments as systemic wholes where all the factors reciprocally affect each other (Salomon, 1994). Capturing complex processes in a schematised manner without simplifying them will represent a considerable challenge for researchers seeking to understand collaborative learning in computer environments.

Supporting productive interaction

Underpinning many of the contributors' interests in understanding productive interaction is the idea that through the study of collaborative interactions we can come to understand how better to support learners' joint endeavours. Throughout this volume we have seen many different visions of how to support and sustain effective collaboration between learners.

Some of the authors stress the importance of identifying particular facets of productive talk in order subsequently to promote or support the occurrence of such types of talk:

> Now that we know what current patterns of performance look like, and how children tend to discuss problems when working around a computer, we can encourage the kind of interaction that will result in the development of their powers of thinking.
>
> (Underwood and Underwood, this volume, p. 21)

A particularly striking example of this approach can be seen in Mercer and Wegerif's sociocultural account of 'exploratory talk'. This type of talk is characterised as the embodiment of critical thinking, and therefore essential for successful participation in educated communities of discourse. Exploratory talk, it is argued, represents a distinctive social mode of thinking and that by encouraging the awareness and use of such talk we may be able to help learners to develop intellectual habits that will serve them well across a diverse range of situations. Whilst acknowledging that there is more to participating in an educated discourse than using talk in an exploratory way, Mercer and Wegerif maintain that their conception of exploratory talk 'embodies qualities that are a vital, basic part of. . . educated discourses' (p. 88). They therefore propose that learners should be encouraged and enabled to practise exploratory talk in the classroom. It is to this end that they describe a programme designed to transform their proposal into educational practice, describing activities directly to support the development of children's capacities for collaborating and using language to reason.

An alternative to coaching learners to practise particular forms of reasoning-in-talk is described by Crook who emphasises bridging the gap between the 'playful' and the 'schooled' deployment of discursive resources. Contending that jointly working at a computer does not *create* discursive capabilities among learners, Crook argues:

> Whichever theoretical gloss is placed on the interactions observed, it is rare that any such features of pupils' talk are novel to the problem-solving activities within which they occur. These are not ways of interacting that are uniquely elicited and nurtured by the classroom tasks that teachers or researchers come up with.
>
> (pp. 104–5)

He argues that what is potent about interactions around classroom problems is that an *existing* repertoire of resources is mobilised for schooled purposes. According to Crook, school-based collaborative tasks afford the opportunity for pupils to appropriate their socially grounded modes of thinking and communicating into domains of knowledge that we value. Seen from this perspective: 'What needs to happen in the end is a redirection of the energy that accompanies playful collaboration into collaborations that arise in school settings' (p. 106) and 'a central challenge for educational practice becomes the successful creation of continuities between pupils' existing concerns and new ones that we are asking them to reason about together in classrooms' (p. 105).

Central to both these accounts is the role of the teacher. Mercer sees the teacher as a discourse guide – a crucial mentor for children's initiation into culturally based discourse practices. According to Crook, the appropriation of discursive capabilities needs to be teacher-managed. Teachers have an important role to play in creating a community in which collaborative activity occurs and is valued. However, when Lewis and Cowie (1993) interviewed teachers about their attitudes towards co-operative groupwork, they found that for teachers one of the most difficult aspects of putting group-work into practice was 'letting go of power'. It is not easy to create a culture of collaboration in the classroom. Building such a culture necessitates a working partnership between teachers and learners and trust in the creative abilities of children and young people (Watson, 1997).

Underwood and Underwood make the point that a sense of trust and ease of working is very important if children are to feel safe in taking the risks which are inherent in opening up their thinking to their peer group. One attempt at involving learners in the creation of 'a culture of collaboration' is described, albeit briefly, by Mercer and Wegerif. Here the children themselves were active in negotiating and agreeing a set of 'ground rules' for collaborative talk. The rules generated by the children highlighted mutual respect, careful consideration of everyone's ideas and opinions, as well as the importance of collective decision making. Through the process of generating and working according to these ground rules, children were 'learning how to learn' together, creating a collaborative community of enquiry.

The specific role of the computer in relation to supporting collaborative activity depends upon the form of collaborative activity we wish to support. If our aim is to support relatively circumscribed interactions *at* a computer (to use the distinctions introduced by Crook), where two or more learners work on a problem together, then there is evidence that the computer can facilitate the process of productive interaction. Such facilitation is often achieved through the delivery and maintenance of a clear task structure and the provision of feedback on joint solutions (Howe and Tolmie, this volume). A different sort of goal, however, may be to support a collaborative community of enquiry. Here the computer can afford unique opportunities for the production and representation of shared classroom experience, offering a powerful classroom resource for supporting collective remembering (Crook, this volume). Clearly, these are but two examples. As Säljö shows, there is a multiplicity of ways in which computer technology can mediate human activity, although these ways may not always be readily apparent or observable. Shared previous experience of a particular computer application or resource can, for example, provide a valuable referent for joint activity undertaken at a much later date. Interaction and discussion *in relation to* computer technology can resource the building of common knowledge even though such interaction may be remote in time and space from the computer itself (Light and Light, this volume).

What is apparent, however, is that students have specific expectations and beliefs about teaching and learning relationships. Learners are still very much accustomed to having the teacher in control of what they do in educational contexts (Cowie, 1994). So despite being given the opportunity to engage in peer discussion in an innovative computer environment, the students in Light and Light's study nevertheless waited in expectation of the 'proper answer' from the lecturer. Computers undoubtedly have the potential to reorganise learning interactions in a variety of significant ways, but experience suggests that established social institutions have a remarkable capacity for 'neutralising' the effects of new developments, technological or otherwise. The established culture of learning can impact significantly on the prospects for new computer-mediated communication initiatives and existing practices will offer resistance to the 'bolting on' of new forms of educational technology (Crook and Light, in press). Computer technology does undoubtedly have the capacity to free students from the constraints of time and place, but participating in activities situated in a particular specific time and place does not necessarily constrain human activity.

We opened this volume by rehearsing concerns about the isolating and dehumanising effects of computer technology. But as Säljö emphasises, in practice, learning with computers is not an automatic process of acquiring 'packaged' knowledge. 'No technology will ever replace the need for learners to participate in ongoing conversations with partners, sharing interests and commitments' (Säljö, this volume, p. 158). Computer technology will never replace communication between learners, rather it holds the potential to resource their collaborative endeavour in new and exciting ways.

References

Azmitia, M. (1997) 'Peer interactive minds: developmental, theoretical and method-ological issues', in P. Baltes and U. Staudinger (eds) *Interactive Minds: Lifespan Perspectives on the Social Foundations of Cognition*, Cambridge: Cambridge University Press.

Barbieri, M. S. and Light, P. (1992) 'Interaction, gender and performance on a computer-based problem solving task', *Learning and Instruction* 2: 199–214.

Bird, L. (1994) 'Creating the capable body: discourses about ability and effort in primary and secondary school studies', in B. Mayall (ed.) *Children's Childhoods: Observed and Experienced*, London: Falmer Press.

Brown, J., Collins, A. and Duguid, P. (1989). 'Debating the situation: a rejoinder to Palincsar and Wineburg', *Educational Researcher* 18(4): 10–12.

Bruner, J. (1996) *The Culture of Education*, Cambridge, MA: Harvard University Press.

Central Advisory Council for Education (England) (1967) *Children and their Primary Schools*, London: HMSO (Plowden Report).

Cole, M. (1996) *Cultural Psychology: A Once and Future Discipline*, Cambridge, MA: Harvard University Press.

Cowie, H. (1994) 'Ways of involving children in decision making', in P. Blatchford and S. Sharp (eds) *Breaktime and the School: Understanding and Changing Playground Behaviour*, London: Routledge.

Crocker, T. and Cheeseman, R. (1988) 'The ability of young children to rank themselves for academic ability', *Educational Studies* 14(1): 105–110.

Crook, C. (1994) *Computers and the Collaborative Experience of Learning*, London: Routledge.

Crook, C. and Light, P. (in press) 'Information technology and the culture of student learning', in J. Bliss, P. Light and R. Säljö (eds) *Learning Sites: Social and Technological Contexts for Learning*, Oxford: Pergamon.

Dillenbourg, P., Baker, M., Blaye, A. and O'Malley, C. (1995) 'The evolution of research on collaborative learning', in H. Spada and P. Reimann (eds) *Learning in Humans and Machines*, Oxford: Elsevier.

Huguet, P., Chambres, P. and Blaye, A. (1994) 'Interactive learning: does social presence explain the results?', in H. C. Foot, C. J. Howe, A. Anderson, A. K. Tolmie and D. A. Warden (eds) *Group and Interactive Learning*, Southampton, Boston: Computational Mechanics

Lave, J. and Wenger, E. (1991). *Situated Learning: Legitimate Peripheral Participation*, Cambridge: Cambridge University Press.

Lewis, J and Cowie, H. (1993) 'GCW: Promises and limitations. A study of teachers' values', *British Psychological Society Education Section Review* 17(2): 77–84.

Liengme Bessire, M. J., Grossen, M., Iannaccone, A. and Perret Clermont A-N. (1994) 'Social comparison of expertise. Interactional patterns and dynamics of instruction', in H. C. Foot, C. J. Howe, A. Anderson, A. K. Tolmie and D. A. Warden (eds) *Group and Interactive Learning*, Southampton, Boston: Computational Mechanics.

Light, P. and Littleton, K. (1997) 'Situational effects in computer-based problem solving', in L. Resnick, R. Säljö, C. Pontecorvo and B. Burge (eds), *Discourse, Tools and Reasoning: Essays on Situated Cognition*, Berlin and New York: Springer Verlag.

Light, P., Littleton, K., Messer, D. and Joiner, R. (1994) 'Social and communicative processes in computer-based problem solving', *European Journal of Psychology of Education* 9(1): 93–109.

Mercer, N. (1995) *The Guided Construction of Knowledge: Talk Amongst Teachers and Learners*, Clevedon: Multilingual Matters.

Mercer, N. and Fisher, E. (1992). 'How do teachers help children to learn? An analysis of teachers' interventions in computer-based activities', *Learning and Instruction* 2: 339–355.

—— (1997) 'Scaffolding through talk', in R. Wegerif and P. Scrimshaw (eds) *Computers and Talk in the Primary Classroom*, Clevedon: Multilingual Matters.

Monteil, J-M. (1993) *Soi et le Contexte*, Paris, Alcan.

Resnick, L., Pontecorvo, C. and Säljö, R. (1997) 'Discourse, tools and reasoning', in L. Resnick, R. Säljö, C. Pontecorvo and B. Burge (eds) *Discourse, Tools and Reasoning. Essays on Situated Cognition*, Berlin and New York: Springer Verlag.

Säljö, R. (1995) 'Mental and physical artefacts in cognitive practices', in P. Reimann and H. Spada (eds) *Learning in Humans and Machines: Towards an Interdisciplinary Learning Science*, Oxford: Pergamon Press.

Salomon, G. (1994). 'Differences in patterns: studying computer-enhanced learning environments', in S. Vosniadu, E. De Corte and H. Mandl (eds) *Technology-Based Learning Environments: Psychological and Educational Foundations*, NATO ASI Series F: Computer and System Sciences, Vol. 137, Berlin: Springer.

Scribner, S. (1975) 'Situating the experiment in cross cultural research', in K. F. Riegel and J. A. Meacham (eds) *The Developing Individual in a Changing World: Historical and Cultural Issues*, The Hague: Mouton.

Scribner, S. and Cole, M. (1981) *The Psychology of Literacy*, Cambridge, MA: Harvard University Press.

Sternberg, R. J. and Wagner, R. K. (eds) (1994) *Mind in Context: Interactionist Perspectives on Human Intelligence*, Cambridge: Cambridge University Press.

Suchman, L. (1987) *Plans and Situated Actions*, Cambridge: Cambridge University Press.

Watson, M. (1997) 'Improving groupwork at computers', in R. Wegerif and P. Scrimshaw (eds) *Computers and Talk in the Primary Classroom*, Clevedon: Multilingual Matters.

Wegerif, R. and Mercer, N. (1997) 'A dialogical framework for researching peer talk', in R. Wegerif and P. Scrimshaw (eds) *Computers and Talk in the Primary Classroom*, Clevedon: Multilingual Matters.

Wegerif, R. and Scrimshaw, P. (1997) 'Computers, talk and learning', in R. Wegerif and P. Scrimshaw (eds) *Computers and Talk in the Primary Classroom*, Clevedon: Multilingual Matters.

Index